I0879387

I Give You Half the Road

Other books by Carol Spindel

In the Shadow of the Sacred Grove

Dancing at Halftime: Sports and the Controversy over American Indian Mascots

I Give You Half the Road

Carol Spindel

THE UNIVERSITY OF WISCONSIN PRESS

The University of Wisconsin Press
728 State Street, Suite 443
Madison, Wisconsin 53706
uwpress.wisc.edu

Gray's Inn House, 127 Clerkenwell Road
London ECR 5DB, United Kingdom
eurospanbookstore.com

Copyright © 2020 by Carol Spindel
All rights reserved. Except in the case of brief quotations embedded in critical articles and reviews, no part of this publication may be reproduced, stored in a retrieval system, transmitted in any format or by any means—digital, electronic, mechanical, photocopying, recording, or otherwise—or conveyed via the internet or a website without written permission of the University of Wisconsin Press. Rights inquiries should be directed to rights@uwpress.wisc.edu.

Printed in the United States of America
This book may be available in a digital edition.

Library of Congress Cataloging-in-Publication Data
Names: Spindel, Carol, author.
Title: I give you half the road / Carol Spindel.
Description: Madison, Wisconsin : The University of Wisconsin Press, [2020]
Identifiers: LCCN 2020017796 | ISBN 9780299330507 (cloth)
Subjects: LCSH: Rural-urban migration—Côte d'Ivoire. | Kalikaha (Côte d'Ivoire)—Biography. | Kalikaha (Côte d'Ivoire)—Social conditions—21st century. | Côte d'Ivoire—Social conditions—21st century.
Classification: LCC DT545.9.K35 S65 2020 | DDC 307.2/4096668—dc23
LC record available at https://lccn.loc.gov/2020017796

First book epigraph reproduced from *The Future Has an Appointment with the Dawn* by Tanella Boni, translated by Todd Fredson, by permission of the University of Nebraska Press. Copyright 2018 by the Board of Regents of the University of Nebraska. Originally published as *L'avenir a un rendezvous avec l'aube*, copyright 2009 by Vents D'Ailleurs.

A portion of the chapter "Just a Word in Our Mouths" was originally published on the *Afropop Worldwide* blog and reprinted as "Women's Songs in Post-Crisis Côte d'Ivoire: 'Ask Gbagbo . . . ,'" Hot Spots, *Fieldsights*, November 2, 2011, https://culanth.org/fieldsights/womens-songs-in-post-crisis-c%C3%B4te-divoire-ask-gbagbo.

The dawn counted its nomadic steps
to the border
the early breeze took over
amid the day's news
the men and the women
weaved a unity cloth
with sympathetic hands

it was ordinary life
between routine and rupture

—TANELLA BONI, "Land of Hope"

The mass graves rot, become humus, the humus becomes compost. The compost of the rotting earth of mass graves is always recommended, good for the Ivorian soil. It's the compost of the humus of mass graves that enriches the Ivoirian soil. The Ivorian soil that produces the best chocolate in the world. *Walahé!* In the name of Allah!

—AHMADOU KOUROUMA, *Quand on refuse on dit non*

Contents

Illustrations

Tamsir Dia, whose artwork is on the cover, is an Ivorian painter whose art has been exhibited in Africa, France, and twice at the Venice Biennale. He lives in Abidjan.

Facts about Ivory Coast

Ivory Coast, officially known as Côte d'Ivoire, is a country in West Africa of approximately 124,000 square miles, about the size of Arkansas and Missouri combined. Ivory Coast gained its independence from France on August 7, 1960. The official language is French.

The 2014 national census counted almost 23 million inhabitants. In 2020 the national statistical institute projects a population of 26.5 million. Roughly half live in urban areas.

Abidjan, located on the Gulf of Guinea, is the largest city. Its ten municipalities, called communes, had a total population of about five million in 2014. The second-largest city, Bouaké, with a population of about 540,000, is located in the center of the country. Korhogo, in the northern savanna, has a population of about 250,000. The official capital is Yamoussoukro, which has about 200,000 inhabitants.

Ivory Coast is home to about sixty cultural/ethnic groups, which belong to five linguistic groups. One-quarter of its inhabitants are non-Ivorian immigrants. Forty-three percent of inhabitants are Muslim, 34 percent are Christian or Catholic, 4 percent are animist, and 19 percent profess no religion.

Ivory Coast is the world's largest exporter of cocoa beans and raw cashew nuts.

In the city of Abidjan, 69 percent of inhabitants are literate. In the northern savanna region around Korhogo, 25 percent of inhabitants are literate. Nationally, half of men and one-third of women are literate.

Just under 3 percent of the population is living with AIDS.

Average life expectantcy is about fifty-seven.

Sixty-two percent of households have electricity. Seventy-eight percent of households cook with charcoal or wood.

Five percent of households have access to a computer, 3 percent to an internet connection, and 80 percent of households have access to a mobile phone. According to the World Bank, in 2018 there were 135 cell phones for every 100 people.

Sources

Institut National de la Statistique. "Recensement Général de la Population et de l'Habitat 2014." http://www.ins.ci/n/documents/RGPH2014_expo_dg.pdf.

World Bank. "Mobile Cellular Subscriptions (per 100 People)." Accessed June 18, 2020. https://data.worldbank.org/indicator/IT.CEL.SETS.P2.

Pronunciation and Spelling

I have created a rudimentary pronunciation guide for the reader using easily pronounced English words and syllables. Although many commonly used spellings for Senari and Julakan words are based on French, publications in English now tend to anglicize their spelling, using, for example, Jula instead of Dyula or Dioula, and I have done the same in many cases. I have made Julakan words plural by adding an "s," which is unorthodox, and used Ivory Coast rather than the official Côte d'Ivoire to make reading easier for English speakers. The Julakan and Senari conversations in this book were translated into French by Ivorian translators employed by me. All French translations are mine. For a more complete list of foreign words, with pronunciations and definitions, see the glossary.

The French *e* or *é* is often used for "ay" (Beh = bay and Chébena = CHAY-ben-nah). The syllable *un* is often used for "oon" (Chékun = CHAY-koon and Lasungo = lah-SOONG-go). The *ng* combination is pronounced as "in" (Ngolo = IN-ga-loe). The *gn* combination is pronounced as "ny" (Gnon = nyon). The *gb* combination can be pronounced as "b" (gbaka = BAH-kah). The *i* is usually pronounced as "ee" (Masita = mah-SEE-tah). Most of the names are accented on the first syllable (Adama = AH-dah-ma and Nawa = NAH-wa). Exceptions are Gozana (go-ZAN-na) and Fonigay (foe-NIH-gay).

Political leaders mentioned in this book are Félix Houphouët-Boigny (HOOF-way BOON-yee), nicknamed le Vieux (leh vewh); Alassane Ouattara (AWL-a san WATT-tar-a); Henri Konan Bédié (en-REE ko-NAN BAY-dee-ay); Laurent Gbagbo (BOG-boe); and Robert Gueï (gay).

Characters

Some people's names have been changed at their request. Main characters are listed in bold with secondary characters who are related to them grouped beneath.

Nawa—oldest daughter of a Muslim Senufo family; moves to Korhogo

Adama, her father, a translator in Korhogo; *Nafini,* her mother, a potter turned market gardener in Korhogo; *Sita,* her grandmother, a potter in Kalikaha; *Zoumana* (nicknamed *Old Man*) and *Djak* (short for Djakaridja), two brothers; *Gozana,* her second husband; *Assiata,* her friend and neighbor; *Masita,* her health counselor

Chékun—oldest daughter of a Senufo family; a teacher in Abobo, a commune of Abidjan

Donni, her father; *Gnon,* her mother; *Chébena,* her uncle; *Bara,* a sister; *Zele,* her youngest sister; *Old Chékun,* her grandmother; *Beh,* her boyfriend and father of *Desirée,* her daughter; *Ngolo,* her husband

Yaya—Jula scrap iron dealer in Koumassi, a commune of Abidjan

Mariam, his mother; *Lonala,* his father; *Abou-lonala,* his older half brother in Kalikaha; *Djeneba,* his first wife; *Aminata,* his second wife; *Lonala,* his nephew; *Khadi,* his oldest daughter; *Moussa,* his cousin and *jatigi* in Abidjan

Abou—Jula younger cousin of Yaya who joins the armed rebellion

Lasungo—Senufo healer and diviner in Korhogo

Zele, his mother, diviner, and brewer in Kalikaha; *Fonigay,* his older brother

Carol—the American author

Tom, her husband, a cultural geographer who does research in Ivory Coast; *Nick,* their son; *Becca,* their daughter

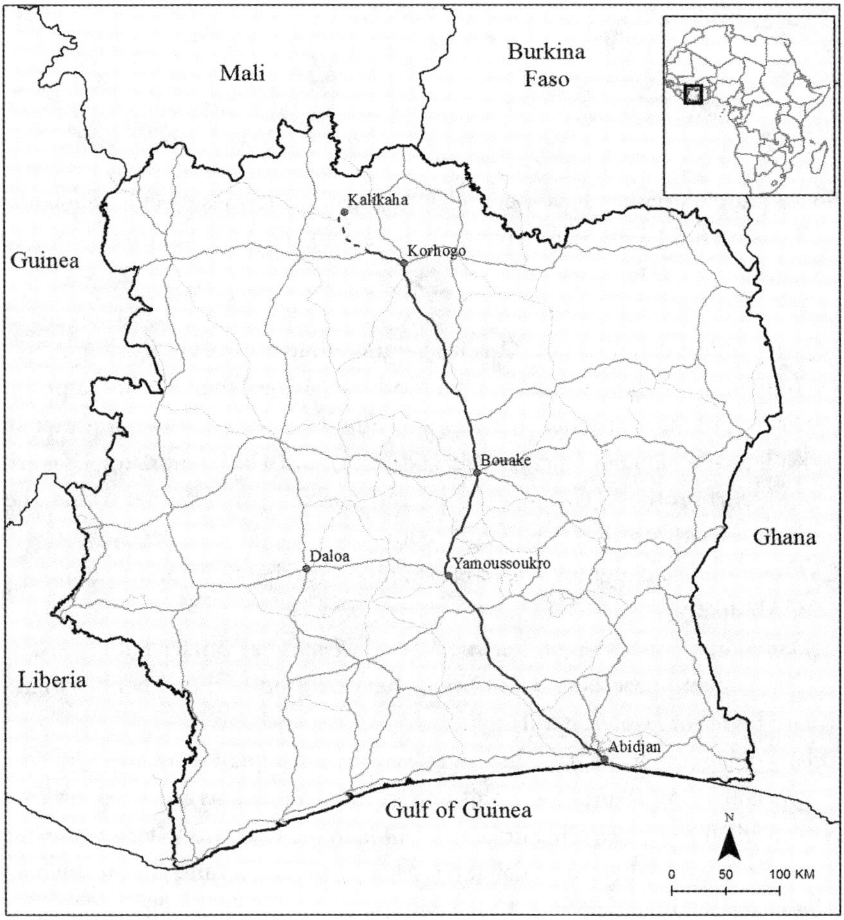

Map of Ivory Coast

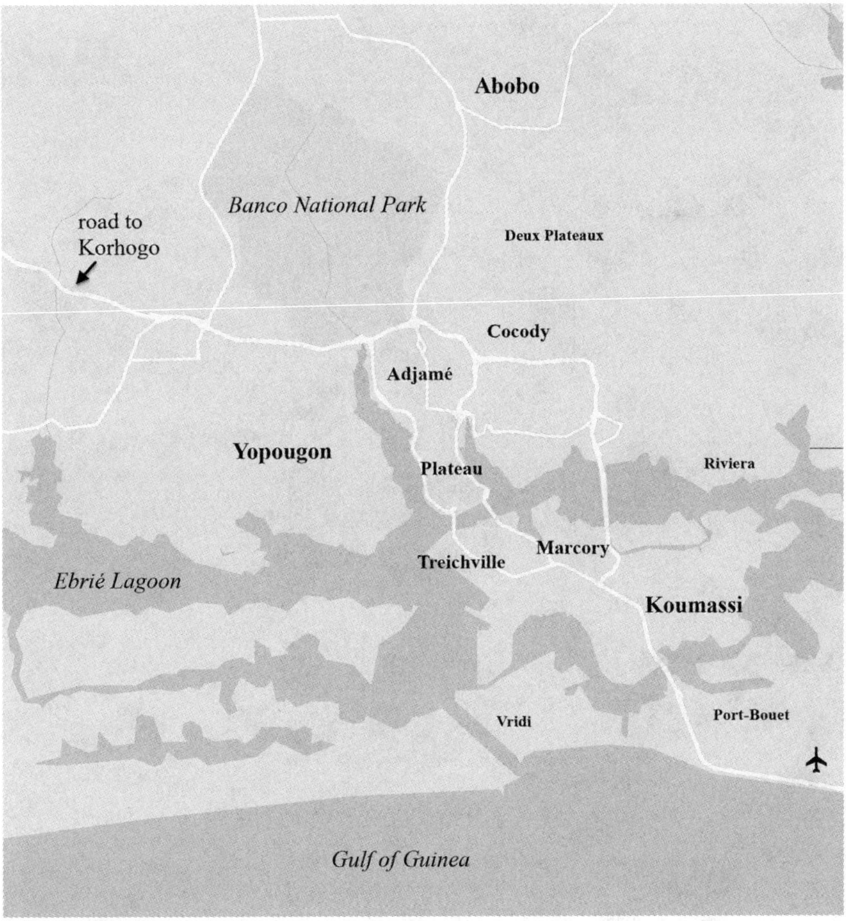

Map of Abidjan

I Give You Half the Road

Prologue

Forty years ago I arrived for the first time in the West African country of Côte d'Ivoire, or Ivory Coast. It was the summer of 1981 and I was young and in love. Tom and I had been separated for seven months while he did research for his doctoral dissertation in geography and I organized a women's writing conference in California. Seventy-seven letters on thin blue airmail stationary flew back and forth between us, numbered so we would know if they all arrived, and they did, although not in order.

I arrived at dusk, and close to the equator, night falls suddenly. When I stepped out of the bustling Abidjan airport, Tom and I leaned against a wall and put our arms around each other. "Ça ne se fait pas ici!" chastised a woman in a sharp voice. "That's not done here!" As we separated, the night city exhaled its damp diesel exhaust and burning charcoal breath and the sky filled with the clink-clink of bats, flying hammers tapping on metal. The thick smoky air closed around me and settled on my skin. I breathed it in and both embraces lasted.

Abidjan is a port city built along coastal lagoons, a lively fusion of French and West African culture, with, at that time, an impressive downtown of glass and steel skyscrapers. The money to build the skyscrapers came from exporting coffee, cocoa, and tropical hardwood, all harvested in the southern part of the country. The Ivorian economy depended, and still depends, on burlap bags of fragrant fermented cocoa beans that are shipped to other countries and made into chocolate. Almost half the world's cocoa is grown there. Ivory Coast, which remained closely linked to France, its former colonial conqueror, was considered the most stable country in West Africa. This combination of political stability and agricultural prosperity was dubbed "the Ivorian miracle." Immigrants from poorer countries, especially the two countries to the north, Mali and Burkina Faso (the former Upper Volta), streamed into Ivory Coast to work and were welcomed because their labor powered the miraculous growth. Although I didn't realize it, when I arrived in 1981 the miracle was over. Coffee and cocoa prices were sinking and the Ivorian economy sank with them. And the tropical rain forest that covered the southern part of the country, one of the largest in the world, was fast disappearing.

Although Ivory Coast's important export commodities were grown in the South, Tom was doing his fieldwork in the North, in the more arid wooded savanna where the cash crop was cotton. No miracle had visited the northern part of the country—roads were unpaved and schools and clinics were few and far between. Like their northern neighbors, the Malians and Burkinabé, many northern Ivorians moved south to work on the cocoa farms or in the cities.

When I arrived, Tom had been living for three months in a rural community of sixteen hundred people that was not even on the main dirt road. The large village was composed of clusters of orange mud-brick houses, some round, some rectangular, punctuated by groups of cylindrical earthen granaries or silos topped with conical thatch roofs. The homes were outlined by narrow winding paths that circled from one family compound to another.

View of Abidjan from downtown Plateau across the lagoon to Cocody, 2013

More than sixty ethnic groups live in Ivory Coast, each with its own language and culture, and like most Ivorian communities, this village is multiethnic, inhabited by three different groups—the Senufo (who speak Senari), the Jula (who speak Julakan), and the Fulani (who speak Fulbe). Julakan is used as a lingua franca between them. The Senufo and Jula farm families live in residential quarters organized by lineage and go out to their fields each day. The Fulani, semisedentary cattle herders and relative newcomers in the region, have settled outside the village in camps with their herds of long-horned hump-backed cattle. In the neighborhood of Senufo farmers where Tom and I lived, each family's compound of small earthen houses was arranged around a courtyard of beaten earth. First thing every morning, the women swept the courtyards clean. Bending from the hips over hand brooms of stiff dried grasses, they swept up the garbage and the goat and chicken droppings, and then, with even strokes of the wrist, used the brooms to create a fan-shaped pattern of lines in the clean dirt.

In my book about our first stay there, I called the community we lived in Kalikaha, to respect its privacy, and I retain that name in this book. Tom decided to focus his research on this one place and try to understand how it was changing over time. We returned as often as possible, and after our son and daughter were born, we took them, too.

One of the chief pleasures of returning to a place is watching the children grow up. Generations are short in Kalikaha, and the idea that each one is a link in a long chain is important to the Senufo. In the past, scarification marks on a woman's stomach—three lines above, below, and on each side—emphasized the center of the universe, a woman's navel. The navel is important because it is the visible proof of a woman's connection to her mother, and through her mother, to the women of all previous generations, and to the ancestor mothers. I see these scarification marks only on the very oldest women these days, but the Senufo still prefer to cut the umbilical cord so what remains swells, a kind of extreme outie we call "herniated." The Senufo admire a protruding belly button because it accentuates the physical proof that the child is one link in a long chain of generations.

Relationships that are not based on blood are also important. Foster kinship is taken seriously and, like blood kinship, involves reciprocal obligation. The most important foster relationship is the bond between host and guest. An outsider like me can't simply move into a village like Kalikaha; without an official host you can't even spend the night. In Julakan, the word for host is *jatigi,* and other groups use the word, too, for they have adopted the practice. But our English concept of host is a poor translation because when someone agrees to be your *jatigi,* they not only feed and house you; they serve as your intermediary. A *jatigi* stitches you to the fabric of the community and, over time, may adopt you as a foster relative. *Jatigiya,* the practice of weaving strangers into guests, and guests into your family, is an important part of Jula culture. This makes perfect sense because the Jula have a long history as both weavers and traders. A trader traveling long distances with his goods across an enormous continent needs a string of *jatigis* so he has places to spend the night. In modern Ivory Coast, a *jatigi* enables children of poor farmers to go to high school in town and to move to Abidjan to take an entrance exam, attend the university, or look for work. A farmer *jatigi* may welcome a Fulani family who will herd his cattle. If we could make the threads of *jatigiya* visible, the lines would radiate out from remote Kalikaha to houses all over Ivory Coast and beyond, like a spiderweb. At each node, someone has been taken in for a night, for many nights, a month, or years. This commitment to a deep and abiding hospitality is an essential characteristic of Ivorian life.

It was my good fortune to land in a place that has a long tradition of accepting outsiders and a cultural practice for integrating them. Our *jatigi*-family's generosity made it possible for Tom, me, and our children to be linked to Kalikaha. We appreciate how unusual it is, this guest-host connection between an American couple and an Ivorian community, an intricate knot we never could have tied by ourselves at the center of our marriage and our family. Holding up our end of the relationship requires us to shoulder responsibilities and obligations, and sometimes we are not sure exactly what they are or how far they extend. Tom and I try our best to fulfill them, for we understand that the *jatigi*-guest web of generosity and obligation is at the heart of Ivorian life. The ethical mandate to take in the stranger has been handed down across centuries and continents from ancient desert crossers to our world through the religious traditions of Judaism, Christianity, and Islam. As much as I admire this ideal, and as much as we have benefited from it, Tom and I have never welcomed anybody into our home as profoundly and deeply as the people of Kalikaha welcome us. In writing about our experiences, Tom in scholarly articles with an unusually deep sense of place, and me in first-person narratives, we hope to share some of what we have learned.

In Kalikaha, the cultural space where my neighbors place me is singular and contradictory. When I first lived there, I was young but was sometimes treated like an elder. I was a woman but often enjoyed the privileges of a man. As a member of the tiny white minority, I stood out everywhere I went, but my minority status came with outsized power and expectations. Most importantly, I had the luxury of coming and going at will, of returning to the United States and the remarkable good fortune I was born into.

When we were young, Tom and I resisted the privileges we were given, insisting we were students who had come to Kalikaha to listen and learn. Nearly forty years later, I can't deny that I am an elder for real with the gray hair to prove it. Although we don't value accrued age in our own world, this is the one status in Kalikaha that we cannot buy or inherit; we must earn it, year by year. I still listen to my Ivorian neighbors, and I learn a great deal from them, but now that my own children are grown, I am more comfortable advising the younger people, sharing my knowledge of the wider world, and helping them out with educational and medical expenses, as elders should if they have the means.

We return to Kalikaha every year if possible, for Tom's longitudinal research and because we want to see our friends. "*Ala i den balo* [May God give your children life]" is the blessing we exchange fervently with our neighbors there. Village parents pray for their children's survival, which is never a given, but like us, they also dream of something more—that their children's lives might be a little easier, a little more secure than their own.

In 1982, when I left Kalikaha after my first stay, I assumed this was inevitable. I imagined my neighbors' children growing up into literate, French-speaking adults who might leave for the city and return as the teachers and health workers the community so desperately needed. I pictured them moving along a linear upward curve of something I would have called, for lack of better words, development or progress.

I had no idea that just as I moved to Kalikaha in the summer of 1981, doctors in Los Angeles published a brief report. They noted with concern that five previously healthy young male patients had contracted a rare form of pneumonia. All five were gay and two had died.

The AIDS epidemic was unimaginable in the early 1980s, but so was civil war—remember that Ivory Coast was renowned for its stability. President Félix Houphouët-Boigny had been president since independence from France in 1960, and every adult belonged to the political party he headed, the only one that was legal. The president, who said he preferred injustice to disorder, was known as "le Vieux," "the Elder," because he was more than just president; he was the patriarch of the country. His death in December 1993 left an enormous political vacuum and instigated a no-holds-barred competition to succeed him.

Less than ten years after his death, in 2002, and six weeks after we had spent the summer with our teenage children in Kalikaha, an armed rebellion split Ivory Coast in two. We were cut off from Kalikaha, reduced to scouring the internet for news of our second home. For six years we did not go back out of fear. Tom moved his research on cotton to Mali and Burkina Faso and friends from Kalikaha traveled there to meet him. When the first list of "failed states" was published in 2005, I was shocked to see Ivory Coast listed as number 1. If the United Nations pulled out, the experts said, the country would completely collapse.

In 2008 we felt the situation was stable enough to return. We found our friends thinner, sadder, and poorer and the clinics, roads, and schools, always basic, in complete disrepair. The farm families had been able to grow enough food to eat, but it had been difficult to get their cotton to market, and their income, always small, had dwindled. The rebels who ran the North taxed everything that moved on the roads but did not put the money back into public services. The United Nations estimated that three-quarters of northern Ivorians were living in poverty.

In every family, a young person had left Kalikaha to move to a town or city. In the past, when they left, it felt like our neighbors' children simply vanished because Ivorian cities had no street names or addresses. But in the six years we had stayed away, something had changed Ivorian life more than civil war: cell phones. Telephone lines had never reached remote Kalikaha and never would, but most people in town had a little plastic cell phone, or access to one, and their relatives in Kalikaha had their number, written down on a fragment of paper stored in a worn plastic bag. The cell phone network enabled me to call up people I knew as children and arrange to meet in Abidjan, a teeming city of millions of people. I wanted to know how they had survived the years of conflict when northerners in the South were harassed by the police and discriminated against by the government. The rural to urban migration stories of four of those people make up this book—two women, Nawa and

Chékun, and two men, Lasungo and Yaya, as well as a few of their brothers, sisters, spouses, and cousins. Many young men from Kalikaha joined the armed rebellion, so I also included Yaya's soldier cousin, Abou the rebel. We live in an era of rural to urban migration, and most West Africans who leave rural areas migrate to nearby cities in their own countries, like the people in this book. Their stories are both so very ordinary and so emblematic.

The form of this book comes from weaving. In West Africa, weavers work on foot-pedal looms, creating long narrow strips of cotton. Sewn together, the strips create fabric, often with complex patterns. With this in mind, I have collected the stories of these daughters and sons of farmers who left their rural home and moved to the city. When Ivory Coast was divided politically and militarily, they were trapped in a violent conflict that cast them as outsiders in their own country. Stitched together side by side, their lives show some of the patterns that emerged when one small West African country attempted to leave behind one-party rule and become a multiparty democracy. In particular, this is the story of northerners during this period.

Their country's political collapse was fueled by anti-immigrant politics based on fear-mongering and ethnic division, but my neighbors' children survived by relying on Ivorian values of hard work and entrepreneurship and by accepting and extending hospitality. When their national political leaders urged them toward tribalism and even ethnic genocide, they refused to turn on their neighbors. They refused to buy into the political narrative that some Ivorians are more truly Ivorian than others. Instead they held fast to *jatigiya*, the guest-host bond, as well as Ivorian values of mutual respect and obligation, tolerance for difference, and forgiveness.

In 2010, in one of the world's most remarkable elections, Ivorians voted to reunite their country under a single president, but the incumbent, who lost the election, refused to step down and tried to hold on to power through force. In this postelectoral crisis, thousands of Ivorians, especially in Abidjan, died needlessly. Some of these people were trapped in that tragedy.

I believe their stories matter, and I believe that to pay careful and sustained attention to the particulars of other lives is one way of showing respect for those people and cultures. Having a second home in Kalikaha and experiencing life in a different society with Tom and our children has been one of the great good fortunes of my life. Understanding the political turmoil Ivorians experienced gave me insights into the risks of exclusionary nationalist and xenophobic politics everywhere, including in my own country. It helped me understand that a democracy is a fragile enterprise that must be continually invented and reinvented, made and remade. This can only be done by ordinary citizens who care enough and feel hopeful enough to step up and take part. The determination of Ivorians to take part in their own government and to reunite their divided country was extraordinarily moving to witness and continues to inspire me. For nearly forty years of hospitality and friendship, I remain deeply grateful.

The South-North Road

The South-North Road takes you from teeming Abidjan to the dusty market town of Korhogo, from the tropical coast to the wooded savanna. Heading north out of Abidjan, you see rubber trees in orderly lines, their slender gray trunks wound round with ribboned slashes. Occasionally you pass stalwart remnants of the tropical forest, giants that tower into the sky and dwarf the groves of teak planted to replace them. Rising tallest of all, all angles and bolts, red and white and gray metal, are the cell phone towers.

For many years, when we traveled this road, it was two-lane all the way. But now, you pay a toll and roll down a modern divided highway. Two hours north of Abidjan, the road transforms into a four-lane boulevard and enters Yamoussoukro, the hometown of le Vieux. Yamoussoukro was a sleepy village until its founding son made it the country's political capital and built administrative buildings, a golf course, a luxury hotel, an impressive mosque, and the world's largest church, whose golden dome floats like a mirage over the town's unpaved streets. But in a rare refusal of le Vieux's wishes, the financial and political action stubbornly stayed put in Abidjan, so Yamoussoukro is doomed to be a stage set, a capital where nothing really happens.

As we continue north and the land gets drier, pineapples and bananas and oranges stacked for sale on the shoulder give way to charcoal and piles of woody brown yams. This is the home of the Baule people, and at thatched roadside stalls, Baule weavers display their cotton cloths woven in narrow strips and sewed together, the dark-blue indigo punctuated by elegant white ikat designs. At midday we reach Bouaké, the second largest city after Abidjan, located in the center of the country. From Bouaké north, the road is two lane and pocked with ruts and deep holes. Along its dirt shoulders, women walk with basins on their heads and men and boys ride bicycles, their machetes tucked under black strips of rubber on the back. Vehicles weave in and out, passing on curves and hills, dodging the people who dart across when the road passes through villages. Long-distance buses filled with passengers pull into the opposite lane to overtake overloaded trucks that list to one side, trailing black exhaust. Gaily painted minibuses stop to load and unload people and their cargo on the dirt shoulder. Enormous logs, lashed to flatbed trucks, roll past, heading south to the port of Abidjan. There is no center dividing line.

This road is a reincarnation of very old trade routes that stretched from the West African coast to Mali and Morocco. Following these routes, traders traveled south from Timbuktu seeking gold and slaves, their caravans of camels loaded with bars of salt. They also traded other goods, bringing beads and metal items south and taking woven cotton fabric and bitter kola nuts, chewed as a stimulant, north. Packed in with these tangible goods, they transported intangibles: Arabic words and the concept of writing them, decorative geometric designs, and Islam.

This road is still an essential commercial conduit. It is the way northern agricultural exports like cashews and cotton reach the port of Abidjan and imports from China like factory-printed cotton and plastic buckets arrive in northern markets. It is also a central artery through the Ivorian body politic, for in Ivory Coast, north and south are not only geographic and economic opposites; they are also the opposite ends of the political spectrum. Who controls this central artery in any location matters. If policemen, gendarmes, or armed rebels block the road with a barricade, the road itself becomes a commercial enterprise and the travelers become customers who must pay to pass.

Ivorians are mobile people. The first president, le Vieux, made a practice of assigning civil servants to posts outside their own region, and many married and stayed. Ivorians use a French word to refer to this—*brassage,* brewed together. People from the North have lived in the more prosperous South for generations, and Ivorians from every part of the country have moved to the largest city, Abidjan. Ivorians are often on the road for business and return to their ancestral villages for visits, funerals, and weddings. When night finds you on the road, you need a place to stay, but more than that, you need a host to take you in, a *jatigi.* And when you are ready to move on, you must request permission to leave by "asking for the road."

"Is it really time?" your host will respond.

"Yes, I have to be on my way."

"Well, then, I give you half the road." This is an Ivorian way of insisting that you must come back.

In the afternoon, the wide blue sky opens in front of us like a pottery basin over our heads, and the baked earth seems to flatten in all directions. We have reached the semiarid North. The wooded savanna is dotted with villages, clusters of red-orange mud-brick houses, cashew and mango orchards, and fields of cotton, corn, and rice. It's late afternoon, so farmers are heading home from their fields on bicycles, mopeds, and foot. The women walk in groups, carrying wide enamel metal basins on their heads; inside are their weeding tools and the pots from lunch, and on top they have piled branches of firewood for cooking dinner. Their long wrapped skirts are faded from many scrubbings and long days in the fields. When, in the afternoon, the blue sky widens, the earth turns terracotta orange, and I see the thatched roofs of the first Senufo village silhouetted against the sky, I feel I've come home.

Nawa

A Village Daughter

When I first lived in Kalikaha, Nawa was five, always dancing or hopping on one foot between the fragile clay jars her potter mother and aunts had set out to dry. She would appear, flash me a look of shy delight, daring me to catch her, and then take off, her heels flying as she disappeared between the mud granaries. She always got away.

When we left Ivory Coast, her parents moved to the town of Korhogo, where Tom's recommendation helped her father land a job for the government livestock extension agency. They took the baby, but five-year-old Nawa and her toddler brother stayed in Kalikaha with their grandmother Sita. "Come here and sit by me and I will show you how to cook," Sita told her lively granddaughter. Nawa was delighted to be trusted with this important task. While she helped her grandmother and worked in the fields, her brother attended the village elementary school, then moved to town to live with his parents and continue his education.

Her parents, Adama and Nafini, had four more children, making Nawa the oldest of seven. Her six brothers and sisters grew up together in town, but she grew up in the potters' quarter of Kalikaha. In the rainy season, she and her cousins worked in her grandfather's fields, and in the dry season she dug clay and her grandmother shaped it into jars. After the firing, Nawa stacked Sita's pots on her head, fastened into a rope net, and trekked with the women to the market in a larger town, a walk of a day and a half. "At the market I always had good luck," she told me. But I suspect that Nawa's luck, the thing that pulled buyers her way like a magnet, was her beautiful smile.

In the rainy season, before she went to the fields, she fetched water and pounded the dried corn into meal. One day, when she was thirteen, she finished her chores and arrived at the field at mid-morning, too late for her grandfather.

Nawa burnishing a large water jar made by her mother in the old potters' quarter of Kalikaha, 1982

"You've been loitering in the village to get out of work!" he accused. He cut a switch and whipped her so hard her back bled. That evening, she ran to her grandmother.

"Just let it go," her grandmother advised. "Put it behind you and go on."

But Nawa refused and said she was never working in her grandfather's fields again. The next day, a Friday, she hid. Her grandfather announced that when he found her, he was going to beat her even harder. Saturday was market day, and every Saturday a little bus, referred to by the residents as the Twenty-Two Places, arrived in the morning from the town of Korhogo and returned in the afternoon. Nawa sneaked out to the road, flagged down the Twenty-Two Places, and climbed aboard. In town she made her way to her parents' house. "I'm never going back!" she declared, showing them the sores.

"If you don't go back, how will our mother Old Sita manage? Who will carry water for her?" her father asked. Nawa stayed in Korhogo, playing with her little brothers and sisters and helping her mother for a few weeks, and then her father put her back on the Twenty-Two Places.

While Nawa worked in the fields, her brothers went to school and learned to speak French and to read, write, and calculate. They studied geography and understood that they were growing up in the late 1980s and early 1990s in the wooded savanna in the western part of the continent of Africa. They studied the history of Ivory Coast—how the entire region had been conquered by the French army in the 1890s and made into a colony that produced raw materials—mahogany, cocoa, and cotton—for France, and how their country, led by Félix Houphouët-Boigny, had transitioned peacefully to independence in 1960 while staying allied with France. They learned about the cells inside every living thing and about invisible microbes that transmit disease.

Nawa learned none of these things. She knew how to plant and weed a cotton field and how to transplant and harvest rice. She knew how to pound and sift dried corn into flour for *toh*, the staple of poor households. She knew just how much water to add and how to whip air into the corn mush with a flat wooden paddle so that when you turned the bowl over and lifted it away, the *toh* stood firm and held the bowl's round shape. She dug clay and helped her grandmother make earthenware jars for water and for medicine, and once the pottery jars were fired, she carried them on her head to local markets. The potters were bilingual, so Nawa could bargain in Senari or Julakan with her customers, but since she hadn't gone to school, she didn't speak the national language, French.

Nawa's Senufo subgroup of potters married within itself, and when she was sixteen, the elder of their lineage called the fathers of the teenage girls together to discuss their marriages. Nawa's father thought of a young man who had been raised by one of his sisters. He didn't really know him, but his sister agreed, so it was arranged. He didn't consult his wife or Nawa. The groom was working as a blacksmith in a town farther north, and after the wedding, Nawa joined him there.

Her marriage started out reasonably well, and she soon gave birth to a son, but when her husband took a second wife, their household changed abruptly. Their marriage had been arranged, but her husband chose his second wife, and after she came into the household, he found fault with everything Nawa did, criticized her, and beat her. "If you aren't happy here, you can leave!" he told her. He even packed her belongings and put them outside, but he didn't give her money for a bus ticket back to Korhogo.

Nawa sent a message to her mother that her husband was beating her, but her mother could offer no help. Since it was a marriage "within the family," husband and wife shared the same extended family, so none of Nawa's male relatives, the only family members who had the power to mediate, would take her side. "This is why I am against this kind of marriage," Nawa says. "Because the woman suffers too much. She has no one she can go to."

She stuck it out for two years, supporting herself and her son as a *yala-yala* food vendor. In Julakan, to *yala-yala* means to meander, to wander, to stroll, or to walk from house to house selling something. From a basin on her head, Nawa sold ginger and hot-pepper-flavored rice porridge for breakfast in the mornings and fried chunks of yam with hot sauce in the evenings. She stayed because of her son and because she did not want to cause trouble between her father and his sister. Nor did she think her father would believe her. "If you want me to leave, you have to send one of your friends with me," she told her husband. "The friend can explain to my father that you have put me out, that this is what *you* want." Finally, her husband agreed to this. Nawa paid for all three bus tickets—round trip for the friend, one way for her and her son.

It's not unusual for women to stay with their parents for a cooling off period when they have conflicts with their husbands, so her father thanked the friend for accompanying Nawa and sent him back with a message: Nawa's husband should come to Korhogo himself so the two men could sit down together and work things out between them. He would instruct his daughter to be a better wife and not to do the things that annoyed her husband. But no answer came back.

Adama continued to send messages, but four years passed and the husband didn't show up. Finally, one day, a response arrived: if his father-in-law wanted him to come to Korhogo and discuss the marriage, he should send the money for a bus ticket. This made Adama furious, and at that point, even he admitted the marriage was over.

In the town of Korhogo, people originally from Kalikaha formed an association, and at the meetings, Nawa chatted with an older man named Gozana. One day an elder from his family called on Adama to extend a marriage proposal. Gozana wanted to marry Nawa. "This man who wanted to marry you, he has nothing," Adama told Nawa later. "I sent him away. You should stay here at home with us."

The next time she saw Gozana, she told him her father thought he was lazy and urged him to find some work, even if it didn't pay much, so Gozana approached a man from Burkina who sold secondhand clothing. The used clothing seller was willing to let Gozana take a few pairs of pants and a few T-shirts and *yala-yala* around Korhogo selling the clothes from a basin on his head. When he brought back the money, he received a small commission. Gozana was poor, but in those days, everyone she knew was struggling to come up with two meager meals a day. "He had very little, it was true, but what he had, he shared." She liked that about him. She told her father that she was too old to live with him and her mother as a dependent, and that Gozana offered to meet the imam, learn the prayers, and convert to Islam. Although no papers had been drawn up, she was now divorced from her first husband and remarried.

Nawa and Gozana rented a room in a large courtyard. In the two rooms next to them lived a family of Fulani *jelis* or griots, professional praise singers by birth and training. The husband limped, leaning on a staff; his wife, slightly older than Nawa, welcomed them warmly. Her name was Assiata and she was originally from Mopti, Mali. When she was twelve, an aunt from Korhogo visited, and since the aunt had only one daughter, she asked if Assiata could live with her. Her father agreed and gave her aunt and uncle permission to arrange her marriage when the time came. She had returned to Mopti only once, for her mother's funeral. Assiata didn't work as a *jeli* herself—she suffered from stage fright when she had to speak in front of strangers. As she and Nawa cooked in the courtyard side by side, they chatted, and their sons, who were the same age, played together nearby. Assiata told Nawa that her husband was a passenger on the night bus to Abidjan when there was a terrible accident. He was the only survivor. Although it had taken years for him to recover enough to walk, she thanked Allah for saving his life and his ability to work. It was their good fortune that he hadn't lost in the accident what a *jeli* needed more than anything: a strong, commanding voice.

Between the vegetables Nawa bought from market gardeners and resold at the neighborhood market and Gozana's secondhand T-shirts and jeans, they were able to pay their rent and buy food. Gozana saved enough to buy a wheelbarrow, which made peddling clothes easier and increased his sales. The man he worked for opened a second stall in the market, and when he sent Gozana to nearby villages with clothes to sell, Nawa managed the stall. After two years, their son, Yardjuma, was born. Nawa was happy living next to Assiata and their courtyard was a harmonious place run by the two friends like one family house.

Chékun

Chosen for School

One morning when she was five, Chékun's father called her to him. "I am going to take you to *laykoli*," he told her. "Even before you were born, I decided that if my first child turned out to be a girl, I would send her to *laykoli*." She had no idea where they were going, but she put her hand in his and they set off.

Chékun had never been to the other side of the town where the six-room elementary school was located. "These are teachers," her father said to her. She had never seen anyone like them. Their clothes were very clean, as if they never worked in the fields. They spoke a strange language that wasn't her language, Senari, or the other village language, Julakan. The teachers were very important people, that she understood. What were they going to do to her at *laykoli*? She felt frightened, but she told herself that, whatever it was, if her papa wanted her to be there, she must accept it.

Chékun had a regulation school dress, blue and white checked. She carried a small slate and a first-grade workbook, although she had no idea what to do with them. "What are they saying?" she wondered. Day after day she sat silently, her eyes on the teacher. When he made a mark on the board, Chékun tried to imitate it on her slate. When she needed to go to the bathroom, she pressed her thighs together and waited for class to end, then ran behind the building to the bushes. This and a bucket of water was the only bathroom they had.

To me it seemed normal for a little girl to go to school and I assumed her father would send her younger brothers and sisters when they were old enough, but he had singled her out. On a trip to the South when he was young, he saw educated Ivorians speaking French and decided that if his first child was a girl, he would send her to school. A boy would work in the fields.

"There go the lazies!" other children called out as she crossed the village in her blue-and-white-checked dress. "You go to school to sleep all day while we go to the fields to work!" Adults taunted her, too. The Senufo admire hard workers and good farmers. Children are praised when they work hard and they know that their help in the fields is not play, that every hour spent sowing or weeding or chasing birds away from the rice and corn fields adds a meal to the stockpile in the mud-brick granaries. On Saturdays, instead of working for their families, the older children worked in the school field or were hired as a group by other farmers and the money they earned went to the school. So sending a child to school incurs a double cost: someone else will have to do that child's household and field chores, and the family, always strapped for cash, will have to buy a slate, chalk, books, a uniform, and shoes, and contribute each year to the parent association that is responsible for the maintenance of the school building. If the child goes on to middle school and high school, the expenses and obligations increase. It's a difficult decision for a father to make—to send even one child to school means less money to buy food and medicine for the rest of the family. And education is a risky investment. To continue from elementary to middle school, every student must take an exam, and Ivorian national education, based on the French system, is set up so that only those students who score the national mean or above move on. In high school there is another exam, and failure to receive a passing score means losing the right to continue at a free public school. At the end of high school, every student faces the daunting exam for the baccalaureate, a requirement for further education or a formal job.

The children were afraid of the teachers—any mistake was punished with a hard whack of a ruler on their open palms. But each time her teacher saw her father in the village, he said in Julakan, the language they spoke in common, "Your daughter Chékun is doing well, she has to go on." When she heard that, she said to herself, This is something I can do.

While we lived in Kalikaha the first time, Chékun started her third year of school. Her father, Donni, who was our *jatigi*, gave me a list and asked me to buy her school supplies when I went to town. I stood in the store in Korhogo a long time, hesitating over which size blue-and-white-checked dress to buy. The dress was long, and later she told me this pleased her because the other children teased her about her knock knees.

When the Senufo say someone has courage, they are rarely thinking of a single heroic act. To be courageous means not to give up. So Chékun, in her quietly courageous way, kept on going to school with her small rectangular slate and broken piece of chalk. Gradually, French began to make sense and she could start to follow the geography and arithmetic lessons.

When the school day ended, she fetched water and firewood for her teachers' wives, and then went home and did the same for her mother. There was no table at her house; the family sat on stools. For light, there was one homemade lantern, a wick floating in kerosene in a small Nescafé can; the women needed it for cooking, and the men wanted it to eat by. After everyone had eaten, she lay on her stomach with her lesson book in front of her to read her assignment by its faint flickering glow. She turned each page in slow motion so as not to put out the open flame.

When she walked to her classroom and took her place on the worn wooden bench, Chékun crossed into a new universe, one her parents would never enter. They could only send her off every morning and welcome her back every afternoon. The teacher continued to tell Chékun's father that she was a good student and he should keep her in school. So he did.

Her last year at the village elementary school, she didn't score high enough on the exam to pass to middle school and had to repeat the class. A year later she failed again and repeated the year for the third time. Chékun was a sturdy

Carol, one-year-old Nick, Chékun in checked dress holding a baby, and neighbors in Kalikaha, 1986 (photo by Tom Bassett)

girl and sunny by nature, but I could tell she was worried that summer as she waited for the exam results. If she failed a third time, her education would be over.

On her final chance, Chékun scored enough points to enter middle school. The nearest middle school was in the town of Korhogo, a two- or three-hour trip over rutted dirt roads in the Twenty-Two Places or on the back of someone's motorcycle. Not only would her father have to pay her fees and buy her books and clothing, he would have to find a *jatigi* willing to take her in for an unspecified number of years. Fortunately, her father, Donni, had a brother who lived in Korhogo, although because their mothers were sisters, we would call them cousins.

Donni's cousin Chébena was about thirteen when his parents both died. He joined the household of an older relative and farmed for him, but this old man cared nothing for him. Chébena was only sure of a meal when he went to Donni's house because Donni divided his dinner in half and shared it. When all the young men hoed a field together, Chébena was the last to finish his row because, although he wasn't lazy, he was small and couldn't keep up. And when the teenage boys got in trouble, his friends' parents apologized for their sons, but Chébena had no one to speak up for him and was punished more severely than the others. Fed up, he ran away to Korhogo. A stranger took him in and agreed to be his *jatigi*; he got a job pushing a wooden two-wheeled cart called a push-push over the rutted dirt roads from dawn to dusk. With the money he put aside, he went into business selling pots and pans at the market, and with those profits he expanded into transport, renting the Twenty-Two Places and driving it to the Kalikaha market every Saturday. So each week, Chébena, still short and slight, returned to the village that had scorned him, a prosperous man who provided an essential service, the villagers' transportation to Korhogo and the world. Chébena was touchy, with a sharp tongue, while Donni was easygoing and affable, but the two were true brothers, so when Donni asked if his thirteen-year-old daughter could live with him to continue her education, Chébena readily agreed. He would be her *jatigi*, house and feed her, and be responsible for her while she went to school in town, although neither he nor her father knew how many years this would entail.

Before she left, Chékun's mother sat her down. "My daughter, the wives at your uncle's house, they are your mothers now, so you must do whatever they tell you and you must treat them all with equal respect. You mustn't do chores for one and not for another." By then, Chébena had four wives, and a grown nephew who lived with him had two wives. And so every day after she returned from school and ate her lunch, her six new mothers asked if she had class that afternoon. Most days she didn't have afternoon class but had been sent home with lessons to prepare for the following morning. Her *jatigi*-mothers were delighted to acquire a daughter old enough to do chores and put her to work. She raised water from the well with a rope and filled the water jars, carried the dried corn to the mill to have it ground into flour, and prepared a huge pot of corn *toh* for the family's dinner, whipping the very large kettle of thick corn porridge with the wooden paddle until her arms ached. After she washed the dinner dishes, she sat down at the table in the courtyard and opened her book to read the lesson for the next day. The teachers called on students to answer questions about the reading and woe to the one who wasn't prepared! Her uncle rented out rooms to traders, and as the renters often slept six to a room, his courtyard was noisy, filled with people who chatted and laughed around her. Her head drooped over the pages and she put down her book, lay down on her mat, and fell instantly asleep. She tried to wake up and finish her homework at four in the morning, but at five-thirty she had to be on her way because her school was at the edge of town and the walk was long.

Three years later, Chékun failed the exam to enter high school. Fortunately, although he wasn't educated himself, her married uncle grasped her dilemma and arranged for her to live in a dormitory. With plenty of time to rest and study, she passed the exam the following year. At her high school there was no dormitory for girls, so she returned to her uncle's house, but older and wiser, she finished her homework each day before she started doing chores. "I really have a lot of work to do for school," she explained, and her *jatigi*-mothers began to understand.

Sometimes the women spread out mats and called to Chékun to come and sit with them because a holiday or wedding was coming up and they were going to spend the afternoon tressing each other's hair. But Chékun refused politely and did homework instead. "I knew why I was there—to get an education. My family had nothing and they were counting on me. My father had sent me to school, only me, and he expected something from that, a good result."

During school vacations, she wanted to go home to see her family, but her father sent word for her to stay in town. Her *jatigi*-mothers sent her to work in their market gardens, where they grew lettuce, tomatoes, and eggplants to sell. When she helped them carry the produce to market, the large basin of washed lettuce on her head was so heavy she had to stop and rest beside the road and was often left behind. She didn't want to ask her father for spending money—he already had to buy her books and school supplies. She knew he had nothing to spare for her clothes and toiletries. So as she walked back from working in the women's gardens, she gathered furry heart-shaped teak leaves, as large as plates. She could sell a stack of leaves to the market women for two cents; they used them to wrap the plantains and yams they fried and sold. At construction sites she asked for the paper bags dry cement came in and sold those to the market women, too. And every six days, because the Senufo week is a six-day week, there is an especially large market in Korhogo, and on big market days she sold cool drinking water by filling a lidded cooking pot with water, buying a chunk of ice, and stacking little cups on top. She made her way through the market with the pot on her head and a bucket of water to wash the cups in one hand. For people from villages without electricity, cool drinking water was a delicious luxury, and she could make a dollar a day this way. During vacations a young man named Beh often chatted with her. He was older than her, already a worldly university student in Abidjan. He came back to Korhogo for vacations, and since his younger brother also lived with her uncle, he spent his evenings there. He had fathered a child with another student in high school, but that relationship had ended, and now he had chosen Chékun. He never called on her parents to make their relationship official, but everyone assumed that once she completed her education, they would marry.

The last year of high school is devoted to study for the baccalaureate, the all-important examination in June. Every evening Chékun sat at the worn plank table and tried to block out the talk and laughter around her. But when the results were posted, she hadn't passed and had to repeat the year. The following year she joined study groups; they met either at school or at the quieter houses of other students. When she came home, she heated water and bathed, ate something, and went straight to sleep. One of her male cousins living at her uncle's house was also studying for the bac that year and he did the same. At midnight, when everyone else was asleep, they woke up, met at the table in the center of the courtyard and studied together until three in the morning. Then they went back to their mats and slept until five. This was the only way they could find the quiet they needed.

As she walked to school or raised water from the well, she thought about her parents, how hard they worked and how little they had. Her younger brother worked in the fields every day. Her sisters did, too, and soon they would have to marry the husbands chosen for them. They had all sacrificed to send her to school, and if she didn't pass the bac this time, she didn't know what she would do.

Lasungo

Champion Farmer

As a young man, Lasungo was at the very center of Senufo life. When I met him in 1981, he was undergoing his seven-year initiation to adulthood and the elders had chosen him as the leader of his cohort. His second-in-command was his best friend, Zana, a hunter's son. The initiation is an important part of the belief system the Senufo call *poro*. For a short period at the outset, youths are secluded in the sacred grove, where they bond with the other boys in their age group and learn about *poro* rituals and values. After that, they perform community service, running errands for the elders and serving at funerals. You can always tell when a teenager is on *poro* duty; he wears only a loincloth made of a strip of cotton and carries a knife in a decorated leather sheath. No shirt, no sandals, all service. If an initiate was skinny or bow legged, the loincloth hid nothing, but Lasungo and Zana were youths to admire. Zana, with his long nose and flat thighs, all planes, looked like the angular Senufo sculptures that inspired the cubism of modernist European artists. Lasungo could also have been sculpted by a Senufo master carver, but one that preferred rounder volumes.

When the young men competed in the fields, bent over their hand hoes, mounding the dirt between their spread legs as they raced down a row, Lasungo nearly always won. It's no small affair to be the champion farmer. The Senufo value hard workers and excellent farmers. The French colonial authorities categorized each ethnic group—some were seen as more intelligent, others as aggressive and difficult to subdue. The Senufo were described as resistant to change but good laborers. Outside Africa, the Senufo are best known for their wooden sculpture—couples carved in angular lines, large birds called hornbills that stand like pregnant women with beaks curving downward toward their bellies, and powerful horned helmet masks. These sculptures are featured

Lasungo as an initiate, carrying corn beer to the elders with granaries in background (photo by Tom Bassett)

in every museum collection of African art, and antique masterpieces can bring millions of dollars on the Western art market.

When he competed in hoeing competitions, Lasungo had power medicines given to him by relatives with supernatural knowledge. He hid his power medicine in the dirt so that whoever came along first and hoed that mound would be afflicted and his pace would slow. He also had medicine to protect him from his competitors' medicines and to make him fast; he washed his body with it the night before a competition and he assumed the other youths did the same.

The farmers of Kalikaha, both men and women, were on intimate terms with the land. The red-orange soil of the savanna was so porous that nutrients leached right through, but by moving their fields every seven years and leaving the old fields fallow, they were able to grow enough corn, rice, peanuts, and vegetables to feed their families. Most families also grew cotton to sell. The land around the village belonged, they explained to us, to the ancestors and the future generations, and was imbued with spiritual power. The Senufo are animists and believe in nature spirits called *tugubele* that inhabit and "animate" particular places, especially waterways, thickets of trees, and clusters of rocks. Some Senufo have converted to Islam or Christianity, which they meld with these beliefs.

Music and dance are integral to Senufo life, and *poro* initiates are trained to perform at funerals. Some initiates wear the carved wooden helmet masks that we display inside glass cases in art museums. Others appear disguised in masquerade costumes of cloth and raffia fiber. Tall feather headdresses on top of their heads transform them into giants, and kazoo-like instruments built into the masks change the young men's voices, so it feels as if apparitions from another world are visiting. Brandishing long thin branches, they serve as guards, keeping the uninitiated away from ceremonies, and a glimpse of one sends children scrambling to safety. On the last afternoon of a three-day funeral, everyone is invited to the funeral grounds and the masqueraders put away their switches and perform as clowns and dancers, to the delight of the crowd.

At these events, Lasungo played a wooden xylophone called a *balafon*. Below a *balafon*'s wooden bars, round gourds serve as resonators. Holes in each gourd are covered with the white woven membranes of spider egg sacs, and when the wooden bars are struck with rubber-wrapped mallets, the spider membranes vibrate. This amplifies the notes and gives the *balafon* its lovely

Lasungo (*second from left*), in white homespun cotton, playing *balafon* in Kalikaha, 1981 (photo by Tom Bassett)

electric buzz. The *balafons* are accompanied by large stringed gourd instruments that thump out the rhythm like upright basses. For percussion, there is often a drummer, as well as the jingle and clink of bottlecaps and bits of tin and the clank of the musicians' ankle bracelets as they step in time to the beat.

Lasungo played standing up for hours, the heavy wood frame suspended across his shoulders by a homespun cotton strap, while the guests danced all night to help the deceased person make the journey from the earthly village to the village of the ancestors. To put their guests in the right mood, the family provided pots of corn beer, local moonshine, and bottles of Le Roi Valpierre, cheap French red wine. Guests were also treated to rice and sauce, and at a funeral, the sauce had beef or goat meat in it, a rare treat. Everyone loved to dance to Lasungo's group because his melodies were complex with a nonstop, driving, dance-til-dawn beat. He was far and away the best *balafon* player in Kalikaha, the village rock star.

Lasungo's mother, Zele, was a diviner who could speak with the spirits. Before Lasungo was born, she lost several boy babies, and when she was pregnant with him, she promised the spirits that if this child turned out to be a boy and lived, he would devote himself to serving them. His name referred to this destiny, for Lasungo means "one who sacrifices to the water."

Shortly after Lasungo was born in 1960, his father died and his older brother Fonigay went south to work on a cocoa plantation. Although it wasn't easy financially, widowhood did afford Zele the rare privilege of having some say over her own life; she got back together with the boyfriend of her youth, and they had two daughters, giving Lasungo two younger same-mother-but-not-same-father sisters. But the girls' father did not farm with them. Zele supported her children herself by growing rice and brewing a large kettle of spicy corn beer every week, the best in the village, people said. If Zele wasn't planting or weeding, she was hauling firewood on her head because the beer simmered for days over an open fire in an enormous, round-bottomed metal pot. After she added handfuls of hot peppers pounded into powder, the spicy steam rising from the pot stung your eyes.

Every Friday morning, Zele's courtyard filled with an assortment of customers—a tiny old woman who carefully unknotted her faded wrap skirt and took out a coin, enough for one gourd bowlful of the unfiltered ochre-colored beer; children carrying well-worn and well-scrubbed plastic containers, sent over by families who could afford to buy takeout beer to drink at home; the drunks and ne'er-do-wells who arrived at midmorning and settled on her benches for a day of gossip and drinking. This was the world Lasungo grew up in.

When he was about eight, his older brother Fonigay came back, but he was not the hard-working young man Lasungo had heard about. He acted strangely and even threatened and attacked people, especially elder men to whom he should show respect. "Sometimes people who are crazy know who made them that way," Lasungo offered as explanation. He was referring to the generational conflicts between young men like Fonigay and their fathers and uncles, who wanted the young men to stay home and work in their fields. But the young men were drawn to the South, where incomes were six times higher, and they sneaked away at dawn without asking permission. Feeling betrayed, the elders made medicines to keep the young men from leaving and to punish those who did; these powerful curses are what made his brother go crazy, Lasungo said.

Unable to control his behavior, the men of the family fastened Fonigay's ankles into a pair of old iron manacles made by the blacksmiths in the days of slavery. Yoked like this, he could not stand upright and had to crawl across the yard to his mother's house to get his meals. If she tried to hand food to him, he slapped her, so Zele set his bowl down a safe distance away. For two long, torturous years, he lived like that and then he died.

The spirits told Zele they wanted Lasungo to play *balafon*, and although he didn't want to learn, the elders insisted, saying he must accept his destiny. His mother hired a teacher, and Lasungo says he learned in a week because the spirits helped him, although it normally takes at least six months. His younger half sister says he played so well because a female spirit came and attached herself to him. The spirit wasn't alone. All the women flocked, dressed in their best outfits, to dance to his music, and when the others had gone home, one young Jula woman stayed. Although she was married, she and Lasungo became lovers, and she had a baby that everyone knew was his.

Lasungo's life seemed to be going well, but when he was alone, he had strange experiences, and sometimes he felt so angry and upset that he got into quarrels for no reason. He wanted to know why this was happening to him, so his mother asked the spirits. She received the reply that one spirit in particular wanted him to become a diviner, as she had promised the spirits when she was pregnant with him. Lasungo went to other diviners in the village, and after they rang their little brass bells, called the spirits, and threw out the cowries, they told him the same thing. But he did not want to give up farming and become a diviner.

Lasungo farmed by himself in a field provided by his mother's brothers. He planted cotton, corn, and rice. But strangely, although he was the champion farmer of the village, he never had a good harvest. This was a curious paradox, and people had three competing theories about how this could be. His half sister said it was because people were jealous of his strength and made supernatural medicines to keep him from working. Another school believed it was the Jula elders who have mystical powers who did this to punish him for his affair with the young married woman from their community. Islamic mystical practices often involve writing, and people say the elders wrote Lasungo's name and then took the paper and put it into water, burned it, or buried it, a ritual that caused him to lose his strength. A third theory is that he was simply too young to be in charge of his own farm. In someone else's field, with others to cheer him on and a competition to win, he was unbeatable, but alone, he lacked direction. Lasungo, although he cited the spirits as the causal force in most other events in his life, agreed with the third hypothesis.

Lasungo was in his late twenties when his strong-willed mother, Zele, died. When he consulted diviners about his future, each one gave him the same answer—that the spirits wanted him to fulfill his mother's promise and become a diviner himself, but he refused. After his mother's death, he passed his *balafon* on to a younger player and left for the closest town, Korhogo, where he landed a job at an open-air garage that repaired tires. But things didn't go well. Lasungo would be taking out the tube and the tube would split apart. He got into confrontations with the customers over trivial things. As if he was watching himself from above, he knew he was in the wrong, but he couldn't stop himself. When he went to a diviner for advice, the diviner said he was being pursued by one determined spirit. He knew it must be from his family's ancestral land, so he returned to the place where his family had set out stones for the spirits to sit on and made sacrifices. He suspected the spirits were jealous of his job repairing tires; they didn't want him to have any other work besides serving them, but he hoped the sacrifices would placate them and reassure them that on behalf of his family he would continue to respect them.

Nature spirits can help or harm humans, depending on their whims. Some are evil. They cause road accidents and then drink the victims' blood; the blood gives the spirits a long life. A spirit like that is always bad, while a good spirit is always good. The spirit that pursued Lasungo continued to interfere in his life, wreaking havoc at the tire repair shop and in his relationships with his friends and relatives. His particular spirit wasn't malicious, Lasungo insists. The spirit was simply pushing at him, nudging, trying to guide him onto the right path.

Finally, Lasungo went to the woodcarvers and commissioned a pair of statuettes, male and female. Every Senufo diviner has a couple like this, carved in the angular Senufo style, the woman slightly taller than the man, a subtle salute to the fertile, generative power of women. Lasungo took the wooden couple to his family fields and made sacrifices to the spirits, but he didn't start divining or declare publicly that he had become a diviner.

When Lasungo traveled to a distant village to attend a funeral, a man who owned a tractor and plowed fields for a fee took a liking to him and offered him a job. The idea of a fresh start in a new place was appealing and he accepted. But the tractor broke down frequently and his employer left for town to find parts, leaving Lasungo without money for food or the means to work. And even in this new village, he continued to find himself entangled in quarrels without understanding why. Finally Lasungo had had enough and he returned to Korhogo and moved in with an older friend named Yardjuma who had worked for us until Tom fired him. Desperate for an improvement in his fortunes, Lasungo gave in to the spirit pursuing him. On his family's land, he promised the spirits he would stay in Korhogo, where he would be close enough to properly attend to them. He vowed that from then on, he would listen to them, and in return, he asked them to give him better fortune. Perhaps he was also giving in to his mother's strong will, for this was the destiny she had laid out for him. Had she been alive, she might not have been enthusiastic about him living with Yardjuma, for wherever Yardjuma went, he spent his money on alcohol and good times and left behind a trail of debts and broken promises.

Nature spirits called *tugubele* are everywhere, Lasungo explains. He couldn't see them in their spirit form. No one can. They are invisible, but they can transform themselves into other forms and appear as humans, either African or white, or as animals. However, if one appeared to him in the form of a certain animal, it rarely reappeared the same way, so he never knew what to expect. If a spirit passed by as we were talking, he didn't see anything, but he felt its presence the way we feel a breeze on our skin.

When a Senufo person goes to a diviner, the client first pays the fee, laying the money down on an animal skin spread on the floor. Client and diviner sit on the floor facing each other, their legs extended, with the animal skin inside the diamond of their legs. The diviner throws out an assortment of cowrie shells and small brass figurines and studies how they fall. Diviners often hold one of their client's hands as they throw out the cowries, and with each throw, they tap the person's hand on their thigh, on the inside, then on the outside, but Lasungo didn't do this. He simply studied the arrangement of the cowries and other objects, often for long silent minutes, and from the way they fell, he could deduce if the issue was a lover, a farming problem, a journey the person wanted to take, or a question of health. As he examined the way the objects had fallen, the spirits put an idea into his head and that was how he knew what the person wanted to talk about. "Every person has problems. They come for help, but they don't explain or name their problems." His job was to figure out what had gone awry and the sacrifices needed to set things right. "The person who comes with his concerns and you can't figure out what it is . . . he won't say anything to you, but afterward, he will say, Oh this guy, he's no good, he knows nothing! Then you lose clients. But if the client is impressed, the word will spread in the neighborhood." Lasungo advised me that if I consulted a diviner and they did not bring up my concerns, I was not obligated to perform the recommended sacrifices. The diviner's fee, however, was not refundable.

In his dreams, the spirits informed him that someone was sick or would soon die. Sometimes the message wasn't clear, but afterward, when something happened, he told himself, That's what the spirits were trying to tell me but I didn't understand. Most of the time, he couldn't share what he learned. "You can't go to someone and tell them they are going to get sick or die." Sometimes in dreams, the spirits taught him how to make herbal medicines, showing him which plants to use for particular ailments and how to prepare them. Although to me he seemed self-taught, from his point of view, he had powerful spirit teachers who trained him in his specialty, protection during travel.

Every journey on the road is filled with danger—potholes that destroy your moped tires, bandits who jump out to rob you, and greedy gendarmes who set up barricades and demand a bribe to let you pass. Lasungo had learned from the spirits the proper recitations to say for protection. Before you set out, you recited what he taught you into your palm and then rubbed your palm over your face; protected in this way you would pass through the dangers of the road in safety.

Paying Attention

Ten years had passed since our first stay in Kalikaha. Tom had a grant to do a follow-up study, and so we packed up and went as a family for three months during the dry season, from January to the end of March 1992. Nick was a six-year-old first grader and Becca was almost four. It was a good time to visit—the year's harvest of corn and rice would already be stored in the granaries, so the farmers of Kalikaha would be in the village with time for us, and the desert wind called the harmattan would be blowing from the Sahel, bringing cool nights.

The big-city hustle and bustle of Abidjan entranced our children, who were growing up on a tree-lined street in a midwestern college town. At every large intersection, a parade of vendors waved or thrust through the windows an assortment of merchandise—ironing boards, television antennas, insulated pitchers, sets of plastic mugs decorated with teddy bears, gold-framed wall mirrors, checkerboards, standing fans, the latest Ninja Turtle video, calculators, watches, baby walkers. If you gave anything a second look, the vendor ran over and tried to strike a deal before the light turned green. At one red light, a vendor proffered a talking calculator with a little girl's voice. "Cinq fois deux égale dix." At the thought of our kids learning their multiplication tables in French, I was sorely tempted. "Park! Park!" shouted the vendor, but I drove away. One man held up two pairs of gray parrots in handmade wire cages. "Let's buy them and let them go at the beach," urged Nick. But when we circled around for a follow-up conversation, we realized some of their feathers had been pulled out and they couldn't fly.

One afternoon the children and I visited the tourist market, where I initiated them into the ultimate bargaining tactic, walking away. Nick loved meandering through the dark aisles, and he was especially drawn to the brass daggers in their hand-tooled leather sheaves. Becca admired the intricate wire toys—trucks, cars, mopeds, and minibuses called *gbakas,* made out of wire, bottle caps, tire tubes, and tin cans—but she found the vendors intimidating. When the young men got too pushy, thrusting things in our faces and pulling at our arms, I drew myself up, pretended to be shocked, and dressed them down in Julakan "Why are you acting so rudely? Didn't your parents raise you properly? Don't you have any respect?" My little drama had an instant effect and their employers, the old men in the booths, stepped in, chastised them, and sent them away. In Julakan the word I used to talk about respect was *mogoya,* literally "humanity" but also "way of life." If you are young in that culture, being a good person means being polite to people older than you. For adults, the right way to live in the world is more complex and refers to the ability to create a social network of responsibility, fellowship, and obligation and to remain connected to the people in it over time.

As we left the market and headed for the bakery down the street, we passed the bookstore, which was filled with a crowd of well-dressed men in suits and women in elaborately tailored African print ensembles. On the window, a poster advertised a book signing. The author was opposition leader Laurent Gbagbo, a former history professor and presidential candidate. A friend of ours had worked with Gbagbo and called him a jerk, but that didn't bother me because Gbagbo fitted my pedagogical agenda nicely. "This guy is trying to make his country more democratic," I explained to the kids. "He works for fair elections, and he has even gone to jail for standing up for what he believes in." Gbagbo sat at a desk signing copies, but we didn't go inside. I wasn't dressed for the occasion, I had two little kids in tow, and the promised *pain chocolats* were waiting at the bakery next door.

Every time we got into the old Peugeot we had rented, the kids bounced in the backseat like astronauts in a space capsule and chanted, "No seatbelts, no seatbelts!" I made them practice crash drills, sliding onto the floor at my command. The two-lane road north to Korhogo was the most dangerous road we had ever taken them on, and I prayed a foxhole prayer as we started the trip. It was a long day of difficult driving, and Nick kept a tally of wrecked vehicles. By the time we stopped for lunch in the city of Bouaké, he had counted thirty.

When we first lived in Ivory Coast, in 1981, twenty years after independence, more than sixty thousand French citizens worked there, twice as many as during the colonial period. They were civil servants, managers, and teachers. In

Korhogo the French expatriate community had a swim club, equestrian club, airfield and flight club, and private school. Boys hawked frog legs in the streets, an Ivorian butcher made paté, and the grocery store stocked wheels of brie, gruyere, and Roquefort.

So closely tied were France and some of its former colonies that their linked political-economic system was called Françafrique. Françafrique, like brunch and skort, is a portmanteau, a word created by combining parts of two other words, named for a type of suitcase that opens into two compartments. Françafrique encompassed a network of secret alliances between businessmen and political elites in Paris and those in African capitals, alliances that ensured France had cheap raw materials for its factories and bases for its military and that French companies had first rights to lucrative contracts in Africa. Under the unwritten rules of Françafrique, government policies arrived in African capitals by telephone from Paris. In Ivory Coast, France maintained a military base near the Abidjan airport, and French companies built the country's bridges and telecommunications networks. There are also stories of actual Françafrique suitcases, filled with money from Africa, passed along to finance the campaigns of French politicians. The hidden linkages of Françafrique benefited French businesses and politicians and French national interests, first, and African dictators and elites, second. The citizens of the independent African countries that made up half of the Françafrique suitcase had little say in their countries' policy decisions.

As the Ivorian economy declined and unemployment grew in the late 1980s, the Ivorian president, le Vieux, took civil service jobs away from French citizens and gave them to Ivorians at lower salaries, a move that simultaneously saved money, decreased unemployment, and enhanced national pride. When we returned in 1992, the French community of Korhogo was gone, most of the stores that catered to them had closed, and in the supermarket, the glass case that had held the big wheels of cheese was empty.

In his final novel, *Quand on refuse on dit non*, published posthumously in 2004, Ivorian novelist Ahmadou Kourouma, no admirer of le Vieux, explains a nefarious consequence of this "africanization":

> This africanization wasn't done at a discount on the intellectual level; the discount was in the salaries. The negro got four or five times less than the white he replaced.

> The negro was stuck in his post. It was impossible for him to support himself and his family. President Houphouët-Boigny was notified of the situation. And the president responded with amusing African proverbs: You don't look in the mouth of the one assigned to shell the peanuts. You shouldn't always be checking the mouth of the one in charge of smoking the agouti. . . . These proverbs meant that whatever work you do, you have to figure out how to help yourself on the sly. . . . These proverbs were well understood by Ivorians at every level. And so corruption was spread from minister to orderly. Everyone got busy seeking the rest of their salaries where they could. Abidjan slang flourished with a thousand juicy sayings . . . : make me; make; make a gesture; make the national gesture; wet my beard; cut my lips; close my mouth.

Thanks to the corruption Kourouma describes, we had the use of a substantial concrete-block house for our three-month stay in Kalikaha. The empty house belonged to the livestock extension agency, which had been closed after an audit uncovered embezzlement and mismanagement at the top. Unfortunately, Adama, our friend and translator, who had worked there for ten years, was out of a job. The extension agent's house in Kalikaha had two bedrooms, a metal roof, a dropped ceiling for coolness, and a concrete-block outhouse—in Kalikaha it qualified as a mansion—and its yard was fenced with barbed wire, another rare and desirable feature that would keep out wandering livestock. All the house needed was a serious cleaning because it had sat empty for a year and a half except for a hive of bees and an owl sharing the attic.

As soon as we pulled up, a group of young men arrived to welcome us and set to work with machetes clearing the weeds in the yard. When I looked up from unloading the car, Nick had acquired a machete and was working alongside them. My American motherbrain flashed: Machete. Danger! But my Kalikaha mindset followed with: Machete. Useful tool. Let kid learn to use it.

Living in Kalikaha as a mother made me realize how alert children are to what we pay attention to. Kids love attention and they're always studying the adults to see how they can get more. What surprised me was how quickly, seemingly by instant osmosis, our children realized the cultural agenda had changed. What mattered in Kalikaha was hard work, generosity, and respect for those older than you. A great deal of positive attention is showered on those who work hard. No one said this outright to our children; no one exhorted them to spend their days helping. They were six and almost four, ages at which village children are just starting to take on chores. The first day, once we had talked to the young men and unloaded our things, we got back in the car to go and greet the chief and the head of the *poro*. I was surprised when Nick asked to stay. He spoke no common language with the young men, but they saw nothing odd about a six-year-old taking up a machete nearly as tall as he was and clearing brush with it, nor anything unusual about a six-year-old who wanted to work with the adults. He was still weeding when we returned several hours later. It was the first time he heard the villagers praise him by saying, "He has really worked hard!"

We hired Nawa to help with household chores, and twice a day she carried several big basins of water from the pump to our house for bathing, drinking, and cooking. At fifteen, tall and lithe, with an angelic, infectious smile, she was enjoying her last carefree days as an unmarried young woman. Soon Becca was trotting on her short legs behind Nawa's long ones and returning with a little bowl of water on her head, trying not to spill it. It was farther than she had ever walked and the sun was hot. In the evening there was a long line at the pump, and they returned in the dark without a flashlight.

"Thank you!" the adults called out to Becca when she tipped her head and poured the water from her little metal bowl into our big pottery water jar.

Nawa and Becca pounding peanuts for sauce in Kalikaha, 1992

"Thank you for your work!" Becca kept her eyes on Nawa, waiting for Nawa's quiet words of praise, and when they came, she smiled proudly. Nick and Becca never opened the box of Legos they had packed. Why build toy structures when you could carry mud mortar to build a real house or weed an old woman's garden and receive genuine appreciation? If she wasn't helping Nawa pound peanuts into sauce, winnow rice, or wash dishes, Becca did pretend work, building stick fires and cooking dirt meals for her teddy bear, which Nawa tied to her back with a scrap of cloth.

In the United States, we pay attention to those who receive—money, honors, publicity, diplomas. Children get a lot of attention on their birthdays when they receive gifts and so they dream of being the birthday child every day of the year. But in Kalikaha, the powerful person, the person who gets the glory, is the giver. Overnight, our kids became more generous than they had been in all their short lives. "Can I give some of this to Salifou? Do we have another bowl of food for Adama? Is it okay to give away one of my slingshots? Can we share the candy we bought in town?" Part of this sudden generosity came from the realization that we had a great deal and these new friends had very little. Partly it came in response to the generosity of their new friends themselves, who although they owned only two sets of clothes and no toys, often turned up to offer something to Nick and Becca: a little bird they had captured in the grass for a pet, a y-shaped fork of wood to make a slingshot, the offer of a ride in an oxcart or on the wobbling handlebars of a too-large bicycle, a bowl of millet porridge, a few eggs from their mother's chickens.

Nick and Becca saw the pleasure their gifts gave to the children who received them—the looks of wonder on tasting chocolate, how a T-shirt was put on and not taken off again for days, the way a strip of rubber from town was made into a slingshot that was carried everywhere. This alone would have motivated them. But an even stronger impetus was the warm approval adults showered over them each time they gave a gift. Even the most important adult conversation was interrupted for a moment, and each person thanked them and gave them a blessing: "May God give you something greater than what you have given." On afternoons when they had no chores, Nick's new friends went on slingshot hunts for lizards or brought down bats sleeping in trees and made bat kebabs, which they roasted and ate for a snack. Since I was willing to provide salt and hot pepper, the boys came back to have their cookout at our house and shared their treat with Becca, who pronounced the kebabs good.

The boys also hunted birds, and when they brought them down wounded but alive, they brought them to Nick and Becca as pets. We turned a large cardboard box into an avian infirmary and had a survival rate of about 50 percent. When they flew away free, Nick was glad, but Becca was sad to see her little friends leave. In the evenings Nawa and I peeled the brown woody bark from yams and made yam fries for Nick and Becca to eat dipped in ketchup we brought from town.

Ten years earlier, I had filled a shelf of bound books about our stay, recording every event and conversation. But my notebook from this trip has mostly blank pages; I had no time to write. Other pages are decorated with child-drawn doodles and games of hangman and tic-tac-toe. I had met with Nick's teacher and our luggage included first-grade workbooks and daily lessons to complete with him, but our stay in Kalikaha was so engrossing and exhausting that most of the time I just read aloud to the two of them from the books I had brought along. We trekked through Middle Earth with Bilbo Baggins and westward in a covered wagon with Laura Ingalls Wilder. Reading by lantern light and plowing with oxen—these activities weren't difficult to imagine because they were happening all around us. Just like in Kalikaha, pioneer life centered around hard work. Later, I would write about stereotypes of American Indians and learn to see these books from the perspective of Native educators. But that larger view of our American past was in my future. When I read these books to my children in West Africa, they seemed to be the quintessential American memoir, one family's restless quest to make a home on the land. In Kalikaha some of our neighbors' children also left home to seek a better living. In 1960, at independence, fewer than 18 percent of Ivorians lived in towns or cities, but Abidjan was doubling every six years, and by 1992, nearly 40 percent of Ivorians lived in urban areas. Laura's pioneer family fled urbanization; my Ivorian neighbors' children were drawn by the opportunities the city offered and disappeared into urban neighborhoods.

Shortly after our arrival, change came to Kalikaha. Two yellow bulldozers cleared a wide dirt road through the center of town. Everything in the way—houses, granaries, old mango trees—was razed. Kalikaha was slated for rural electrification, but first its streets had to be platted into a grid pattern. The old paths wound through courtyards and neighborhoods, but any family that wanted electricity had to buy a lot on the new right-angled streets. Entire neighborhoods, each composed of a single lineage, relocated together. New houses had to be put up quickly, so instead of the familiar architectural plan of separate houses, round for women, rectangular for men, most families built one long, narrow house with a single row of rooms, like a motel. There were rooms for the men, their wives, elderly relatives, and for storage; each room had a wooden door that opened to the outside. Those who could afford it bought corrugated metal for the roofs; everyone else gathered sheaves of thatch.

Nawa and her relatives lived outside the village proper in a circle of houses on a rise next to a grove of mango trees. There was always a breeze out there, and dense shade under the mango trees, but they were moving to a bare and dusty new neighborhood next to the road. "We can't live out here alone, without the young people," the women told me, on one of our last afternoons in the old place. "And the young people want electric lights and boom boxes." Only Nawa's grandfather refused to budge. A tall, thin man, he wove at his loom in the mornings and napped in the afternoons on a lounge chair made of sticks. For the rest of his life, he remained in his small sturdy concrete house next to the mango grove.

Nick and I helped our *jatigi* Donni build a new house. As the walls rose, Donni stood on a scaffold and Nick and I scooped up handfuls of mortar and threw the mud balls up to him. His oldest son, a young teenager, transported the dried earthen bricks in an ox cart, and Becca played in the middle of the construction site baking mud muffins. Even we joined the construction frenzy and bought a double lot across the wide new dirt road from Donni. Our architectural style was female, nostalgic, and American influenced: we built a mud-brick round house with a conical thatched roof supported by a central pole. Over the mud bricks, the masons spread a thin layer of cement to make the walls more durable. We opted for the more expensive five-year thatched roof rather than the three year and insisted on two large windows, which we ordered at a woodworking shop in Korhogo and covered with screen cloth. Village houses had one tiny window with a solid wooden shutter that latched at the bottom. Our neighbors warned us that our big windows were a bad idea: we would be vulnerable to sorcerers at night and they would leak in the rainy season. But we were determined to have a house with a breeze. Of course our neighbors turned out to be right, at least about the rain. The windows did leak, causing cracks in our mud walls.

Our new next-door neighbor was Dinaba, who we had known since he was a boy. When we first lived in Kalikaha, he often came in our house and sat on our bench, watching everything we did without saying a word, so we nicknamed him the Benchsitter. We preferred his little brother, who attended school and spoke a little French. When we ran out of kerosene or matches at night, we sent the little brother to buy more; he delivered messages for us, did his homework by our kerosene lantern, and often fell asleep on our front porch. His older brother, Dinaba, would appear, cuff him a few times, and drag him off to bed. I thought Dinaba a bit of a lout.

Ten years later, Dinaba had grown up into a sturdy farmer and was married with a toddler son of his own. This was one of the great pleasures of returning to Kalikaha, to see our neighbors' children grown up and assuming adult roles. What kind of people were they turning out to be? As I came to know Dinaba as a young man, I realized I had underestimated him. Dinaba wasn't stupid; he was shy. Nick and Dinaba had no language in common and didn't need one. If Dinaba had corn to husk or thatch to weave into mats for a roof repair, he walked over, and without exchanging a word, the two of them reached an agreement, and Nick followed Dinaba home. Their special relationship lasted through many years of visits and I came to trust Dinaba completely. Nick often spent the day in Dinaba's fields, which were a long way from the village and seemed to have an unusually large number of poisonous snakes. Somehow I felt sure that if there were any possible way to bring Nick home safe, Dinaba would do it.

One day Nick heard us talking about an old man who was ill and coughed constantly. We were concerned he might have tuberculosis, but the old man told us he was worn out because sorcerers used him as a horse, riding him all night long. "Why can't we just sit beside him for one night and watch to find out if any sorcerers come?" Nick asked. Like the village boys, he wore his slingshot around his neck at all times and he offered to take it with him to the old man's house and, if the sorcerers showed up, to chase them away with pebbles. I appreciated his pragmatic approach and his bravery. If only our questions about the spirit world, which permeated the everyday world of Kalikaha and affected everything that happened there, could be settled by a night vigil with a slingshot. But I didn't okay Nick's plan; our neighbors' relationship with the spirit world was complicated and I tried to keep my distance. A web of beliefs, fears, and suspicions underlay their world, and in response, a cottage industry that anthropologists call the "occult economy" marketed protections and treatments. In the past, when I wrote about Kalikaha, I downplayed sorcery out of fear that non-African readers would find my Ivorian neighbors backward and superstitious. But in the intervening years, I have come to feel that my avoidance of the supernatural painted a partial picture of Kalikaha and Ivorian life and sabotaged my goal to depict my neighbors in all their complexity. We speak positively about mysticism in other contexts; I feel it's important to acknowledge its role in daily life in Ivory Coast. The spirit world explains illness, failure, and death and helps people cope with the fragility of life, something we in the United States try not to acknowledge. Ivorian life expectancy averages fifty-seven years. Children are particularly vulnerable to disease, and nearly 10 percent do not live to the age of five. In poor rural communities, the percentage of children who do not live to fifteen is much higher; in Kalikaha it is close to a third.

This is a reality the parents of Kalikaha comprehend only too well, and once I had children, I came closer to understanding the need the spirit world fulfilled, for once my children were in it, the world became a much more dangerous place. To manage our fear, my neighbors had their protective amulets and I had mine. Theirs were made of beads, leather, or cowries, often tied around their children's wrists or waists; they also bought protective creams from healers and rubbed them on their children's skin to prevent disease. I too had purchased and brought with me tubes of cream to rub on Nick and Becca's skin to prevent disease. I also had, thanks to the luck of where I was born, vaccinations, malaria prevention drugs, antibiotics, and bike helmets.

The parents of Kalikaha try hard to satisfy the spirits' demands, consulting diviners for advice, then making the necessary sacrifices and buying the recommended amulets. The more money you have, the more supernatural precautions you can afford. Parents in the United States do the same thing: those who can afford them purchase organic food, better health insurance plans, and houses in areas where the air and water are cleaner and the streets are safer. But rarely do the parents in either place come together to make society safer for all children.

By 1992 Tom and I knew, from published studies, that the rate of HIV infection was extremely high among sex workers in Abidjan. I thought Kalikaha, which wasn't even on the main dirt road, was remote from the contagion, but one day Adama and I happened to be sitting outside our house when a young man strode by with a door on his back. Adama, who was always curious, asked where he was going with it.

A traveling prostitute had arrived in the village for a week, he explained, and needed a *jatigi*. He had offered her the empty house next to his, but the house had no door, so he was installing one. I knew what I was doing went against every cultural norm in Kalikaha and usually I tried to respect these, but I felt I had to say something. In an attempt to make my words less awkward, I didn't speak directly to him. "Adama, there is something our little brother should know. Many of the prostitutes have a disease now and anyone who sleeps with them will catch it and they will get sick and die." With the heavy slab of wood balanced across his back, the young man listened politely. Then he went on his way.

Kalikaha finally had its own small clinic, staffed by a nurse, who often came over to chat with us in the evenings. That evening I asked him what he was doing to educate the villagers about AIDS. Had he convened the elders and warned them that sleeping with the itinerant prostitutes was extremely risky? "I could never do that," the nurse said quietly. "It would be very rude for me, a young man, not even from this village, to talk to the elders about something like that."

The conversation gnawed at me, and if the subject came up, I warned men I knew. These women carried a disease and should be avoided. They would get it, their wives would catch it from them, their children would be orphaned. As I spoke, I was aware how much like the villagers I sounded. An invisible disease that you caught by sleeping with someone—it sounded like sorcery, exactly like the curses men bought from diviners to place on their wives so that any man who slept with them would become impotent or suffer a strange illness and eventually die. Years later, when the young man was thin and weak and his two wives had died, the image of him carrying the door across his strong young shoulders would haunt me. After antiretrovirals arrived in northern Ivory Coast, he regained his strength and remarried a woman from town. He told me he had suffered from a severe case of parasites.

Saturday was market day in Kalikaha, and every Saturday morning we gave Nick and Becca each five hundred CFA francs, about a dollar. Becca came home with a leather amulet to wear or a tiny bottle of nail polish to share with Nawa. Nick bought fried fish and *attieké*, fermented cassava pounded into grains, to share with his crew of boys, but he ignored the trinkets and saved most of his allowance. What he wanted to do with his savings, he announced, was buy thatch—a big pile of it, and on our last night, he wanted to set the thatch on fire. Everyone around us was building houses and I wasn't sure we should let our son burn up roofing material for the fun of it. But Dinaba was on board with the plan, so Nick handed over his savings, and a few days later, Dinaba unloaded an enormous pile of thatch in our yard. Nick and Dinaba cleared the ground of dried weeds and they piled the thatch up in a tent shape twice as tall as Nick. The last night, after dinner, the moment came, and Dinaba told Nick to ask us for the matches. The flames whooshed up as if they were alive and would fly away into the sky, and we watched, rapt, as the fire burned away to glowing ashes and then to cinders. Nick was sooty and smudged with black, but he and Dinaba were both grinning, and we all felt a sense of satisfaction. The fire had given a ceremonial ending to our stay.

Our days in the North had been peaceful, but disturbing news arrived from Abidjan via our shortwave radio. Students had played a key part in the rising opposition to le Vieux and his government, and because of their political activity, the army had attacked a student dormitory the previous May. An investigation into the attack had been ordered, and the report detailed rapes, beatings, and arbitrary arrests. The opposition called for someone in the army to be disciplined, but President Houphouët-Boigny made it clear he wasn't going to punish anyone, and the officer in charge was promoted to general. In protest, opposition leaders organized a nonviolent demonstration in Abidjan. Twenty thousand people turned out to march peacefully, but one small group armed with clubs and rocks smashed windows and burned cars, and the government security forces responded with tear gas and brutal beatings. More than one hundred opposition and student leaders were arrested, although there was no evidence to link them to the violence. Laurent Gbagbo was sentenced to two years in prison but was released after two months. Seventy-seven other demonstrators remained in prison and the following July, Amnesty International named them "prisoners of conscience" and called for their release. In principle, Ivory Coast had become a multiparty democracy with a free press, but in practice, le Vieux and his party still controlled the government, including the judicial system.

At the end of our stay, we drove south toward Abidjan, stopping in the town of Yamoussoukro. Yamoussoukro was le Vieux's birthplace, and in 1983 he declared it the political capital. That day, as usual, the wide streets of Yamoussoukro were deserted. I remembered a story Adama, who loved a good story and told them well, had recounted to us. In 1978 Adama had been hired for $2 to go to Yamoussoukro to welcome the French president Valéry Giscard d'Estaing when he landed in a supersonic jet for an official visit. Adama was one of sixty people sitting on benches in the back of a truck, and his truck was one of ten that had left from Korhogo. As they rode along, they imagined how this important guest would be welcomed and what they would see as they stood in the crowd at the ceremony.

In Yamoussoukro, they climbed down and waited. Eventually a helicopter circled overhead and they were told the French president was inside. As soon as the helicopter disappeared, they were ordered to climb back into the trucks for the return journey. The helicopter didn't even land, Adama told us indignantly. We could only conclude that le Vieux wanted his hometown and future capital to look like the kind of lively, populous place where six hundred people would come out to watch a helicopter fly over.

Since our last visit, le Vieux had built a monument in Yamoussoukro that outshone all the others—the largest church in the world, a Catholic basilica called Our Lady of Peace. We know Rome wasn't built in a day—it took over a century just to build St. Peter's—but le Vieux's basilica, resembling St. Peter's but slightly larger, was built in three years between 1986 and 1989. This feat was only possible because the artisans and laborers worked seven days a week. Le Vieux claimed he paid for the basilica with his personal fortune and although he refused to disclose the exact amount, he mentioned a figure of $130 million and insisted that meager sum wasn't enough to do any real good to get his country out of its financial crisis. Observers estimated the basilica's cost at well over twice that. To detractors who pointed out that only 15 percent of the population was Christian and that the country could not pay its international debts, the information minister retorted that the critics were racists who did not think Africans deserved anything big, beautiful, and lasting. Ivorians said le Vieux built the church to have an opulent setting for his own funeral and nicknamed it Our Lady of the Treasury. After some hesitation, Pope John Paul II consecrated the basilica in 1990, after le Vieux agreed to build a charity hospital on the grounds and to leave the cross off the dome, keeping the height just under that of St. Peter's. But once the pope had come and gone, an enormous gold cross was installed on top.

When we arrived on a Sunday afternoon two years later, the place was deserted except for a bottled drink vendor and some boys selling booklets about the pope's visit. As we hiked through the enormous fluted columns and crossed the marble esplanade, I felt like a mouse trekking across a ballroom floor.

"I will explain everything to you, and at the end, whatever has not been explained, you may ask," proposed our guide, who looked Lilliputian standing in the doorway. We accepted, and he took us up the aisle and showed us the two air-conditioning vents in the back of each pew, one pointing out, the other up. Only the lowest fifteen feet of air was cooled, he explained, although most days the air-conditioning was turned off. Had it been on, curtains of cool air would have flowed upward at the open doorways. The church could seat at least six thousand worshippers, although if some stood in the aisles, eleven thousand could squeeze in, and the seven-acre marble esplanade out front could hold three hundred thousand. The pews had been filled only once, when the pope came for the consecration. We admired the bank of gleaming organ pipes, the way the elevators were hidden inside the massive columns, and the luminous stained glass windows with their explosion of crisp modern shapes and brilliant colors. "Four times more stained glass than the cathedral of Chartres," our guide informed us, "and four thousand different colors." One window showed Jesus entering Jerusalem on a donkey, and kneeling beside the road, our guide pointed out the artist who created the windows, the architect, and the pious patron, le Vieux himself, President Félix Houphouët-Boigny.

In an elevator we rose to the second level, the height of a thirteenth floor. Pink and blue sunbeams sparkled on the floor from a dome of stained glass above us. In the center was a white dove in flight. On the polished marble floor, the kids found a dead bee and a dead butterfly; they must have flown in, mistaking the colored glass for flowers and the church for a garden.

As we stood outside on the high terrace, our guide said the time had come to ask our questions. Nick wanted to know how many people fell off and died building the basilica. The answer was three. Tom asked about the charity hospital, and pointing to an empty field, our guide assured us the hospital would soon be built there. It would stand next to the papal residence, kept ready at all times in case the pope wanted to spend the night in Yamoussoukro. It was time for us to leave, but Nick had one more question. "If the church is for peace, why do the guards have machine guns?" Our guide nodded thoughtfully before he answered. "That is because of the current unrest," he replied in a sober voice. "There is a concern that someone might come here and throw stones at the windows."

Yaya

The Most Stubborn

Yaya's family was the poorest of the seven households in Tom's original farm study, and each week we questioned every family member, children included, about the farm and household work they had done. Sometimes we visited their fields, riding our motorcycle along muddy trails, then crossing the river on foot over a bridge made of vines. "When you and Tom came to our fields," Yaya told me years later, "I put on a little show and pretended to work hard. But I wasn't really working much." He slapped his long thin leg, chuckled, and admitted that when he was supposed to be weeding, he snuck away to hunt lizards with his slingshot. An eleven-year-old boy who shirks his work knows he has a beating coming, and Yaya's father gave them out after the evening meal. As soon as the women placed the bowls of corn *toh* and sauce on the ground in front of his father, Yaya sat down next to him, scooped palmfuls of food into his mouth as quickly as he could, and bolted. "My father was old and I was fast!"

Yaya's father, Lonala, had two wives. The first was old and tiny like a shriveled little bird; she was the mother of Yaya's tall, broad-shouldered older brother Abou-lonala. Yaya's mother, Mariam, was middle-aged, fair-skinned and tall, with a husky voice and laugh. After the rainy season ended, Jula women like Mariam grew tobacco, which they dried and pounded into snuff to sell. When I passed Mariam's tobacco plot on my way home, she would be lowering a large gourd pierced with holes into a shallow well and swinging the gourd back and forth, so the water sprayed out in thin streams. Mariam was fond of chastising me, but her husky voice always held a half chuckle between syllables. "Night is falling. You should be home cooking for your husband! What if he gets home and there is no dinner for him?" she teased.

"Maybe Tom is already home and he is cooking dinner for me," I countered.

Yaya as a boy (photo by Tom Bassett)

"Greet him for me, and may Allah give him a long life," she said with her deep laugh.

When Yaya's father was young and forced labor was the official policy of the French colonial regime, he was sent to a logging camp in the tropical forest. The laborers attacked the enormous trees with hand-held saws, and once a tree went down, it took more than a hundred men pulling together on ropes to move the huge trunk out to the road. One crew did nothing but dig shallow graves and bury the men who died. In Kalikaha, a deceased person is carefully wrapped in layers of new fabric donated by friends and relatives, and forty years later, when he recounted his experiences, Lonala was still outraged at the way Ivorians were buried at the lumber camp. Your only shroud, he said sadly, was the dirty sheet you slept in.

The family was so poor that they often went without dinner. "We had nothing. Not even tools to farm with—no cart, no oxen," says Yaya's older brother, Abou-lonala. To help his family, Abou-lonala migrated south to work for a man from Kalikaha who had acquired ten hectares of forest land near the town of Daloa and was growing coffee and cocoa. Abou-lonala was paid $100 a year plus room and board. After several years, he thought about staying and trying to get some forest land of his own, like so many northerners were doing. The forest soil was rich, there were two rainy seasons a year rather than one, and you could support a family growing cocoa. But he knew his parents were getting too old for farm work and needed him at home, so he bought a bicycle, a radio, and new clothes, and returned to Kalikaha to give the rest of his earnings to his parents. That was in 1979, two years before we arrived. Abou-lonala never left again, but the experience gave him new ideas. Courage—that's what helps you get ahead, he told himself, and he decided the family would grow cotton, the cash crop of the North. The cotton company provided its growers with fertilizer on credit and farmers could divert a little of this valuable fertilizer to the fields where they planted corn and rice together. They could also get a plow, a cart, and a pair of oxen on credit, although this was risky because it was a big debt to take on.

They moved to new fields on the other side of the river where the soil wasn't worn out. There was no bridge yet, so for the five months of the farming season, Lonala and his sons slept in an open hut in the field. Yaya couldn't run back to the village to play with his friends; he didn't know how to swim. On Fridays, his father went to the mosque for the midday prayers, and so he slowly walked into the water. He patted one shoulder and told Yaya to hold on there. He patted the other shoulder and told Yaya's brother Sori to hold on there. Then he started swimming. As they crossed, Yaya laughed out loud; he felt just like a fish.

Only one cotton company, co-owned by the Ivorian and French governments, along with private investors, operated in the area, and after the harvest, Abou-lonala sold their cotton back to them. They weighed the cotton, subtracted the cost of the seeds, fertilizer, and pesticides, and kept back an additional sum to reimburse their debt. Abou-lonala had to trust the few literate farmers in his cooperative group that the figures on his receipt were correct. It took three years to pay off the oxen, the plow, and the cart.

When Yaya was fifteen, the cocoa farmer, assuming he would be a hard worker like his brother, offered him a job at the same salary, $100 a year plus room and board. To Yaya it seemed like a fortune, so he went to work on the same ten-hectare cocoa farm near Daloa. The first day the wooden handle of the machete rubbed his palms raw and his hands stung so fiercely he sat down under the trees and cried. But when he stopped crying, he understood something—hard work was a necessity; there was no way around it. This is what I have to do, he told himself. Once he made up his mind to work hard and his hands toughened up, he became the second-fastest worker on the farm.

Three years later, the farmer went into town and ran into one of Yaya's relatives. "Tell my younger brother Yaya his father has died and we are about to hold the funeral," the man told him.

"Ayyy!" exclaimed Yaya, when he heard. "My father has died and no one has told me?"

"Pack your things," said the cocoa farmer. When they got to town, he helped Yaya bargain for what he wanted, a pair of shoes and one of the bicycles so sturdy they were nicknamed "Americas." The farmer gave Yaya the remaining $200 and put him on the bus for Korhogo. From there, Yaya rode his new bicycle to Kalikaha for the funeral.

After three years as a hired farmhand, Yaya, who was eighteen, was glad to be home. The late 1980s were tough years, and their neighbors had very little cash to spend, but Yaya, riding his bicycle from village to village, managed to get a higher price for his mother's tobacco than his older brother ever had. "I was the most stubborn but also the best at buying and selling!" The Jula have long been traders, and finally he had a skill his elders valued. Referring to his relationship with his mother, he placed his two long index fingers next to each other and said, "We were like that."

Yaya had three loves: soccer, politics, and a girl named Djeneba. All three were forbidden. The Jula elders disapproved of soccer—all that running around for no reason—a young man could get hurt and then who would do the heavy work in the fields? They decreed that Muslims should not play soccer, but Yaya, tall, long legged, and fast, sneaked away to join the afternoon matches on the field next to the school.

He noticed Djeneba on a full moon night when the Jula teenagers formed one large circle and danced for hours. "I was playing drums, she was dancing. I liked her. But in our world, you don't choose, you are given." The drum Yaya played was made out of a metal barrel; he struck it with his hand on one side and a stick on the other. When his drum group was invited to play in surrounding villages at weddings and campaign rallies, he always accepted; it was another way to make a little cash. But as much as the money, what drew Yaya to the political rallies was the excitement, the crackling feeling that something big was about to happen. And it was. The presidential election of 1990 was coming up in October. For the first time the elections would be competitive because for the first time, there was more than one political party.

When the opposition party came to Kalikaha to campaign, Yaya's drum group played to welcome them. The man who dared to run against le Vieux was a round-faced professor named Laurent Gbagbo. "Support me," he urged, "because Houphouët is a thief! When you look around at the North, what do you see? The roads are bad and you aren't paid well for your cotton. If I win the election, we are going to buy the cotton at two thousand CFA per kilo!"

This was more than twenty times the current price, and Yaya enthusiastically joined the chanting: "Houphouët-Thief! Houphouët-Thief! Thief! Thief! Thief!" Why shouldn't a cotton farmer in the North be represented in Abidjan? Why shouldn't he have a say in who ran the government? Voting was one thing; everyone voted. Even immigrants from other West African nations could vote in presidential elections, but every candidate was from the Democratic Party of Ivory Coast and le Vieux always won by a landslide. For thirty years, Ivory Coast had been a one-party state, and even in remote Kalikaha, the party secretary was a powerful man. Yaya was impatient for change, and multiparty politics—this was an idea he liked. He wanted to know his vote counted. "Isn't that what elections are for?" he demanded. "Or what?"

His steady older brother worried that Yaya was going to get himself in trouble. It was true that le Vieux had allowed independent newspapers to spring up and opposition parties to organize, but how long would it last? What if le Vieux decided things had gone too far and cracked down, as he had done before? But Abou-lonala, who could not speak French or write his name, had no idea about changes in the world and how the ripples from those changes were reaching Africa, Ivory Coast, and even Kalikaha. The Berlin Wall had fallen, and in a significant speech in June 1990, French president François Mitterand gave Africa a clear warning that times had changed, and in future, France would make it a priority to distribute aid to and trade with those countries making democratic reforms and holding free and fair elections.

No one knew exactly how old le Vieux was, but officially he was eighty-five, running for what must surely be his last five-year term. Many Ivorians believed their president was imbued with mystical powers and would stay in the presidential armchair forever. But of course, inside his luxurious walled enclave, where it was rumored Chagall tapestries decorated the walls, le Vieux must have known his days were numbered. As the leader who successfully fought to end forced labor in the French colonies and the father of Ivorian independence, his legacy was secure. He had also been admired as the steward of the Ivorian economic miracle, until cocoa prices fell and the Ivorian economy slumped with them, and his attempt to stockpile the cocoa harvest and negotiate a higher price failed disastrously. Perhaps le Vieux wanted to add another positive line to his biography, perhaps he had no choice if he wanted to maintain the relationship with his country's former colonial master, France. Whatever his reasons, independent newspapers sprang up and opposition parties became legal.

The only candidate willing to run against le Vieux in 1990 was Gbagbo, a Bété from cocoa country. He was unknown in the North, but he garnered support there for opposing Houphouët-Boigny. Northerners were tired of the way the South and the center (home to Houphouët's own ethnic group, the Baule) had benefited from the years of prosperity but not them. Now that there was less money to distribute, the paved roads, schools, and clinics they saw in Baule country galled even more because there didn't seem to be any money left to build equivalents in the North. Gbagbo's ethnic group, which hailed from the tropical forest, were hunters rather than farmers and had a reputation for feistiness, for refusing to be put on, and Gbagbo certainly seemed to live up to the stereotype. Ivorians agreed that running against Houphouët took balls and Laurent Gbagbo had them.

In Kalikaha, Yaya was Gbagbo's most fervent supporter. He persuaded many of his relatives and neighbors to abandon the old single party and support Gbagbo's Popular Front, but no one was surprised when le Vieux won more than 80 percent of the vote. One afternoon after the election, Yaya's younger sister went to the well with her basin. A group of girls from the Koné family were there. Their family had stuck with Houphouët, and the girls surrounded Yaya's sister and taunted her. "If you want water, call Gbagbo to help you dig a well and get some! This well wasn't dug by Gbagbo. It was dug by Houphouët!" When she put her basin under the pipe and started to pump, one of the Koné girls pulled it away. Yaya's sister grabbed the girl and they scuffled. The Koné girl ran home and told her family that Yaya's sister beat her up over politics.

A group of her relatives came looking for revenge, armed with sticks and machetes. They found Yaya's sister and a younger cousin named Abou at home and gave the two a beating. At their cries, Yaya's family came running, carrying whatever they could grab. They chased the Konés off, but one of them, an old man, came out of the fracas with a broken arm, and the Konés went to town and filed a complaint with the police.

"The ones who are guilty should speak up and admit it," urged the police, but no one confessed, and there were no neutral witnesses. The police put four members of Yaya's family in jail. Questioned again, the Konés settled on Yaya as the culprit, and he was summoned to the police station in town. "Who broke the arm of the old man?" the policemen asked him.

"I don't know, I never saw the old man." Yaya was pretty sure that in the melee he had done it, but he wasn't about to admit it. Every evening the police let him leave the police station to sleep at the house of a man who had offered to be his *jatigi*. Every morning Yaya reported to the police station. "Was it you who broke the old man's arm?" the police asked, and day after day, Yaya denied it.

After a month, they put Yaya in jail and let the others go home, and a week later, they held his trial. The old man testified that Yaya had broken his arm, and he had two witnesses, men from his family who had been in the fight. The first swore it had been Yaya. The magistrate asked him what weapon Yaya had used and the witness said an iron rod. He left and the second witness came in. This witness also named Yaya as the culprit. Asked what Yaya committed the crime with, he said a stick. The court condemned Yaya to three years in prison.

The local head of Gbagbo's Popular Front Party, a member of a prominent Korhogo family, had come to court as Yaya's lawyer. "But these two witnesses contradict each other," he pointed out. "One says the weapon was iron, the other says wood!" In response to this defense from an influential person, the judge shortened Yaya's sentence to two months. After Yaya had spent a week in jail, Abou-lonala came and offered the warden $50.

"Are you going to run off?" the warden asked Yaya.

"No, I am not going anywhere."

The warden agreed to let Yaya out during the day, but he had to be back by eight o'clock to sleep in the jail. When the two months were up, Yaya went home.

In French, a *palabre* is a discussion, usually a long protracted one, and is related to our word "palaver." *Palabre* can have a positive connotation and refer to a real sit-down to listen to others and reach consensus, but in Ivorian French, a *palabre* is just the opposite—it means a dispute, a fight. And after he returned home from serving his two months, Yaya kept getting into *palabres*. "You need to leave the village," his mother told him. "These *palabres* of yours are no good. Go, I give you the road."

But Yaya didn't want to leave home again. He and Djeneba were seeing each other on the sly, and Yaya decided to flout custom—to call on Djeneba's family and ask straight out to marry their daughter. His mother was horrified. "You can't do that! You can't speak to the elders that way!" Yaya went anyway, with his older brother, Abou-lonala, as his intermediary. Djeneba's family heard them out politely, but the elders said they couldn't possibly agree because Djeneba was promised to another family.

Former presidential candidate Laurent Gbagbo toured the North again, and when he arrived in Kalikaha, Yaya's drum group again played to welcome the entourage. "We have to keep on!" Gbagbo told the crowd. "We can't give up! Houphouët stole the election but we will keep fighting, so continue to support me!" After his speech, he asked, "The young man who went to prison because of me, where is he?"

Yaya, sitting outside, heard people calling him. Inspired by a poster of the Ivorian reggae musician Alpha Blondy, he had bought himself a pair of curved sunglasses and was feeling cool as he greeted his hero. "Are you the young man who went to prison for me?" Gbagbo asked. Yaya said he was. "Listen," Gbagbo said. "Let me give you some advice. When someone important calls you and you are wearing dark glasses, you should take them off. Otherwise they will think you are disrespecting them, that you are some sort of bad guy." Yaya took off his sunglasses. "Now let me give you some more advice. Keep your courage but calm yourself down. Everything will work out eventually. There is no need to get into fistfights." After that, Yaya was even more enthusiastic about Gbagbo and he got himself a membership card for Gbagbo's party, the Popular Front.

When it became obvious that Djeneba was pregnant, his mother said, "Yaya, I give you the road. Run away now! Her family is going to kill you!" But Yaya stayed. His mother scolded him loudly, but he sensed this was mostly a dramatic performance she was putting on for the neighbors. She couldn't condone his behavior openly, but he knew she liked Djeneba and wanted him to be happy. After the baby was born, a girl they named Khadi, Djeneba's milk didn't come in. A man explained to Yaya that babies couldn't drink cows' milk, only milk made from an expensive powder you bought in town. Yaya set off on his bicycle to find some. Djeneba's mother had died giving birth to her and her father was a truck driver in the city, but she had plenty of female relatives determined to keep Yaya away, so his sister delivered the powdered formula and a bottle. "Our families were not happy with us, so who was going to go and buy milk? No one!" Yaya told me. The formula kept the baby girl alive until Djeneba's milk came in.

Almost every day, his mother said in her husky voice, "Yaya, you have to leave this place. You have gotten into too much trouble here. I give you the road." But Yaya had left Kalikaha once and he knew life in the world beyond was not easy for someone who didn't speak French. He didn't want to leave home again. Yet he knew he had disgraced his family's name and upset his mother by getting Djeneba pregnant and, worse, for going to jail for fighting. He had saved about $40 from drumming, so he asked for the road and bought a bus ticket to Bouaké, the second-largest city, half a day's bus ride south. He stepped off in a new urban world and went to work for a man he knew who sold groceries from a stall near the market. Djeneba's father, a truck driver, worked out of Bouaké, and once he had earned a little money, Yaya went to see him. Away from the village and the family elders, Yaya hoped he might have more of a chance, but her father explained that he had promised her to someone else and couldn't go back on the agreement. Of course, he wasn't sure if the other family still wanted Djeneba, now that she had a baby girl that everyone knew was Yaya's.

Back in Kalikaha, Yaya's older half brother, Abou-lonala, continued to call on the elders of Djeneba's family. "Listen," he told them each time, "I am very sorry and I ask your forgiveness for all the trouble my brother has caused, but these two, Yaya and Djeneba, they are going to be together no matter what we say. The best thing is to let them marry."

The answer was always, "No, no, absolutely no."

After six months, Yaya had to admit to himself that things weren't working out in Bouaké and that he and the grocer didn't get along, so when he was offered a job on a rubber plantation farther south, he took it. He and the other workers planting rubber trees had to bring their own rice to cook for lunch and there was no well; to quench their thirst they dug a hole, scooped up the slurry, filtered out the sand and dirt, and boiled the water to make tea. After two days, Yaya was fed up and bought a bus ticket to Abidjan.

When he got off at the frenetic main bus station with his small sack of possessions, he had no idea where to go. He didn't speak French, and he knew only one person in the enormous teeming city, his cousin Moussa. He thought Moussa worked in a part of the city called Plateau, but he had no idea how to find him. People bustled in all directions trying to find the right bus, the drivers' young assistants called out destinations loudly, and vendors carried basins on their heads piled with plastic bags of water or peanuts or with bananas, oranges, or flip-flops. "Ji! Ji!" the water vendor girls called out in Julakan. "L'eau, l'eau!" they repeated in French. Men pushed wooden handcarts filled with merchandise and loaded and unloaded sacks of goods from the tops of the buses.

Then Yaya had a stroke of luck. In that seething crowd of strangers, a man walked by that he recognized, a man from Kalikaha. Yaya called out to him and told him he had just stepped off the bus.

"Where do you want to go?"

"I want to find my older brother Moussa, the son of my mother's sister. He works in Plateau."

"Moussa lives in Koumassi," the man told him. "I know the place and I will take you there. But first, I'm hungry, so come with me while we eat something."

This was a polite way of offering Yaya a meal so he would not arrive hungry. They sat down at a small stand and ate bowls of rice and sauce and then the man shepherded Yaya all the way across Abidjan, past the skyscraper-dotted downtown, Plateau, and across the bridge to Koumassi, a sprawling, densely populated neighborhood on the southern side of the lagoon.

Moussa and his wife were living in a dark two-room house in a neighborhood of dirt paths and small wooden shacks on the bank of the lagoon. Moussa had a good job, but it wasn't downtown in Plateau, as Yaya thought. He worked in a small hotel in an upscale residential neighborhood. Moussa is only a few years older than Yaya, but except for the flicker of affectionate teasing that passes between them, it is hard to tell they are first cousins. Yaya is tall, Moussa is short; Yaya has a long thin face, Moussa's is round. Yaya's long body is packed with compressed energy while Moussa gives off an air of genial patience.

"When he arrived, did Yaya ask if he could stay with you?" I asked Moussa once.

"This is Africa!" Moussa replied with a laugh and a shrug. "You don't ask—you just stay!" So Moussa, his slightly older cousin, became Yaya's *jatigi* in Abidjan. He took Yaya to a mill that ground corn into flour, and the miller took Yaya on, offering him $20 a month, plus lunch. When the man gave him a $3 advance, Yaya sent it with someone going home, to give to his mother.

A few months after Yaya arrived in Abidjan, President Houphoüet-Boigny died. Yaya didn't feel sad—he wanted change, and he was just where he wanted to be when it happened, in Abidjan at the center of the action. He was disillusioned with Gbagbo, his old hero. Gbagbo was too ready to go along with exclusionary tactics when they benefited him and his party. So when someone told Yaya there was going to be a meeting in his neighborhood to form a new party that would represent northerners, Yaya went. The leaders didn't give their speeches in French or Julakan; they spoke in the Senufo language, Senari, a language only northerners understood. They were going to create a new party because it wasn't right that northerners couldn't be part of Ivorian politics. Listening, Yaya felt happy. Why shouldn't a northerner be president? he thought. As soon as the new party was official, he signed up and got a membership card. The party was named the Rally of Republicans, and its leader in absentia was Alassane Dramane Ouattara.

Alassane Ouattara was Jula like Yaya, although he seemed to live on another planet where everyone was educated and had plenty of money. But Ouattara was being disqualified from running for office because he was a northerner, and Yaya could identify with that. Yaya was often treated badly in Abidjan because he was a northerner, and this made Ouattara his candidate. Whenever the Rally of Republicans sent out the word to come to a meeting or a demonstration, Yaya didn't hesitate. He went.

The End of an Era

Many Ivorians believed President Houphouët-Boigny would remain in the presidential armchair forever. He not only had the most powerful African supernatural medicines; he also had a European "battery" that had been inserted at a health spa in Switzerland and was recharged on his frequent visits. At least that's what some people told me. But le Vieux was suffering from prostate cancer, and in May 1993 he flew to France to have surgery. He never recovered and in November he was flown back to Yamoussoukro to die at home. We don't know precisely when le Vieux was born or died or where he is buried. According to rumors, as he lay on his deathbed in the halls of his walled enclave, his two potential successors, Henri Konan Bédié, president of the national assembly, and Alassane Ouattara, the prime minister, sparred, while advisors circled anxiously, trying to broker a peaceful transition. On December 7, 1993, the death of President Houphouët-Boigny was officially announced and the country plunged into mourning. Le Vieux had become an ancestor, the chief of all Ivorian ancestors.

His passing ended an era. The country lost more than its president, more than a founding father; it lost its government, its patriarch, its compass. No future Ivorian president would have his stature, and without him, it was harder for Ivorians to see themselves as one Ivorian family. Yet despite his age, health, and political sagacity, he had left his most important task unresolved: his political succession. Who would take le Vieux's place for the two remaining years of his term? The constitution had recently been amended to say that if the president died in office, the president of the national assembly should succeed him until special elections could be held, but thanks to another recently passed law, Prime Minister Alassane Ouattara had legally been serving as head of state in the president's "absence." This left just enough ambiguity for Ouattara to challenge Bédié's succession. Bédié, like le Vieux, was Baule, and since the Baule dominated the old single party and the government, Bédié made a suitable crown prince. Ouattara was an American-educated economist who had instituted two unpopular polices for le Vieux—the World Bank's stringent belt-tightening called structural adjustment and resident cards that immigrants were required to purchase. He was viewed as an effective administrator, but since he was Jula from the North, his cultural and geographic origins were less suitable in the eyes of the party elite.

Bédié won the battle and sank into the armchair for the remainder of le Vieux's term, which would end in 1995. Ouattara accepted a post abroad with the International Monetary Fund. The struggle had taken place within the old ruling party, which, for the first time, split into factions. Le Vieux's absence left a dangerous black hole, a swirling vacuum of potential chaos and instability.

One month after le Vieux's death, even before his state funeral in the grandiose basilica, the French government took the step the old president had managed to stave off for years. The value of the West African currency, the CFA franc, used by multiple West African countries, had always been pegged to the French franc at a rate of fifty to one. With le Vieux gone, the French government devalued the CFA. One day it had its old value, fifty CFA francs to one French franc; the next day it took one hundred CFA francs to make a French franc. As if the rope supporting the climber below had been sawed halfway through, Ivory Coast's economy dangled by a fragile thread. Imports like fertilizer, pesticides, and gasoline became twice as expensive, and for city dwellers, it was suddenly even more difficult to make ends meet. Cotton and cocoa were traded on the world market in dollars, which meant that the public-private companies that sold them actually received higher prices in CFA francs for their exports after the devaluation. But these extra CFA francs did not make their way back down the economic chain to the farmers. The standard of living of ordinary people declined even further. Bédié, a weak and corrupt president, did little to solve the economic crisis while he prepared his campaign for the election in 1995. His campaign strategy was to change the constitution to disqualify his old rival, Alassane Ouattara.

Ivoirité

Being Truly Ivorian

From 1990 to 1993, Ivory Coast was a political contradiction—a multiparty democracy controlled by an authoritarian leader. When le Vieux died, he left behind a nation with legal political parties and a fledgling free press, but none of the other institutions a democracy requires—no independent judiciary, no strong legislative branch to oversee the executive, no civil society organizations to act as watchdogs. Many Ivorians felt orphaned and grieved; others, like Yaya, welcomed the opportunity to choose a new leader by casting a ballot in the election set for September 1995.

In the post-Houphouët era, as the country tried to steady itself on wobbly new legs, two questions were threaded through every discussion and were the unwritten subtext of every newspaper article. Who should be an Ivorian citizen with the right to vote and run for office? Who should be able to own land? (And, as the devil is always in the details, *which* Ivorians should be able to own *which* Ivorian land?)

Le Vieux had solved his country's labor problems by encouraging immigration, and one-fourth of the population was made up of immigrants, many of whom had resident cards and voted legally in presidential elections under le Vieux's unusually welcoming rules. The largest number of immigrants were Burkinabé from Burkina Faso, followed by Malians and Guineans, but all the West African nations were represented in the pan-African stewpot le Vieux had simmered for three decades. The immigrants had always voted for le Vieux, and President Bédié and his party tried to keep it that way. But Laurent Gbagbo, the opposition leader who ran against le Vieux in the first multiparty election in 1990, and his party, the Popular Front, lobbied to revise the rules for voting to limit the power of the old ruling party and won.

The new electoral code adopted in December 1994, one year after le Vieux died, withdrew the vote from non-Ivorian African residents. The rules for citizenship remained the same—if you had one Ivorian parent, you were an Ivorian citizen. But under the new code, to run for president, a candidate had to have not just *one* parent who was Ivorian, as in the past, but *two*. Another article enforced the same rules for deputies in the national assembly. Before, every candidate needed an Ivorian mother *or* father. *Mère ou père.* Now it was *and. Mère et père.* This change was intended to bar former prime minister Alassane Ouattara from running for president because his parents had been born in the North when it was a colonial district of French West Africa and he could not prove that both were born inside the 1960 boundaries of Ivory Coast. People called the law "the *and* instead of the *or*." If you draw both French words out, *et* and *ou* sound like mournful exclamations of pain, and in Ivory Coast that is what they became.

As part of le Vieux's open-door policy, some non-Ivorian residents had farmed Ivorian land for decades. "Let the land go to those who cultivate it," he had said, an approach to land ownership linked to traditional African land use practices, in which there is no private property. Land, the elders of Kalikaha had explained to us, belonged to the ancestors and future generations, not to any particular individual. Any one piece of land might have several authorized users—a farming family, a hunter, and women who gathered nuts and pods from trees intentionally left standing in the fields. In Kalikaha, one elder, the land priest, was the highest authority; he arbitrated land use disputes and mediated with the nature spirits. No one, not even the land priest, had the right to sell land. To compensate for the poor savanna soil, the farmers practice a system of rotational farming. After farming a field for about seven years, the family clears a new field, leaving the first one fallow so the soil can recuperate. Cotton is an especially demanding crop, and without long fallow periods, cotton would destroy the soil, rendering it useless for growing rice and corn.

This system worked because there was plenty of available land around Kalikaha. Land in the North was not the issue. At issue was the much more valuable land in the forest region where there were two rainy seasons per year rather than one and the soil was fertile. This was the land Ivorians were fighting over, the land that could produce low-grade arabusta coffee beans that could be turned into powdered instant coffee and, more importantly, high-grade cocoa beans, which grow in pods on small bushy trees. Ivory Coast is the single largest producer of cocoa and grows more than a third of the world's supply. The flat brown cocoa beans are fermented, dried, and then exported to Europe and the United States, where they are processed into chocolate.

In the 1980s, with the economy in the doldrums and unemployment at 40 percent in the cities, many young men returned to their rural roots. Those from the cocoa and coffee-growing region, in particular, hoped to make a living as owners of small plantations. But when they arrived back in their family villages, they found the land all taken. Immigrants from Burkina Faso and other countries and Ivorians from the center and North were already farming cocoa there. These "outsiders" had obtained land rights from the young men's fathers and grandfathers, who were hunters rather than farmers. The farmers had local *jatigis* and paid rents in cash, a share of the crop, or both. Many farmers had been there for years, spoke the local language, and had unofficial papers to prove they had obtained the land legitimately. In Ivory Coast, selling land is frowned upon; it goes against the ethos of communal land ownership. But in some cases, the returnees discovered their elders had done just that, sold away the family land for cash. Unable to express their anger at their own elders, the disinherited young men, living hand-to-mouth in Abidjan, turned their resentment on the immigrants. They wanted to kick out the Burkinabé and take back their land. They viewed even Ivorians from the North, like the Senufo farmer Yaya had worked for, as outsiders who should not be allowed to own farmland in their region. It was localness taken to the extreme. Politicians, including Laurent Gbagbo, a native of the region, exploited the young men's desperation and resentment to gain a political following and campaigned on promises to return their ancestral land.

Closing some of le Vieux's wide-open doors to land ownership had to be justified in some way, and so President Bédié and his intellectual supporters at the university turned to identity politics and came up with a philosophy of Ivorian supremacy they called *ivoirité* or "Ivorianness." They held conferences and published books filled with lofty philosophical ideals about affirming Ivorian cultural identity. Ivorians needed, they claimed, to protect native Ivorian culture from the homogenization and globalization sweeping across the world. *Ivoirité* was elegantly decked out in intellectual language and in the national colors of green, white, and orange, but woven into its philosophical designs were threads of a dark, politically motivated anti-immigrant xenophobia. As disturbing as that was, *ivoirité* went further, declaring that some Ivorians were more truly Ivorian than others. Real Ivorians were those from the South, and the true Ivorian culture that *ivoirité* celebrated and promoted was the Ivorian culture that sprang from southern ethnic groups. Its political purpose may have been disguised with intellectual rhetoric, but no one was fooled: it was a rationale for disqualifying former prime minister Alassane Ouattara from running for president in 1995. According to *ivoirité,* Ouattara, and by extension all Jula people like him, and by a further extension, all northerners, were *less* Ivorian than southerners. They might be Ivorian citizens, but they were not *real* Ivorians.

Ivoirité was a risky game played with highly flammable substances, designed for short-term political advantage, and national cohesion turned out to be every bit as combustible as the brown savanna grasses in the dry season. President Bédié lit the fire to disqualify his political rival. Gbagbo benefited, gaining the support of the disinherited, landless young men, so he fanned the flames. Excluded from running, Ouattara withdrew from the old ruling party and formed a new political party, the Rally of Republicans.

The Gendarmes on the Road

Beside the dirt road between Korhogo and Kalikaha, an old mango tree created a wide circle of shade, and lying in the shade on cots were always two or three gendarmes, the soles of their black boots facing the road. The tree was their regular place of business. Double-sided signs on round bases in the road ordered vehicles to HALTE. The gendarmes were a national police force, often southerners working in the North; they should have been fighting bandits because the country was experiencing a crime wave, but instead, they extorted passersby. For the old men who left their villages on their mopeds to sell a few chickens or visit relatives in town, passing the tree meant running a gauntlet. The gendarmes rose from their cots, pulled them over, examined their faded papers, and invariably claimed that something—their registration, their insurance—wasn't in order. The old men were illiterate and had no way to know what their faded papers said or should say, so they handed over a bit of their valuable cash. No tickets were ever issued. Day after day, this was the regular roadside racket; the gendarmes had taken to heart le Vieux's advice to find the rest of their salaries where they worked.

But when we passed in the summer of 1995, the big mango tree was dead and the gendarmes were nowhere to be seen. "One day the gendarmes looked up and saw their signs walking away, just like that, all by themselves," Adama told us with that pregnant gleam in his eye that meant he had a story to tell. This was serious supernatural medicine and the gendarmes didn't wait to find out what would happen next. They jumped on their motorcycles and drove away. After that, even the tree that shaded them died. "It was the revenge of the old men," Adama explained. "They were the ones, of course, using their special powers to turn invisible, who paid the gendarmes a little visit and carried off their signs."

For the first time that summer, we were living across the wide dirt street from Donni in our own round, one-room thatched-roof house. There was just enough space across its diameter for our folding cots and mosquito nets. Three years had passed since Kalikaha's new streets had been laid out for rural electrification, but the promised electric wires hadn't arrived, so we were still using a propane two-burner stove and kerosene lanterns. Chékun was waiting for the results from her second baccalaureate exam. If she passed, she could apply to the university in Abidjan, but for the moment, her life was on hold and she was glad to accept my offer of a job as a translator. The older Senufo women I wanted to interview spoke only Senari.

Chékun and I made regular rounds every morning to visit our old ladies. Most still raised a little rice, so it was best to catch them before they left for their fields. Fridays were hopeless; they were too busy drinking corn beer with their friends to bother with us. Rainy days were excellent—stuck in their houses, they were glad to reminisce and answer our questions. We arrived with aspirin and two stimulants—powdered snuff in black plastic film canisters and red heart-shaped kola nuts. Some of our informants were toothless and grated the kola on graters made by punching holes in sardine cans.

Our old ladies agreed that girls these days were poorly brought up, not as hard working or as respectful to their elders and their husbands as they had been. They had been whipped frequently by their fathers and husbands for being late to the fields or slow to cook dinner. Some thought the changes were for the better, others that things were going downhill. They had farmed with short-handled hoes—no oxen then, they reminded us. One old woman told us, gleefully, about a memorable day when she was bent over her hoe, clearing a field with a group of teenagers. She passed all the girls, kept hoeing and reached the boys, and even passed the slowest ones. But she didn't slow her pace! When she passed the fastest boy and reached the end of her row, she stopped work and sang, dancing with her hoe until the others caught up. For those few minutes, it was as if she were the champion farmer, singing her victory song. When the young men returned to the village that evening, they were teased for letting a girl show them up.

After they married, the old ladies worked in their husbands' fields five days a week and in their own rice and peanut fields the other two days. On the days they worked in their husbands' fields, their husbands provided them with corn or rice from their granaries, but on their two "rest days," they had to feed themselves and their children. Women also had to come up with money to buy clothing for themselves and their children and ingredients for sauce to serve with the corn or rice. Some had managed by buying cotton from their husbands, spinning it into thread by hand with drop spindles, and selling the thread to weavers. They also sold some of their rice or peanut crop, a calculated risk.

The way Senufo couples divided their household resources and responsibilities hadn't changed. Chékun's friends, cousins, and younger sisters were marrying, and they faced the same challenge as their grandmothers: trying to raise enough rice to feed their children on the days when they didn't work in their husbands' fields and trying to come up with money to buy sauce ingredients and clothing for themselves and their children. There was a clinic now, and you could go yourself or take a sick child for treatment, but what was the point if you had no cash to buy medicine? And if, as was usually the case, the clinic didn't have the medicine, a woman needed money to get to the pharmacy in town or to pay for gas for a male relative to make the trip on his motorcycle. School had its own additional costs—uniforms, sandals, workbooks, slate, and chalk. Some fathers paid, but clothing was a mother's responsibility. And both parents lost a schoolchild's labor. Girls, in particular, were a big help to their mothers and grandmothers. They carried water, gathered firewood, pounded corn into flour, hulled and winnowed rice, and took care of younger children.

When they reminisced about their youth, our old ladies always returned to the same subject—the work they were forced to do under the French colonial regime. The French district commander employed a police force of Ivorian guards; they were the face of colonialism in Kalikaha and their methods for ensuring compliance were often brutal. Chékun's grandmother, Old Chékun, and the other teenagers were put to work building a road to a nearby town. "You had to leave at the first cock's crow because if you arrived after the guard, he beat you. And if he didn't think you were working hard enough, he beat you for that, too!" They brought their own rice, which one woman cooked in a big pot. When it was time to eat, the guard blew his whistle. "But you couldn't eat normally! In an instant he was whistling again to go back to work. You had to eat as fast as you could!" They worked all day, every day, until that section of road was completed, and while they built the road, it fell to older people to do their work in the fields.

To supply the French textile mills, the farmers were ordered to grow cotton. They already grew a perennial cotton tree at the edges of their rice and millet fields, but the guards ordered them to grow an annual variety as a monocrop. The size of the field to be planted was specified by the district commander and enforced by the guards. Women were conscripted to remove the cotton seeds by hand, and Old Chékun was sent to work at the gin in Korhogo three times. She walked there, two long days, carrying her supply of rice on her head and stayed a month each time. Another woman told us that after she pulled the seeds from the fluff, she placed red ones in one basket, white in another. She had no idea why, but it was likely to separate different varieties. The colonial administrators were constantly experimenting with new cotton strains, trying to find one that gave higher yields and worked well in French mills, and once they decided which strain would be grown the following year, all the farmers had to plant those seeds the way the guards specified.

In addition, the district commander requisitioned rice, peanuts, millet, and corn, and young women were the porters who delivered the food on their heads. They made the two-day trek in groups, their babies on their backs, walking all day with only a brief rest stop to eat cold millet flour mixed into water. At night, when they stopped at a village midway, they could build a fire and cook the rice they carried.

When they wanted you to do something, you had to do it, the old ladies explained. If the head of a family refused to send the number of workers they demanded, they put him out in the hot sun and made him stay there all day without anything to eat or even water to drink. The guards also conscripted young men to cut timber in the southern forests and they beat the fathers who didn't consent. While their sons and nephews were gone for six-month stints, the older men had to do the heavy work in the fields. Novelist Ahmadou Kourouma called forced labor "slavery without the name."

Once a year the guards came to collect taxes. They had to pay with money, not food, so their fathers had to sell rice and peanuts after the harvest. "Taking the grains out of the cotton wasn't so hard; it was our parents who suffered the most. If they couldn't pay the money they owed, they were forced to carry a large stone all the way around the village, then the guards put them in a hut, built a fire, and threw red pepper on it. They left them there until someone came and paid their tax!"

One day a messenger came to Kalikaha and announced that forced labor was over, but no one celebrated because they didn't believe it could possibly be true. But after a year passed and no guards arrived to make them work, they knew the man had spoken the truth. After hearing these stories firsthand, it was easier to understand why le Vieux, who was instrumental in ending forced labor, was still held in such high regard.

That summer we spent our evenings sitting outside, chatting with visitors who stopped by, while Tom, who was learning to play the banjo, practiced his clawhammer technique. He was bringing his new instrument back to its continent of birth, for early forms of the banjo came to America with enslaved Africans. If we were lucky, a storm blew up and the wind cooled us as the lightning flashing on the horizon moved closer. The kids fell asleep on mats, looking up at the creamy sweep of the Milky Way and watching for shooting stars. Some of the young men who dropped by to chat were supporting the old ruling party in the upcoming elections, while others had joined Gbagbo's or Ouattara's opposition parties. The opposition parties were talking about boycotting the election, to show it wasn't democratic and to demand reforms.

We left Ivory Coast in early September 1995 as the country prepared to hold its first presidential election without le Vieux. Since Alassane Ouattara had not been allowed to run, his new Rally of Republicans party and Gbagbo's Popular Front joined forces and called on their supporters to boycott the election. But as political strategy, the boycott was a disaster, enabling Bédié to sail into office with more than 96 percent of the vote. Bédié's party also took most of the seats in the national assembly, which had limited powers. Two years after le Vieux's death, the old ruling party was still running the country, including the press and the courts. Ivory Coast, President Bédié announced, had become a peaceful democracy.

Yaya

A Northerner in the South

Yaya went back to Kalikaha to see Djeneba and their daughter and to plead his case once more with her family. He barely scraped together his bus fare, so he wasn't in a position to impress them with gifts, and although he stayed more than a month, they didn't change their minds—Djeneba's marriage had already been arranged.

When he was laid off at the mill, he told Moussa he wanted to work with the scrap metal dealers who had their scrapyards under the electric power lines. Jagged mountains of scrap metal sat there, waiting to be sorted and sold, and in open-air workshops, men cut and shaped metal sheets to make watering cans, funnels, presses, and other useful items. When the owner of the hotel where Moussa worked died suddenly, he lost his job, so he was working in a stall there himself, fixing radios and televisions. The air clanked and gonged with the sounds of metal being loaded and weighed and dumped, banged and hammered, and men came and went, wheeling and dealing, buying and selling, searching for the size rebar or wire they needed. It was just the kind of bustling place Yaya liked.

"Apprentices work for nothing," Moussa said. "Do you think you can handle that?"

Yaya said he could, so they went to see a scrap dealer Moussa knew. "If you take me on as an apprentice," Yaya told the dealer, "there is just one thing I ask. I would like to stay for two full years so I truly, truly learn this business."

The man agreed and Yaya went to work for him the next day. At midday, he often gave Yaya a few coins to buy a plate of rice and sauce, but if he didn't, Yaya had to manage for himself. Now that he was in a place where he heard French all day, Yaya started to pick it up. His employer bought and sold iron, aluminum, tin, brass, and copper. Yaya helped with the weighing and transporting and learned how to tell the metals apart, what to buy, and how to negotiate a good price. He was still determined to marry Djeneba, but since he was a penniless apprentice, he knew he didn't have a very strong suit. To avoid the marriage her family planned for her, she had gone to live with her brother in another town.

Djeneba's family was a bit exceptional because her parents had married across ethnic lines. Her father, the truck driver, was Jula like Yaya, but her mother's family was Senufo. Djeneba had never known her mother, who died when she was born, but she was close to her mother's sister, who lived in Korhogo. She was the only person in her extended family who was sympathetic to the young couple, and when Djeneba came for a visit, this aunt took matters into her own hands and sent a message to Yaya: "Come here to Korhogo and get your wife. She is at my house and she should be living with you." He went, and Djeneba and their little girl, Khadi, came back with him to live in Abidjan.

When his two years of apprenticeship were up, Yaya asked his mentor for the road. The man gave him his blessing, and Yaya rented a stall nearby and went into business. He made the most money from scrap iron, so he focused on that.

Mariam, Yaya's mother, sent a message that he should come home and marry, but the bride she had in mind wasn't Djeneba. Years before, their family had given Yaya's oldest sister to a family, and now, in return, that family had given them a thirteen-year-old girl.

"No way!" Yaya told his older brother. "It's impossible. I'm just starting out in business, I already have Djeneba and Khadi to support, and Djeneba is pregnant again. We live in a little wooden house I pay fourteen dollars a month for. You know what you call it? A 'go-in-and-sleep' because that's all you can do there—it's one room. Our younger brother isn't married. Why not give the girl to him?"

The girl's parents, explained Abou-lonala calmly, were the sort who poked their noses into other people's business and made trouble for everyone, and Yaya's mother, Mariam, felt sure that if this girl married her younger son in Kalikaha, her parents would always be interfering, their household would be one long *palabre,* and the marriage would be a disaster for them all. They couldn't refuse the girl, so the only solution, according to Mariam, was for Yaya to marry her and take her to Abidjan. She was young enough that Djeneba would be like a mother to her, the two would always get along, and Yaya would have the good fortune of a harmonious household. He gave in and returned for the week-long wedding.

Aminata was afraid when she arrived in Abidjan, but Djeneba taught her to find her way through the dirt streets of their neighborhood and how to avoid being taken advantage of. The two divided the household chores amicably, and soon Yaya and Djeneba's second child was born, a boy.

Back in Kalikaha, Yaya's older brother hadn't given up as Yaya's ambassador. He brought in reinforcements, enlisting a family friend, the Big Marabout-la, known not only for his skill in mediation and his spiritual prowess but also for his sheer bulk. "I know she is promised to someone else, but since she and Yaya have two children now, wouldn't it be best if they married?" the Big Marabout-la asked Djeneba's family. And they finally said yes. Eight months after Yaya's wedding to Aminata, he and his two wives and two children returned to Kalikaha to say the prayers and "tie the kola" inside the little mosque. At this ceremony, kola nuts are tied up in packages and exchanged to represent the bond between the two families. Djeneba was carried into her house, dressed in her best, and stayed inside for a week. As a bride, she was treated to special porridge every morning. Normally, Jula women make their breakfast porridge by reheating cooked rice and adding ginger and a touch of hot pepper. It's mushy but tasty, and you sip it from gourd ladles that add their own woody flavor. But a bride is served thick millet porridge with flavorful dark honey. Like so many ritual meals, this one is nostalgic. Millet is the grain of olden times, before upland rice varieties were promoted and rice became the preferred staple. Although millet is more drought tolerant and more nutritious than rice, it has fallen out of favor. But Jula families planning a wedding plant a small field of millet because for one week, the bride is royalty and must be served millet porridge every morning like her mothers and grandmothers. Just like an American bride, a Jula girl begins her marriage pretending to be the princess she will never be in real life. Her house party lasts for seven days, and dressed in her best clothes, her eyes outlined with kohl, she does nothing but receive friends and visitors while she is feted and pampered with good food, music, and dancing. To each well-wisher who calls on her, she gives a little gift, a kola nut or, these days, a wrapped piece of hard candy. This is how Yaya and Djeneba were married in Kalikaha. On the last night, the seventh night, all their friends were crammed into the one-room house, dancing, when suddenly flames crackled above them. The thatch was on fire—and everyone was pushing and screaming and shoving to get out the door. Yaya dove back in through the tiny window, all long skinny arms and legs, to make sure their children were not still inside. Everyone got out safely, but a woman's wedding is the moment when she acquires possessions, and all Djeneba's gifts, kitchen utensils, fabric for clothes, sandals, wooden stirrers, the large pile of baskets and pots she had been given for her new life—every single thing burned.

It was a bad omen, some people said, Yaya's fault, because he was just too stubborn. God did this, others said, to punish Djeneba and Yaya.

"God did it, all right," Yaya retorted. "I wasn't burned, Djeneba's not burned, Aminata's not burned, the two children—we are all still here!" The wiring that ran from a generator to the lights on the house, set up for the celebration, had caught the thatch on fire. Yaya paid for the burned wires and took his family back to Abidjan, where Djeneba was, and always would be, first wife and senior wife.

The next time Yaya's mother, Mariam, sent a message, it was to exercise her rights as a grandmother. Ivorian grandparents often raise one of their grandchildren, a practice that weaves generations together, but she had none of his children living with her, she reminded Yaya, so Djeneba took the bus north with their little son and left him in Kalikaha with his grandmother.

Two years later, Yaya's older brother, Abou-lonala, called to tell him that his mother was seriously ill. Yaya left money with Djeneba for the household, hid another sum in his clothes, and took the bus north. His mother was so weak she couldn't get up from her mat, and he sat beside her and they talked quietly. One day she asked him about the money he had brought, if there was much left. He had given it to Abou-lonala when he arrived, to buy medicine and the only thing Mariam could still eat, smoked fish. Abou-lonala had told him that morning the money was nearly gone. "You should leave then," she said. "Go back down to Abidjan to work. If we don't see each other again, it's all right, because we have said everything there is to say between us." And if the family had to borrow money for the funeral, he should be sure to pay it back. He promised he would. Then she gave him a great many blessings, for a long life for himself and his wives and his children, to prosper in his business, and to do good for others. And then, although he hadn't asked for it, she gave him the road.

When he told his family he was leaving the next day, they were surprised. Perhaps they were thinking he should stay for the end and the funeral. "It's her wish. She gave me the road." In Kalikaha, his brothers could grow food, hunt for meat, and earn enough from tobacco and cotton for the little expenses, but Yaya was the real breadwinner for the extended family. His ability to turn scrap iron into West African francs was a lifesaving alchemy. Fifteen days after he left, his mother died. He didn't make the trip again because he knew that although she wasn't his mother, Abou-lonala would make sure the burial and prayers were carried out just as they should be.

After seven years in the one-room go-in-and-sleep house, Yaya had saved up enough to buy an empty lot at a cost of $1,200. Housing, whether you bought or rented, was expensive in Abidjan, even in neighborhoods with unpaved streets and no running water or sewage systems. Yaya built a concrete house with three rooms that opened off a hallway and a courtyard behind where the women could cook and wash and the children could play. He and Djeneba and Aminata and their children, of whom there were five at home, moved in. On the front wall, he built a tiny shop with a window, which he rented out.

Their neighborhood, Koumassi, was filled with Jula northerners and immigrants from Burkina and Mali who greeted one another in Julakan, and the call to prayer rang out five times a day from the mosque. But in the era of *ivoirité*, being Jula or northern made you a second-class citizen, and when Yaya spoke Julakan at a government office where he went to get some necessary paper or pay his taxes, the officials looked at him disdainfully and said, "Only French is spoken here!" When he presented his ID card, he was told, "Kalikaha? Never heard of it. Must be in Mali." He found himself having to explain that he was Ivorian. "It's in Ivory Coast. I was born there! Just like you—this is my country, too!" Returning from a visit home, Djeneba was thrown off the bus outside Korhogo. She had a ticket but only a photocopy of her identification card, not the original, so the gendarme said she must be a foreigner. The two children traveling with her were allowed to stay on the bus and made the trip back to Abidjan alone. Djeneba had to buy a second ticket and take the bus the following day.

One day Yaya was returning from a visit to Kalikaha. At the city limits of Abidjan, all the bus passengers had to get down and line up to file into the little office and stand, one by one, before the gendarmes. When Yaya arrived in front of their table, they took his ID and refused to return it.

"What is the problem with my card?"

"No problem," the gendarme replied.

"Well, if there is no problem, give it back to me."

"Watch yourself! Do you want a beating?"

"I just want my ID back."

A young man standing behind Yaya whispered, "Older brother, just leave it or else you will get a beating as a present for free. You should just leave." It was the last roadblock before the bus station and Yaya had a photocopy of his ID at home, so he walked away and left the original with the gendarmes. If they wanted money, they didn't ask for it. It was harassment. "My card, it didn't do them any good. It was only good for me. But those gendarmes—look at them wrong and they would kill you for free. . . . They didn't come to make things work; they came to wreck them!"

Chékun

So This Is How It Is

On her second try, Chékun received her baccalaureate. The uncle who had helped her move into the dormitory said he knew someone who could get her into the national police academy for $100. It was a huge sum, but he somehow came up with the money, and she went straight to Abidjan and took the exam, but she wasn't accepted. She also took an exam for health training, as she had always wanted to be a nurse, but wasn't accepted for that either. She applied to the university and went to the university gate the day the list of accepted students was posted, but her name wasn't on the list. "Maybe you should check over there," a person standing near her told her, pointing to the list for national teacher training. Although she hadn't applied, she found her name. Education schools were located all over the country and she slid her finger across the line. Assigned location: Korhogo. Back to Korhogo! She felt like the door to the future had been slammed in her face. As her bus pulled away from Abidjan, she turned to the window and cried silently. People would say she must have lied about getting her bac because here she was, back again at her uncle's house. She also worried that her boyfriend, a university student in Abidjan, would forget her because he was spending a lot of time with another girl.

Her two-year teacher training program consisted of one year of classes and a year of internships in nearby schools. The second year, in the classrooms, facing a room of children on benches, she felt useful, and at her uncle's house, she was treated differently. As a teacher, she had a status even the older men respected, but her sisters were not so fortunate. The patriarch of the family arranged a marriage between her next youngest sister, a stolid girl of few words, and a cousin working in Korhogo as a mechanic. The groom didn't want to marry his broad-shouldered, uneducated country cousin, but to the patriarch, the young mechanic said only, "I accept." To his friends, Chékun overheard him say, "You'll see! I won't tell her to go. She will leave of her own accord!" He didn't attend his own wedding, so the family put the bride on the Twenty-Two Places with her cooking pots and a large bag of rice and one of corn.

When Chékun visited, she found her sister living on plain boiled corn because her husband didn't give her a single franc to buy ingredients for sauce. Her husband ate at work or at his friends' houses, but her sister admitted that the only time she ate a real meal was when she visited their uncle's house, where Chékun lived. She was also expecting, although she hadn't told anyone. As soon as she got home, Chékun wrote a letter to the patriarch in Kalikaha, their great-uncle. "My sister, even while pregnant, is neglected and starving," she explained. She knew one of the young men who went to school would read the letter to him. He responded by sending money for her sister to come home on the Twenty-Two Places. The marriage was over, but the men quickly arranged to give Chékun's pregnant sister to a friend of her father's in a neighboring village; her second husband was older than her father. Chékun was waiting for her assignment to a school where she would student teach for a year under the supervision of the principal and an experienced teacher, and if the inspectors found her teaching satisfactory, she would receive her credentials. If she became a certified teacher with a salary, her uncles could no longer force her to marry. Unlike her sisters, she would have a chance to decide the terms of her own life.

A young man named Ngolo from a small village near Kalikaha came to her uncle's house one day. Slightly older than she, he had been a good student, first in his class in math, and now attended the university. Short and stocky, with a round face, he had a jovial smile. They exchanged news and then he turned serious. "For a long time, there is something I have wanted to say to you."

"Oh? Yes?"

He had always liked her in high school, he told her, and hoped they could be together someday.

"But you never told me," Chékun replied. "Me, I am already with someone, our older brother Beh. We have been together seven years and we plan to marry." Ngolo said he understood and was glad she had someone to look out for her. He didn't want to start a quarrel with an older brother, but he did want her to know how he felt.

She received her assignment and packed her bags to student-teach in the southern part of the country. When she arrived at the bus station, she told someone she was a new schoolteacher and needed to report to the district education office. Finding out she was Senufo, some young men said, "Oh, Aunty, come with us, we'll take you to the chief of the Senufo here. It's not far at all." The Senufo elder welcomed her and offered her a place to stay, and just like that, she had a *jatigi*. At the office, she learned she had been assigned to a school in a smaller village, and the next day she took a minibus there. Her house had a living room, kitchen, and three bedrooms, all for her! As soon as she got back to town, she called the uncle who had helped her on several occasions and offered to host his oldest daughter for the school year. She had so much space she could be a *jatigi* herself.

Sawmill Village had been built around a sawmill, which closed once the tropical forest had been turned into lumber. But many immigrants who had come to work in the sawmill stayed after it closed to farm cocoa. The little town was about the same size as Kalikaha but less remote, as it was connected to the world by a post office, a paved road, and regular bus service. After Chékun unpacked, she took the bus to Abidjan to buy school supplies and see her boyfriend.

At her boyfriend's house, there were always other students visiting, and whenever a Baule woman was there, he acted as if he barely knew Chékun. When she and another young woman were alone in the kitchen, the young woman said, "My sister, I can tell you straight out—this one is not going to marry you. You should go out and find yourself another man."

Find herself another man? Chékun's mind whirled. She didn't understand. Was she saying Chékun should have other boyfriends besides Beh? She wasn't that kind of girl! Beh had told her he wanted to marry a girl from home, a Senufo girl, so she knew the young woman was wrong—he might like the Baule girl, but she was the one he intended to marry. That night, she and Beh went to a hotel and spent the night together.

The school year began and she was busy teaching her first-grade class. She called Beh and left him a message. "Strange, ever since we were together in Abidjan, my period hasn't come." But he didn't call back. The only phone was at the post office, where you could be overheard, so she wrote him a letter but received no answer. When her Christmas vacation came, she went to Abidjan to see him. She explained that ever since they had been together in October, she hadn't had a period.

"Why are you coming to me?" he asked.

Chékun was too taken aback to answer.

"You should go and talk to the father about it, not me. Go and find the real father of your baby."

"Listen, it's your child."

"But we haven't even been in the same town."

"We were together in Abidjan."

"One night only!"

"But it's yours. I know it."

"After the baby is born," he told her, "I'll have a paternity test done, and if it turns out I am the father, I will take responsibility then."

Ah, bon, she said to herself, so this is how it is. That night she cried all night. She thought about her parents, who had nothing and yet had managed to send her to school. She would have to tell them she was pregnant and the father was not willing to support her. At the teacher training school, each time she received her small scholarship, she put a little sum away. That was how she had managed to buy bus tickets and teaching supplies. But her savings wouldn't go very far, and she would receive no salary, only a small stipend for expenses, until she finished her practice teaching. How was she going to survive her pregnancy and support a child? After her sleepless night, she dressed and went to the bus station. To her surprise, Beh was waiting there for her.

"Listen," he said. "If I have a little something, I will help you, and after the child is born, we will do the test, but for now I can't take responsibility."

Chékun had heard about doctors at the hospital who performed abortions on the side, and that was the simplest solution, she knew. But what if something went wrong and she was left with health problems? What if she wasn't ever able to have another child? At the end of the year, if I get my teaching certificate, I'll have a salary and I'll be able to support myself and my child, she told herself. She decided she would keep the baby and raise it alone, and although it went against her forthright nature, she kept her pregnancy a secret from her family.

She had been raised in the Senufo spiritual tradition with its powerful masked figures, diviners, sacrifices to the nature spirits, and *poro,* centered in a sacred grove of trees. She belonged to the founding lineage of Kalikaha, and her mother's uncle was the land priest and the head of the *poro* society, the most powerful man in the village. Senufo society was matrilineal, which meant that men inherited from their mother's brothers rather than their fathers; that didn't prevent it from being firmly patriarchal. If she told her family about her pregnancy, the men would summon her boyfriend's father and uncles and arrange their marriage. But it was a marriage she no longer wanted, so she kept her secret. Alone in a strange town, pregnant and no father in sight, someone else would have invented a story of a fiancé working or studying elsewhere, but Chékun was too honest even to think of that. Her women neighbors often came by and invited her to join them at church, and one day she accepted. She found it made her feel better to sit in the service and give her problems up to God, and she appreciated the way the church women dropped by her house in the evenings to chat, brought her food, and included her in their circle of warmth and support.

Once she had decided to keep the baby, in her straightforward way, she went to her school superintendent and explained her situation. As long as she did her work satisfactorily, she was entitled to maternity leave like anyone else, he told her. In February the superintendent and the committee of inspectors arrived to evaluate her teaching. She wore a long tunic over pants to camouflage her pregnancy. "It seemed as if the children understood how much was at stake for me that day and how nervous I was because they behaved perfectly. That day they knew every answer!" She still laughs happily at the memory. That very day she received her certification to teach, and the school held a little celebration for her.

When she had given her first graders their end-of-year exams and filed their grades, she telephoned Beh. "You should go home to Korhogo to have the baby," he told her. But Chékun didn't want to return pregnant and unmarried to her family. "You are free to go anywhere you want," he said, "but if you come to Abidjan, you can't stay with me."

Chékun needed someone to look after her while she gave birth, someone who lived in a town large enough to have a maternity clinic. In desperation she wrote to a man she called an older brother, although they were not related. He was from Kalikaha, a successful magistrate who knew her and Beh well and was posted to a city not far away. In her letter, she laid out her predicament. The magistrate wrote back immediately and invited her to his house; she stayed with his family for a month, and in July her daughter was born.

The baby girl looked exactly like her father, as if, as they say in Ivory Coast, he had just vomited her out. But of course, he hadn't. And although it's customary for a father to contribute financial support to the mother of his child, he hadn't even done that. Despite his promise at the bus station, he never sent her a single franc.

"What are you going to name her?" the magistrate asked Chékun.

"You have accepted me into your home and you are my older brother, so I would like you to give my child a name."

"But the father should name the baby. I'll call him."

"Why do that? He said it wasn't his! We haven't done the paternity test, so we can't say it's his child."

"Let's not dwell on that," said the magistrate soothingly, and called Beh without her knowledge.

"I can't name the baby," Beh told him. "It's not mine." But eventually he gave in and gave the little girl his last name, his mother's name as a middle name, and for a first name, "since Chékun wanted this baby so much . . . Desirée."

A few weeks later, Chékun took Desirée to Abidjan. She didn't tell Beh she was coming, but the magistrate called him, and by the time she arrived at her relatives' house, he was already there, waiting. When she walked in, he came and took the baby from her, as if nothing were wrong between them, and she, not wanting to react in front of everyone, let him. He looked at Desirée's face. "He never talked about the paternity test again!" she said, with a pained little laugh. "Never one other single word!"

Chékun learned that he was living with the other young woman, but as far as she was concerned, it had been over between them the moment he refused to recognize her pregnancy. She took the baby to her uncle Chébena's house in Korhogo, and to her surprise, Beh followed her. He came to the house again and again, and each time he held Desirée and played with her, bitter thoughts flew through her head: He says she's not his! He hasn't sent me a single franc! Inside, Chékun was seething, but the family had no idea anything was wrong and assumed they would soon marry.

She went to Kalikaha to see her parents and show them their grandchild. It was a happy visit, and in response to their questions, she told them frankly what had happened between her and Beh and how they would take the baby to the hospital and look at her blood to see if it was the same as his. The school in Sawmill Village had hired her as a teacher, but she needed someone to care for Desirée while she worked. She was no longer a *jatigi* because her young cousin had passed the test to enter middle school and returned to her parents' house. When her parents said her sister Bara could come with her to help with the baby and the housework, Chékun was delighted. Bara was thirteen, lively and outgoing, with a wide smile that lit up her face.

Bara adjusted easily to her new life. With Desirée on her back, she walked through the village selling shea butter from the North. She set up a pan of hot oil in front of the school and fried little round doughnuts to sell, and after Chékun bought a refrigerator, she also sold plastic baggies of cool water. She picked up French phrases quickly and attended church services with Chékun. "It was an easy life," Bara says. "I always had enough to eat and even money to spend."

By the time Beh finally came to visit them, Desirée was walking. His best friend came with him and, on Beh's behalf, asked for Chékun's forgiveness. Beh wanted them to start over, and this time, he promised, he was serious about their relationship.

"The way things have turned out," Chékun told him, "it's fine. Let's leave it at that."

Chékun should forget everything that had happened, the friend suggested, so the couple could start over at zero.

"I could never do that. After what I saw of you, I could never go back."

The two men talked all night, trying to persuade her.

"You already have a wife," she told Beh. "Now I will start looking and I will find my own husband." She had loved him from a young age, and she knew he didn't believe she was serious about never seeing him again, so after he left, she sat down and wrote him a letter. She wanted to be sure she had made herself perfectly clear, so she spelled it out: everything was completely and totally over between them. And, finally, she felt fine with her decision.

As she taught school, ate dinner with Bara, played with Desirée, and sang hymns in church, Chékun sometimes wondered what lay ahead for her. If she let her uncles and her father choose, they would marry her off to an illiterate farmer who had worked in their fields or done them a service. The only man who had suggested marriage was Ngolo, but she hadn't considered him as a possible boyfriend, more like an older brother. He was probably married by now to some young woman he had met at the university, but on an impulse, she wrote him a letter and explained that things had not worked out with her and Beh.

One moment after she dropped the letter into the slot at the post office, she regretted it. He would probably do just what Beh had done, lead her on although he wasn't serious about marriage. She wanted to find a husband, but writing Ngolo and asking straight out if he were married—why had she done such a foolish thing? With Beh she had been young and naive and she had learned a hard lesson, but here she was, supposedly older and wiser, foolishly walking right back into trouble. She wished she could call the letter back!

It didn't take long for a response to arrive from Ngolo. He had left the university and given up his plan to become a pharmacist because even though he didn't have to pay tuition, the small expenses added up—the books, the course packets the professors sold, food, and transportation. Instead he was learning to be a specialized mechanic. He had always liked technical things, so he wasn't unhappy about it. And he wasn't, he added, married.

After they corresponded for a time, he asked if he could come and visit her on a weekend and Chékun agreed. He arrived with gifts for her and Bara, and food, including a large sack of rice. In person he explained why he had been glad to leave the university. His first year he had taken the required introductory class for health sciences, held in the largest amphitheater, where there were never enough seats. There must have been a thousand students, and to be sure of a seat near the front, he had to leave his *jatigi*'s house at four in the morning. Although they were learning anatomy, among other subjects, there were no images during the lecture, and if you sat at the back with the students who were repeating the class and had already taken notes, you couldn't hear a thing over their chatting. At the end of the year, all the students in the class took a week-long exam. Only the highest-scoring students would be accepted into the health education programs, but if you didn't make the list, you could take the class again and try a second time. They had completed two days of the exam when a high school friend called him. "Come over," she said. "I want to give you something, some *petrole-petrole*!" She wasn't in the class, but she had a wealthy Abidjan boyfriend who was.

Ngolo had heard of *petrole-petrole* and he was curious. Her boyfriend and all his friends had this, so she wanted him to have it, too, she told him, handing him a photocopied study sheet for that afternoon's physics exam. The sheet contained sample problems and solutions.

When he sat down in the amphitheater that afternoon, opened the test booklet, and read the first questions, Ngolo recoiled. The questions were the exact ones on the study sheet, the same physics problems written in the exact same order! A wave of discouragement hit him so powerfully that he slumped in his chair. "No matter how much I study, I can't compete against this," he thought.

So many students were caught running to the little photocopy stall around the corner to copy the answer sheet that the university had the owner arrested, as if it were his fault. They also annulled that day's test results. It was rumored the wealthy students had paid professors an enormous sum for the answers. A large group of students went on strike and demanded the annulment of the entire exam, and Ngolo joined them, but the university refused to give the entire exam over. They threw out the results from the physics section but kept the results from the two days before that. Ngolo took the rest of the exam but he had no hope, and neither he nor anyone he went to high school with scored high enough to continue.

He had no idea what to do next, but then a cousin called to tell him about a navy program that trained mechanics—the entrance exam was coming up, although it wasn't publicized. Ngolo took the exam and sailed in easily. Once you bought a uniform and a workbook, the government provided nearly everything else—tuition, lodging, and subsidized meals. He studied for two years, learning about all sorts of motors, how they worked and how to repair them, and then began the required paid internship.

Chékun had regretted missing out on a university education, but as Ngolo filled her in on the young men they knew in Abidjan, she realized she was lucky to have a job. Most of their friends who had university degrees were unemployed and dependent on the generosity of relatives.

Ngolo won Bara's approval right away with his gifts, and he played with Desirée and carried her around. But even after many weekend visits and letters, Chékun just couldn't bring herself to trust him. She did not want to repeat her mistake, so Ngolo went to Kalikaha, called on her parents, and asked to marry their daughter.

It was Chékun's decision, her father replied, and if she said yes, the marriage was fine with him. When Chékun heard what he had done, she put aside her doubts and fears. They agreed about most things—both valued education, and neither wanted to have more children than they could support. The exception was religion. "I am a Senufo man," he told her. "Christianity—this is a Western belief system that Europeans brought here along with slavery. The Christians worked alongside the slave dealers and the colonizers, telling Africans to accept their enslavement and their poverty because they would be rewarded in heaven."

"That may be true, but that time is over," Chékun replied. "We are living our lives now." She wouldn't coerce him, but she hoped he would consider joining the church because she had no intention of leaving its path. Since he hadn't worked in her father's fields, Ngolo paid her father a dowry and gave the family gifts. In Senufo terms, they were married. Their marriage was still long-distance because Ngolo was living in Abobo, a district of Abidjan, a city of one million within the city, and Chékun was living with Bara and Desirée where she taught school. When Chékun was pregnant with their first child, they traveled north to the administrative office near Kalikaha to do something unusual—obtain an official marriage certificate. When they stepped off the bus, a man from Kalikaha recognized Chékun and asked if she had come for the funeral.

"What funeral?"

"Your mama has just died."

Chékun could barely breathe, but she managed to get out the question, "Which mama?"

He named an elderly relative and she exhaled. After they completed the official forms at the subprefecture, they attended the funeral. Her father told Chékun that Bara would soon have to return to Kalikaha to be married. She was sixteen.

Now that she was legally married, Chékun applied to transfer to a school in Abobo, where her husband lived. "If I get my transfer, you can come with me," she told her younger sister. Bara now spoke basic French and could even read and write a little, thanks to Chékun's tutoring, and her outgoing personality made her a popular vendor of cold water, shea butter, vegetables she grew, and fried round doughnuts. Both sisters liked to dress well, Chékun traditionally in a long straight skirt and matching blouse made by her tailor out of brightly printed cotton, while Bara was more adventurous and sometimes wore pants and a T-shirt like a city girl. Once Chékun was assigned to a school in Abobo, the two sisters and little Desirée moved to an apartment Ngolo had rented. When she received her paycheck, Chékun handed the money over to Ngolo. Now that they were living together, she thought this was what a wife should do. She assumed he would return some of it, so that she would have spending money for herself, but he kept it all. After several months, she stopped giving him her paycheck and went back to how it had been between them before, each with their own separate accounts.

Their father sent word from Kalikaha that Bara must come home. Bara had been raised to be a dutiful daughter and had always been especially close to her father. To disobey him was hard for her even to contemplate. When the sisters walked down the street in their crowded new neighborhood, it seemed to Chékun that everyone knew Bara and greeted her warmly. She made friends easily, but she missed her family in Kalikaha and the idea of her own household and her own children sounded appealing. "Think it over carefully," Chékun advised her. When summer vacation arrived and they went home for a visit, Bara stayed and was quickly married, becoming the second wife of a relatively young farmer.

Santa Claus in Uniform

The Bédié government, elected in 1995 for a five-year term, continued to light sparks of xenophobia and exclusion. Sometimes the rumors claimed Ouattara's father was born in Burkina Faso, so he had the *ou* but not the *et*. Sometimes it was Ouattara's mother who was born in Burkina Faso, so he had the *ou* but not the *et*. Foreigners, especially the Burkinabé, were playing too large a role in the economy of the country, and Jula northerners were not really Ivorian; they had moved across the border to take Ivorian land and Ivorian jobs. And many of them had falsified ID cards and were voting illegally in Ivorian elections! The country was being destroyed by voter fraud!

Newspapers proliferated, and each one was affiliated with a political party and spread the rumors that buttressed that party's point of view. The papers that supported the government and the old ruling party published article after article repeating the charges against foreigners and northerners and the rumors about Ouattara—the sparks of *ivoirité*. Ivorians read the newspaper aligned with their political affiliation, so everyone was persuaded their side was right. Of course, when Ouattara's parents were born, birth certificates were rare and neither Ivory Coast nor Burkina Faso (the former Upper Volta) existed, but the partisan press was not interested in ambiguities or in facts. Ouattara had been an unpopular prime minister who had overseen the World Bank's stringent structural adjustment program and required immigrants to apply for and buy residency cards. He had spent his adult life in the world of international finance, rising to become deputy head of the International Monetary Fund. His suits were always immaculately pressed and his demeanor was stiff. In middle age, he married a highly successful widowed French businesswoman, and the power couple hobnobbed with the French business elite. For all these reasons, Alassane Dramane Ouattara, nicknamed

ADO, seemed an unlikely person for poor people from underdeveloped northern Ivory Coast to identify with, but by excluding him from running, his political opponents gave him a viable political identity. Northern Ivorians were marginalized and excluded in many small insulting ways; he was excluded in a large public way from the presidential armchair. Northerners called him Alassane, as if they were on a first-name basis with him. If Alassane wasn't Ivorian, they weren't either, they declared. By changing the constitution to keep him from running, his opponents breathed life into his starched suits and gained him a loyal following. His detractors often called him "the Mossi." The Mossi are the largest ethnic group in Burkina Faso, and there is nothing inherently pejorative about the name, but his political rivals used it as an insult, meaning he was Burkinabé rather than Ivorian. When they heard the vilifying rumors about him and the insults on the radio and television, immigrants and northerners, who lived in every part of the country, flocked to his party, the Rally of Republicans.

On December 24, 1999, a bloodless military coup overthrew the Bédié government. Bédié fled to France, and General Robert Guéï became the transitional president. "Santa Claus in uniform," the Ivorian press dubbed him. The Bédié government had to go, the general announced, because of its ethnic intolerance, financial mismanagement, and widespread corruption. He had no personal interest in the office, he declared, and would stay just long enough to sweep the house clean. Once democratic elections had been organized and the people had voted, his government would step down.

Yaya and his cousin Moussa had gone North for a funeral, and the day after the coup, they were on the Twenty-Two Places headed for Kalikaha when gendarmes stopped the bus. Using the first coup d'état in Ivorian history as a pretext, the gendarmes stole the passengers' money and left them at a village along the road while they returned to town in the Twenty-Two Places. Yaya and Moussa were stranded until their relatives heard what had happened and came on motorcycles to pick them up. Of course, gendarmes took advantage of any excuse to fleece people. That aside, Yaya felt happy that Bédié was gone. Soon there would be a real election and Ouattara would win! In Abidjan, people would be out in the streets, dancing and celebrating; he was disappointed that he had missed the excitement.

The general's first statements and the new constitution that turned the *and* back into *or* pleased Yaya and other northerners. But the sweeping general found that once the house was tidy, he liked living there. And when he contemplated his fellow political leaders as rival candidates, he saw the utility of the *and* instead of *or*, so he amended the new constitution to add it back in. "After five months, we saw that the road we thought we were on," said Yaya, shaking his long finger, "and that wasn't it. A new road had come up and we were headed in a different direction. He said, I've come to sweep, but after he swept, he didn't put the trash outside the door. He left it in the house! You sweep, then you have to pick up the disorder and put it outside. Him, no, no, no! He left everything he had swept up inside! Now the house was dirtier than before!"

When the political parties began to organize for the 2000 presidential campaign, it was clear that the general intended to renege on his promise and run. Since no party would nominate him, he declared himself the people's candidate, but the people tore down his campaign posters. Ivorians had been shocked by the Christmas Eve coup of 1999; this kind of thing happened in other African countries all the time—but not in theirs. Generals ran other countries—but not Ivory Coast. And yet many welcomed General Gueï and his broom because they felt something needed to be done to check Bédié's government. It had been rolling down a slope like an overloaded truck with faulty brakes, way too tolerant of no-holds-barred scarfing of public finances and top heavy with a flammable cargo of xenophobia and discrimination. It seemed like no one was at the wheel until General Gueï jumped into the cab and steered the truck to the shoulder. But the general's decision to run for president made most Ivorians uneasy. Le Vieux—an authoritarian founder who ended forced labor and fought for independence—was one thing. A military dictator was another.

Calamitous

The Election of 2000

A supreme court appointed by General Robert Gueï, the sweeping general, disqualified the important opposition candidates except Laurent Gbagbo, who wasn't considered a serious contender. But faced with the prospect of electing a military dictator, many Ivorians were inclined to vote for Gbagbo. Fuming over Ouattara's disqualification and the anti-immigrant, anti-northern rhetoric that went with it, Ouattara's Rally of Republicans Party urged its supporters to boycott again rather than lend legitimacy to an undemocratic election. This time, the Democratic Party of Ivory Coast, the old ruling party, joined the boycott. Many people believe the two candidates struck a deal—the general would be declared winner and Gbagbo would recognize his victory and be appointed prime minister.

Elections are always held on a Sunday in Ivory Coast, and Election Day, October 22, was peaceful. In the North and in neighborhoods of Abidjan dominated by northerners and Rally of Republicans supporters, turnout was low. Yaya, much as he loved politics, stayed home, and insisted everyone in his family do the same. In Korhogo, fewer than 10 percent of electors voted. On Tuesday, General Gueï claimed victory, but if they had made a pact, Gbagbo didn't keep it. Gbagbo declared *he* had won and called on all patriots to go into the streets to force Gueï to back down. The following day, the streets of Abidjan filled with hundreds of thousands of people. "When you looked around, you would say no one lived here!" said Yaya. "Not a soul! We had all gone out into the streets! I was in the big stadium. We marched there! No one stopped us. No one said anything. There weren't any police that day! We were all mixed together—those for Alassane and those for Gbagbo." Soldiers from the presidential guard loyal to Gueï killed at least nine demonstrators the first night, but Ivorians continued to fill the streets on Wednesday, demanding that Gueï stand down. When he looked up and saw a helicopter flying away, Yaya felt relief. The general had fled the city, vanquished by the people. "We thought now they would wipe away the election and start over. Now we would vote in a real election and Alassane would be a candidate!" But a second set of election results was released on Thursday, and although only 37 percent of the electorate had voted, Gbagbo, who had received the most votes, declared himself president.

France, where Gbagbo had influential political allies, remained silent while the African Union, United Nations, United States, and South Africa supported a new election. The Rally of Republicans called on its supporters to demonstrate peacefully for a democratic election in which every candidate could run, but Gbagbo's young street fighters had no intention of giving up what they had just gained, their man in the presidential armchair. The Abidjan streets, having shown their power, now divided into two factions, those for Gbagbo and those for a fair election. When Yaya and his friends tried to reach downtown Abidjan to demonstrate, they found their route to the bridge across the lagoon blocked by the security forces, who had rallied behind Gbagbo.

In Abobo, on the northern side of Abidjan, Chékun's husband, Ngolo, was tired of the way it had become acceptable to insult northerners and discriminate against them in painful little ways. The southerners in his program had completed their internships and taken jobs, but he was still waiting to receive his certificate. At work, when some southerners insulted the Jula and the Mossi, no one spoke up anymore to defend them or decry that kind of talk. When they heard about the march, Ngolo and a friend decided to go. At seven in the morning, the two young men walked through Abobo, joining a crowd headed in the same direction. On the wide main road, in front of a burlap sack factory, the demonstration formed up. "No stones, no sticks, no machetes, and don't vandalize anything!" the leaders instructed. "We are going to march peacefully!" Looking back, Ngolo couldn't see the end of the march. It stretched to the horizon.

As they walked toward central Abidjan, he saw military trucks ahead blocking the road. This was a familiar tactic—bottling people up in their neighborhoods so they couldn't reach central Abidjan to demonstrate. But this time, when the marchers reached them, the trucks drove straight into the crowd. Panicked people ran in all directions—toward the safety of side streets and into the Banco National Park. Ngolo was on the side of the road by the park, a protected reserve of dense tropical forest, but he didn't want to run into the trees; the Banco was a place where bodies were dumped and criminals had their hideouts. Since he had a military ID because of his job, he decided to take a calculated risk and walked with measured steps to the side of the road and sat down.

"What are you doing here?" a policeman asked him brusquely.

"I was on my way to work." Ngolo tried hard to sound calm. "Since the buses weren't running this morning, I had to walk. The people who were marching came along and surrounded me, and I got mixed up with them, so I came over here. I will show you my ID card." A military identity card was larger than a civilian ID and had two sides. Ngolo's photo filled one side and his information was printed on the other. He handed it to the policeman in a two-sided clear plastic case.

When the policeman turned the card over, he saw his northern name. "Ngolo!" His tone hardened. "You're one of those who wants to put Ouattara in office!"

"These are all Ouattara's people!" added another gendarme. "I saw this man this morning in front of the sack factory carrying a pistol!"

"It couldn't possibly have been me," Ngolo replied carefully. "I have never in my life had a pistol in my hand." They searched him, took the $60 in his pocket, and ordered him to undress down to his underwear. They kept his clothing and ID card and turned him over to another policeman. As he walked the line of prisoners toward the military trucks, now parked on the side of the road, this policeman asked Ngolo, not unkindly, how he had ended up there.

Ngolo repeated his story about trying to get to work. It was midday and they were walking down the road in the scorching sun, Ngolo barefoot and wearing only his underwear.

"Frankly," said the policeman quietly, "I don't like to let you go with this group because you're one of us. I swear, those trucks you see over there, everyone you see in them—look at their faces carefully! If you see them again, you will know you are not in this world." The policeman added, "Now, though, it's very complicated for you."

It was very complicated. Ngolo knew it.

"What I am going to do for you," the policeman continued in a low voice, "I am going to talk to our commanding officer. If he agrees, you are going to leave. If he doesn't agree, here is what I can do. I will put you at the end of the line. You will be last and when I tell you to run, run! They will shoot at you, I guarantee you. But if you are a real Senufo, the bullets won't touch you. So those are the two things I can propose to you. I am going to talk to the commander first."

Ngolo began to tremble. Gendarmes were beating some of the men with batons and pistol butts. "You sons of whores!" yelled one as he struck them. "You want to make that foreigner president!"

The sympathetic policeman walked over to his superior and asked him to let Ngolo leave. The officer agreed. But the gendarme who had beaten and insulted the men had Ngolo's ID card and refused to hand it over. Annoyed at this insubordination, the officer reached over and took it out of the gendarme's breast pocket himself. The one who had interceded for Ngolo came back and handed Ngolo his clothes and his ID. "There is still the business of the money," he said.

"Never mind!" Ngolo replied quickly.

"Put your clothes on, you're leaving." He gestured to a little lean-to nearby. "You are really lucky. These others, you will never see them again."

"Please, please, let us go, too!" pleaded the other prisoners. "Have mercy on us! Pardon! Pardon!" Their faces were bleeding and one man's scalp was peeled back. "Help me, please help me!" he called to the gendarme who had interceded for Ngolo. But the officer turned away. Ngolo put on his clothes and walked as quickly as he could back toward Abobo. He hadn't seen his friend since the panic and he hoped that meant he had gotten away.

When he reached the sack factory where they had joined the march, piles of tires were burning, set on fire by the demonstrators, and plumes of black smoke and the smell of burning rubber filled the air. Men in uniform were pulling over the *gbakas* from Abobo and making the passengers get down and hand over their ID cards. Men with northern names were ordered to put out the fires by pissing on the burning tires; when they stopped, the uniformed men beat them. The northern women were forced to undress, get down on the road on their hands and knees, and clean the road by picking up the bits of burning rubber and putting them into oil drums.

Since he was heading in the opposite direction from the demonstration, they glanced at his military ID and let him pass. A young woman in her underwear on her bare knees was sweeping the street with her hands and crying. He walked away as quickly as he could, his mouth and throat burning with thirst.

When he reached a friend's house, his friend gave him milk to drink and urged him to spend the night and go home in the morning, when it would be safer. Although his friend refused to give him the road, he insisted on leaving.

Avoiding the main roads, he made his way through the side streets. When he emerged at a large rotary, a group of women called out in Senari, "Watch out! Be careful! The trucks are picking up people!" He turned back into the side streets, but it was an area he didn't know, and he realized he was in a neighborhood of Attié and Abé people. These southern ethnic groups were staunch supporters of Gbagbo. Ahead of him, a group of young men with red scarves on their heads had barricaded the road, leaving one narrow passage. They stood around the opening armed with sticks, machetes, and hatchets. One examined the ID of each person who wanted to pass, and some people were waved through; others were sent into a partially built house with an open door.

Ngolo took all this in quickly. He was in hostile territory, but it was too late to turn around. The young man glanced at the ID Ngolo held out, and when he saw it was a military ID, he waved him through. But after Ngolo had gone a few steps, he called out, "Wait! Wait! Stop! You are which ethnic group? What's your last name?"

He hadn't seen Ngolo's name because Ngolo had carefully held the ID with the photo side up; it showed his picture crossed by a diagonal stripe in the national colors of green, white, and orange. The information was printed on the other side, the side Ngolo had kept turned down. If they saw his name, it would be all over.

"You saw my card," he called back. "You know already. Why are you asking again?"

"Look at his face," one of the men called out. "He doesn't have the face of a northerner. Let him go!" People sometimes said this about Ngolo, that he looked Baule. He walked away, his arms covered with goosebumps. He had escaped again!

Around four that afternoon, he finally reached home to find his friend, who had come back hours before, distraught and his friend's wife in tears. They had seen trucks pull up to the hospital morgue with bodies, and since Ngolo hadn't returned, they thought he must be among the dead. His friend was trying to summon the courage to go to the morgue and look.

Ngolo thought about the men who had been caught and put into the truck; he didn't know any of them, so he couldn't tell their families what had happened to them. And the half-built house with the open door—who knew what would have happened if he had been sent in there?

That night and the next day, Gbagbo's street militias, armed with machetes and clubs, rampaged through the city's Jula neighborhoods, turning on anyone who looked Jula or had a Jula name. If you wore a boubou or were named Koné or Diabaté or Ouattara or had a northern Senufo name or a northern birthplace on your ID card, you were a target because you must be a supporter of Ouattara. The security forces also picked up people thought to be opposition activists. When the street violence ended, 155 people were dead, 316 wounded, and 50 missing, according to one count.

A group of Ngolo's friends who were active in the Rally of Republicans Party were drinking tea at their little shack in another part of Abobo when a military truck pulled up. Before he moved, Ngolo had lived nearby and often sat with them, drinking innumerable little glasses of strong sweet gunpowder and mint tea and talking politics. The seven young men were picked up that day by security forces; he never saw them again.

Thanks to his "patriots" in the streets of Abidjan and the support of the security forces, Gbagbo held onto the presidential armchair. The international community stopped calling for new elections. In November, a mass grave of fifty-seven bodies was discovered in the district of Yopougon. All had died from gunshot wounds at close range. The Rally of Republicans and the victims' families claimed they were Rally of Republicans supporters shot by gendarmes loyal to Gbagbo. When he heard the news, Ngolo thought once again about the men in the truck. He could not forget their faces, though he never saw any of them again.

A military coup d'état, then an election even Gbagbo, the victor, called calamitous. An ethnic witch hunt against the Jula. A mass grave. These things happened in other countries, it was true, but in Ivory Coast? Ivorians against Ivorians? They didn't think of themselves like this, but somehow they had reached this point. Even Gbagbo seemed frightened, and under international pressure, he convened a national dialogue. He chose novelist Ahmadou Kourouma to serve as leader of the national reconciliation forum; Kourouma was well suited for the position since he was a northerner and ostensibly Muslim (he described himself as practicing but not believing) and had a well-honed sense of irony about Ivorian politics. However, in newspaper interviews, Kourouma spoke frankly, saying there was no doubt Ouattara was Ivorian and that Bédié's *ivoirité* was "a perverse doctrine that had divided the country." This was too frank for Gbagbo's taste, and Kourouma was out. He spent the rest of his life in Lyons, France.

What people wanted was a top-down reconciliation; they wanted the big four—Laurent Gbagbo, Henri Konan Bédié, Alassane Ouattara, and Robert Gueï—to make peace. Ordinary people lived side by side in relative harmony most of the time while their political leaders battled for power. Some politicians struck matches and fanned the flames of division and exclusion, some looked the other way while their allies did it, but in every case, ordinary people, most often northerners, suffered the consequences. The mass grave of Yopougon tipped Ivorian politics over an invisible brink into overt violence, and since no one was held accountable and the big four did nothing, there would be no going back.

Powderkeg

2002

Two years after the calamitous election, in the summer of 2002, Tom and I returned to Ivory Coast with our two reluctant teenagers. In Korhogo, Nawa's younger siblings were also growing up. She had four brothers. The oldest had taken the baccaleaureate exam and was waiting for his results, the next had quit school and returned to Kalikaha to farm with an uncle, and the two youngest, Old Man and Djak, were in high school. Both were good students. Old Man, called that because he was named after his grandfather, was tall and gentle. He tutored neighborhood children and went everywhere on a ten-speed bike he had bought with his earnings. The three girls had not attended school; Nawa's two younger sisters helped their mother at home and in her market garden. Nawa was living on the other side of town with her second husband, Gozana, and came to see us with her two little boys, beaming her lovely smile.

In 2000, eight years after the bulldozers platted Kalikaha's streets into a grid, electric power lines had finally reached Kalikaha, and our round thatched house was now equipped with two lights, one inside and one outside, and electric outlets. I no longer had to hold a flashlight while I cooked, and fans made it much easier to sleep on hot nights. Telephone poles and wires hadn't reached Kalikaha and never would. Already, in the cities and towns, businesspeople had cell phones, and those who couldn't afford their own cell phone patronized the little stalls on every corner where you could top up your minutes or pay to make a call.

As soon as we had our house unpacked and set up, Tom asked to meet with the elders so he could report to them on his research; the meeting was set for the following morning at eight under a large mango tree. Tom started the meeting by thanking everyone for coming. Using the polite form of indirect address, Tom spoke not directly to the elders but to Adama in Julakan and French. To my surprise, Adama passed Tom's words on to a Jula elder elegantly turned out in a white boubou and turquoise plastic oxfords for the translation into Senari for the Senufo. Like most Ivorians, the Jula elder spoke two languages (indeed, many speak three or four).

Since the elders had given him the authorization to count everyone, Tom explained, he had done so the year before. The 1998 government census had counted eighteen hundred people, but he and his student had counted twenty-six hundred in Kalikaha proper, and even more living in camps outside the village (another six hundred), so thirty-two hundred in all. Despite being one of the largest towns in the area, Kalikaha was not a subprefecture, which is like a county seat; it had no public buildings and was under the administrative authority of another town. With a stick, Tom drew three large circles in the dirt. "Imagine that Kalikaha is composed of three large quarters. But the government only saw two of them." He covered up the middle circle with his clipboard. If they approved, he would go to the government administrator in the town twenty miles away and present his census results. The men agreed immediately. It was to the benefit of Kalikaha, politically and economically, to have its true size recognized. At the end of the meeting, one of the elders addressed our teenagers, sitting next to us on the bench. When we were gone, he said, it would be their responsibility to continue our relationship with Kalikaha. This is not something I would ever ask of our children. Tom and I had come to Kalikaha, and it had become a central knot in our lives and our marriage, but I wanted our children to find their own passions and their own roads, and now that they were teenagers, the day when they would leave to seek them was not far off. Ever since our arrival, they had complained about how boring Kalikaha was, so I was pleased when they answered the elders politely.

One morning I walked down to the potters' quarter to visit an old friend, Na, a tall, thin, big-boned woman about my age. Becca, fourteen that summer, came with me. Na's youngest daughter, playing on her lap, was two. After we exchanged news, Na said to me, "You had two children and then no more. Did you take medicine?"

I said I did.

"Well, give me some of it," Na said. "I don't want to have any more children. These children are killing me." She lifted her thin muscular arms and shook the loose skin at me.

I asked her how many children she had given birth to.

"Ten, but five died. Five left and five stayed." As we talked, Na kept coming back to children and how it was a good thing to have only two. Several other women joined our circle, including a high school girl home on vacation. I suggested Na see the nurse at the clinic, but she said she didn't have any money to buy medicine. "Could you tell your husband to buy Prudence?" I asked her. Prudence was the brand of condoms sold everywhere as part of the HIV-prevention program. Even the little stores in Kalikaha stocked the subsidized Prudence condoms.

"The men won't agree," another woman said.

"They won't spend the money!" added others.

"Just lock the door to your house," I told Na teasingly, "and when your husband comes, tell him he needs Prudence before he comes in. If he has it, open the door. And if not, keep it locked!" The high school girl looked embarrassed and the older women chuckled. But Na was perfectly serious, and she was right. Women needed to be able to space out their children. Fewer pregnancies would improve their health and they would have more money to sustain each child with better nutrition, medicine, and schooling. Prudence condoms were available in Kalikaha, but their price, which probably seemed so cheap to the people who organized the anti-HIV campaign, made them a luxury. Besides, what Kalikaha husband would be willing to limit the number of children he could have? Every farmer-father dreamed of a field full of young workers planting, weeding, and minding the oxen. I wondered, for the thousandth time, if rural development professionals in Abidjan, Paris, and Washington, regardless of whether they were educated urban Africans or from other continents, had any notion about women's lives in places like Kalikaha. I had been a young woman when I first came to Kalikaha, and now I had a daughter facing her own young womanhood. In my world, women's opportunities had expanded dramatically in those twenty years. But in Kalikaha, women still faced the most basic problems, especially once they were married. They had no control over their own bodies, and they were not treated as autonomous adults with the same rights as men.

Departmental elections were set for Sunday, July 7, and we went into Korhogo the day before. On Saturday afternoon, supporters of the candidate for the old ruling party, the wealthy owner of a transport company, paraded down the main street in company buses singing and playing drums. Young men had taken the mufflers off their mopeds and decorated them with leafy branches and campaign signs, and they roared back and forth, doing stunts for the crowd. The candidate waved from inside a limousine, so we couldn't see him well, but on his campaign posters he looked dapper. His black-and-white houndstooth sport coat was draped rakishly over one shoulder, and he wore suspenders, a fedora, and the confident smile of a candidate who had the funds to run a competitive campaign. Having prospered under the old ruling party, he had stuck with it. But the Rally of Republicans dominated the North, and their parade was even larger.

President Gbagbo announced on the radio that only voters in possession of the new green national identity card would be eligible to vote, but the government admitted that seven hundred thousand cards still had not been distributed. At dusk, the evening before the election, two men stood outside a government building with a stack of the new ID cards calling out names. Since there are five main Jula surnames and five Senufo ones, many of the names were repeated. It was like hearing someone call out, "John Smith, Robert Smith, John Smith." If no one stepped up, the man handed the card to an assistant. President Gbagbo announced that if you hadn't received your card, you could still vote by showing the receipt you received when you registered.

Sunday evening, I quizzed everyone I met up with—had they voted? Adama had not received his new green card, so he had gone to his polling place with the receipt, but he hadn't been allowed to vote. Kass, a broad-shouldered young man from whom we rented our car, also had only the receipt; he didn't try. "The army, the police, gendarmes—they're all there . . . and this is *not* the United States of America where they will just chat with me about it," he said, giving me a pointed look. "They might just turn me over to the army." Kass thought I viewed Ivorian elections naively, with rose-tinted American lenses, and later events would prove him right. An ardent Rally of Republicans supporter we knew had not received his new card, so he took the receipt to his polling place, where he was asked his father's and mother's names. His name was on the list of eligible voters, so he was given a ballot. "I would have insisted because I had registered. How can the government require a card that hasn't even been distributed?" In my small sample, he was the only one who had successfully voted with a receipt, and I wondered if he had been treated fairly because he was educated, something you could easily tell by the way he spoke French.

We returned to Kalikaha the following day. "How did the voting go?" I asked everyone. "The voting went fine," said a Jula elder who had stuck with the old ruling party and had a poster of its dapper candidate pasted to the earthen wall of his house. "If people were not on the list, it's because they didn't take part in the census as they were supposed to."

"How did the voting go?" I asked our *jatigi* Donni. "Did you vote?"

Donni shook his head. He had his green card, but when he arrived at the polling place, his name was not on the list. "Even the chief—his name wasn't on the list either. And the business with the Jula women . . ."

"What happened with the Jula women?"

"Their names weren't on the list," Donni said. "Have you talked to Natagoura?"

"No. Why?"

Natagoura, a Jula woman who lived next to the marketplace, was a diehard supporter of the Rally of Republicans and known for her sharp tongue. Men tried to stay out of her way. "You should go and talk to her yourself," he said.

"The government took the names of the Jula women off the list so there would be fewer Rally of Republicans voters!" said one of our neighbors. "They know the Jula women turn out and they know they vote Rally of Republicans!"

That afternoon, Adama and I found Natagoura bent over a large kettle, scooping out a serving of rice for a customer. Her sharp eyes brightened. "It's good you have come to ask about the election," she said, even before I asked. "How is Tom?"

"He is well."

"And the children?"

"They're there." It was a standard reply, perfect for the mother of two teenagers who complained constantly about having to spend their summer in a boring African village. "They have gone out to the bush with Tom to visit cattle herds."

"May Allah give them a safe return and a long life."

"Amina," I replied contritely. Amen. It *was* best not to think annoyed thoughts about your teenagers until they were safely home. She handed her ladle to a daughter and offered me a stool. "I walked down to the school to vote—with my new green ID card. But that teacher said my name wasn't on the list! They found my parents' names, but not mine!" Natagoura drew herself up and raised her index finger to the sky. In a dramatic voice, she continued, "I told them, 'Look at me! Look! I was born in this village! I am leaving here and going back to my house right now. I will wait there. And I want someone to come and tell me you have found my name. And when that person brings the message, I will come back and I will vote.'" I could picture her sweeping out of the school, a thin woman in a white headscarf who walked with quick determined steps.

Natagoura called out to a woman nearby. "Come over here and tell Carol your story!" The woman scooted over, holding her stool to her bottom. She had her green card, too, but when she got there, her name wasn't on the list. "More than ten people in my family went and only two were able to vote. Two!" She sighed. "We didn't speak up like Natagoura."

"I wasn't the only one who argued with them," Natagoura added. "Some others did, too. But they weren't as forceful and so nothing happened."

"And did they find your name?"

She nodded and jabbed at the air. "Now do you think my name suddenly appeared, just like that, where it wasn't before?" They couldn't find the chief's name, either, she pointed out, and turned him away, but one of the local young men found it later and sent for him. It didn't surprise me that the teachers, who weren't Senufo, had trouble with the multisyllabic Senufo names. I struggled with them daily. But the Jula names were easier. "The Senufo came to vote one at a time," Natagoura added. "But the Jula really turned out in groups."

When I talked to the poll workers, they said 113 people had voted. It seemed a small number for a community of more than 3,000. The nurse, who had worked in one of the three polling places, said there were 151 names on his list, but only 42 votes were cast. Three ballots had to be thrown out because they were not completed correctly. Thirty electors voted for the Rally of Republicans and nine for the coalition created by Gbagbo's Popular Front and the old ruling party.

After the election, people in the North went on with their lives. It was the rainy season, and the farmers were in their fields from daylight to dark, determined to have a good harvest and fill their granaries for the year ahead. But their resentment lingered. The new cards and voter lists had been created, they felt sure, to exclude them.

At the end of the summer, when we drove south to Abidjan, the tension in the city's crowded streets was palpable. Northerners were furious at Gbagbo's government because their names had been left off the voter lists. The new green identity cards were a government conspiracy, they said, to exclude them from the political process because they had northern names and would be likely to support Ouattara and the Rally of Republicans. Over and over, we heard the same bitter refrain: "I was born here and this is my country, but I have no rights here anymore. I am Ivorian but I am treated like a foreigner in my own homeland!"

When I thought back over the summer and tried to make sense of what was happening, two moments stood out: one was the anger and resentment after the departmental election. The other took place on a dirt road as we left the North. We drove up to a barricade, a piece of rope tied across two poles. The gendarme was holding a machine gun and he walked over to Tom's window. Once we greeted him, he responded politely, lowered the rope, and waved us through.

"Did you see that?" Tom asked me soberly after we drove away.

"A machine gun!"

"And before he walked over, he took off the safety!" We had never seen a machine gun in northern Ivory Coast. We had seen shotguns, some made by local gunsmiths, others imported, as well as the antique flintlock muskets hunters carried. But a gendarme wielding a machine gun on a remote dirt road in northern Ivory Coast? If bandits had attacked vehicles in that area, we would have heard about it and we hadn't. It didn't make sense.

Resentment over political exclusion. Machine guns. Six weeks later, the two merged and exploded. On September 19, 2002, while President Gbagbo was on a visit to the Vatican in Rome, an armed rebel group tried to take over the country. The rebels, led by northern soldiers from the Ivorian army, attacked government security positions, gendarmeries and barracks, in three cities at once—Abidjan, Bouaké, and Korhogo. The rebels took Korhogo and Bouaké, and in the North they gained the support of the local population, but they failed to capture Abidjan, the seat of power and wealth. From Bouaké they announced their goal—to end exclusion and *ivoirité* in Ivory Coast. They wanted Gbagbo out—to be replaced by a civilian transition government that would hold fair elections.

Who was behind the rebellion? Who had financed it? Where had the soldiers been training before they suddenly appeared on September 19? No one knew, but many fingers pointed north toward Burkina Faso. Many thought President Blaise Compaoré, who had assassinated his childhood friend Thomas Sankara to become president of Burkina Faso in 1987, must be the mastermind and the financier behind the attempted coup. In the wave of anti-immigrant violence and harassment that had swept Ivory Coast, thousands of farmers and business owners from Burkina had fled home, losing their investments and even sometimes their lives.

Showing no fear, Gbagbo returned to Abidjan. He wanted the French to help him put down the rebellion and reunite the country because he was, after all, an elected president, and because the two countries had a long-standing mutual defense agreement that included a French military base near the Abidjan airport. *Long live Françafrique,* which he had so often criticized. But instead of fighting the rebels, the French military formed a boundary line between the Ivorian forces in the South and the rebel army in the North. To punish the rebellious North, Gbagbo's government cut off their cell phone networks and electricity. His street militias, who called themselves Young Patriots, ruled the streets of Abidjan, railing against the foreigners who were behind the rebellion and the neocolonial French, who refused to come to the aid of their elected president and oust the rebels.

In January, representatives of the political parties of Ivory Coast and the rebels, who had renamed themselves the New Forces, met in a suburb of Paris. In addition to a cease-fire, they agreed to end *ivoirité,* to revise the rules for citizenship and candidacy, and to form a government of national reconciliation. This accord reduced Gbagbo's powers and gave the New Forces and the opposition parties seats at the government table, which outraged Gbagbo's supporters. After this, the country was suspended in a strange stalemate, a divided purgatory—neither outright civil war nor genuine peace and reunification. The New Forces controlled the North while Gbagbo's government retained control of the South, which included Abidjan with its all-important port, three-quarters of the population, and most of the cocoa revenues.

The political leaders on both sides dragged their feet and failed to enact the reforms they had agreed to. A series of other agreements was signed and ignored. After several African-led initiatives failed to resolve the conflict, in 2004 the United Nations created a peacekeeping mission to help Ivory Coast implement the peace process. The UN mission, called ONUCI (United Nations Operation in Côte d'Ivoire), included more than six thousand blue-helmeted peacekeepers who patrolled a buffer zone between North and South. While a small group profited from the instability, most people, on both sides of the line, became poorer than ever.

Lasungo

Protection

No northern soldier went into battle without supernatural protection. That would be like going naked and unarmed. In Lasungo's dreams, the spirits taught him what ingredients to put into a goat or sheep horn so bullets would pass right by, what recitations to say, how to spit into the horn before he closed it up. They taught him how to make bulletproof undershirts, and since bullets were not the only danger, they taught him how to make amulets that protected against the other perils of war.

Although Lasungo lived in a secluded thatched-roof house next to a stream on the edge of Korhogo, the young rebels found their way there. Because he knew they would be in a hurry, he kept a stock of horn amulets and bulletproof undershirts ready. The shirts were made out of narrow bands of homespun cotton he bought from a weaver in a small village. Lasungo cut the hole for the neck and sewed the bands together himself. The horns were priced at $50 each, the shirts $100. The recruits didn't have this kind of money, so he told them to pay whatever they could, even if it was just enough for his tobacco or kola. This was what he could do to support the rebellion. Other diviners and healers also offered their services for the northern cause.

When the young soldiers came to him, he sat with them on the floor of his spirit hut, threw out the cowries, and recounted what the spirits had shown him in a soft persuasive voice. The undershirts, he promised the young men, would protect them. No bullet, no machete blade would pass through. And the sacrifices of chickens, kola nuts, and sheep he prescribed would keep them safe from less predictable dangers. He also had herbal power medicines he had brewed in ceramic jars. These the young rebels could wash themselves with for strength and safety. When they got their orders to leave, he worked the ingredients into shea butter, easily transported in a little plastic tub or bag.

At night, anxious about the dangers of the day to come, they could rub the mixture on their skin. These power medicines came with strictures—they weren't activated until the young man received the blessing of his elders and would deactivate if he stole from innocent people. With some, the user had to abstain from sexual intercourse for twenty-four hours each time he rubbed the medicine on his skin. Later, if he were killed, other soldiers would say he must not have obeyed the conditions to the letter or that whoever killed him had a medicine stronger than his.

After a rebel commander visited him, Lasungo's reputation grew. The commander promised that after the war was over, if the bulletproof shirt worked, he would come back and give Lasungo its true value, plus a car. Cars were one of those other dangers the young rebels needed to be protected from. They commandeered all sorts of vehicles and went careening through the dusty, pedestrian-lined streets of Korhogo in a risky game of dodge-ems. They crashed into buildings, into people, and into each other, and quite a few of them died that way.

During the rebellion, Lasungo prospered. His young clients wanted to stay on good terms with the spirits. They often returned with some eggs or a chicken for him to sacrifice, and after he cut the chicken's throat and put its blood on the shrine behind his house, the spirits wanted him to cook and eat the meat so he could serve them well. The young men dropped by and sat on the bench outside his little house, chatting and drinking. They looked up to him and sought out his advice; Lasungo liked the feeling that he was looking after and protecting his younger brothers, who were fighting for the rights of northerners like him.

Abou Joins the Rebels

When they failed to take Abidjan, the rebels took off their uniforms and evaporated into sympathetic neighborhoods—Abobo, Koumassi, Adjamé, and some parts of Yopougon. Gbagbo's security forces took revenge on these places and people disappeared—Rally of Republicans activists, immigrants from Burkina Faso, and imams, Muslim religious leaders. When Gbagbo's supporters spoke about the rebellion, they construed it as being composed of people they conflated into northern-Jula-Muslim-foreigners-for-Ouattara. They rarely mentioned the other northerners who supported the rebellion, like the Senufo, although the New Forces leader, Guillaume Soro, was a Christian Senufo.

Shortly after the rebellion, one of Yaya's younger cousins came to see him at the scrapyard. Abou was twenty-seven, tall and broad-shouldered. He had gone to school with Chékun for three years before his family took him out of school to work in the fields. He was joining the rebellion, he informed Yaya, who didn't discourage him.

Like Yaya, Abou went south as a teenager to work on a cocoa plantation, then moved to Abidjan, where he worked as an apprentice driver on a *gbaka*. In Abidjan, hundreds of brightly painted *gbakas* follow set routes from one point to another. They start out as white Renault vans, then are retrofitted with windows and rows of seats, some of which fold to let passengers squeeze in and out, and finally are decorated with names and mottos—Destiny, Allah knows all, Chicago, TGV (after French high-speed trains)—and portraits of guardian heroes from Nelson Mandela to soccer stars like Yaya Touré to musicians like Tiken Jah Fakoly and Alpha Blondy. Heedless of traffic rules, *gbakas* veer in and out, crossing lanes to load and unload their passengers at appointed landmarks or intersections, often the busiest, most crowded places.

The apprentice driver hangs on the back barking out the destination, collects the money, opens and closes the back doors, helps the passengers in and out, and when everyone is in, thumps on the roof to let the driver know he can take off. The ideal apprentice has a strong voice, is as agile as a gymnast, and has not yet realized he is mortal. Abou was a teenager when he started. On Sundays when there wasn't much traffic, he was allowed to drive, and as soon as he was twenty-one, he earned his *gbaka* license.

That was in 1996 in the early years of *ivoirité*. His job put him in constant conflict with the police and the gendarmes, who barricaded the roads and collected tolls, augmenting their salaries as le Vieux had advised. "They stopped us, hassled us, racketed us, gave us shit!" On his route from the northern outskirts of Abidjan to the main mosque in Adjamé, about ten kilometers, there were always three and sometimes as many as six police checkpoints. When he was an apprentice, he would have to fork over fifty cents at each checkpoint. When he became a driver, it was a dollar, and that was if your papers were in order. If they found something missing or expired, you paid more. "You didn't have time to argue, so you paid and took off. Your apprentice was yelling the desination—*Adjamé! Adjamé! Adjamé mosquée!*—and everyone was always in a hurry!"

But when the political situation heated up and Ouattara's Rally of Republicans Party started organizing demonstrations, Abou said, "That's when the real problems started!" The gendarmes harassed the passengers they viewed as northerners. "If you had a Jula name like Coulibaly, Ouattara, Koné, you had a thousand problems! But if your name was a Baule name like Kwakou or Kwadjoe, or if you spoke Baule or Bété to them, you passed—even if you didn't have all your papers. But if you were Jula or Senufo, or if you wore a long boubou or a white hat . . . hehhhh . . . they wore you out with their shakedown!

"When the passenger had a problem, we would wait a little, but if they wouldn't let the person go, we had to leave them there. If the passenger hadn't paid and the driver or apprentice was a good person, they wouldn't ask for anything and they could take another *gbaka*. But often we collected the money for the trip at Banco. So if there were problems between Banco and Adjamé, the trip was already paid. You have to get off, the driver has his money, and if you take another *gbaka*, you pay again."

The *gbaka* he drove belonged to a southerner who owned several, and all the papers were in order, but even so he ended up paying. "The gendarme would say there was a problem with the red emergency triangle or my first aid kit. If you say, 'Hey, I know my rights!' you will never get away—so you give them the dollar and you take off. A *gbaka* man has no time—you show your papers, he doesn't even look at them, you pay, and you keep driving!"

Friday mid-morning was always a busy time as Muslim elders headed to the mosque for the midday prayer. One Friday, gendarmes stopped the *gbaka* and went down the narrow aisle, picking out passengers they thought were northerners and checking their papers. An old man in a long white boubou and white skullcap didn't have an ID card—it was possible he was Guinean or Burkinabé or, like so many Ivorians, undocumented. After they left, Abou looked back and tears were running down the old man's face. "What's the matter?"

"They took my money." When they got to the mosque in Adjamé, he was still sitting there in despair, his face damp. Abou pulled out $2 and gave it to him so he could get home.

The security forces got *gbakas* themselves, the same white vans but without windows and seats, and drove around Jula neighborhoods to shake people down. They came nearly every day to the Jula enclave where Abou lived and hassled the women. One day they picked up Abou's wife at the market and took her to the police station. Since she wasn't yet eighteen, she didn't have an ID card, so although she was pregnant with their first child, they made her spend the night in jail. After that, his heart hardened against the police and gendarmes. Every time they stopped him, a wild rage rose in his chest. He hated everyone in uniform.

He became active with the Rally of Republicans, and when Gbagbo forced out Gueï in 2000, he went into the streets to demand new elections. When he heard that Alassane Ouattara was coming to Yopougon to give a speech, Abou put on his orange Rally of Republicans hat and scarf and filled the *gbaka* with supporters. "I was 100 percent Rally of Republicans! And people were on top, people were inside, all wearing orange, all waving and shouting for the Rally of Republicans."

When he returned to the garage that evening, he was told to park the *gbaka*. "What's wrong with it?" he asked. "Sorry, just park it." When Abou called him, his boss said, "This *gbaka*—it's not Alassane who bought this for me, it's not the Rally of Republicans who paid for this. It's mine." The owner took the keys from him and gave them to another driver. After that, Abou worked as a relief driver eight or ten days a month. In addition to his scheduled relief days, he would stand around waiting, and when the *gbakas* pulled in, the drivers would give him a few dollars to drive while they took a break.

He worked security at all the Rally of Republicans meetings, linking arms with other men and standing around the crowd to protect them. "'March!' That's all they had to say, and I was there at the front." After the rebellion, the police and gendarmes and CECOS (Centre de Commandement des Opérations de Sécurité), a paramilitary anticrime unit that had a reputation for harassing anyone they suspected of not supporting Gbagbo, started coming around. "'You foreigners, you rebels, we are going to kill you!'—that was how they talked to us. They were picking up people, one by one. I had a wife and child, and my wife was pregnant again. When I saw them taking people like that, I knew I needed to leave. They know me, because I am always at the front of the marches, and one day they are going to come for me."

His friends were calling from Bouaké. "We have uniforms, we are training, you should come!" He told Yaya he was leaving and asked him to provide for his wife and child if he couldn't get money to them.

Yaya had heard the security forces shot young men if they thought they were going to join the rebels.

Abou reassured Yaya he had a way to cross safely—he would be ferried across in a Red Cross ambulance, disguised as a Red Cross worker. Abou denies he actually did this. He says he dressed in a T-shirt and jeans, hid his money in his pocket, carried nothing, and got down from the bus just before the line. "If you weren't lucky or you looked frightened, you had problems." Some of the young men on the bus were taken away by the police and never turned up in Bouaké. But no one asked him anything, so he started walking, and men on motorcycles appeared to ferry him and the others to Bouaké. At the first roadblock, the first rebel he saw was from his neighborhood. "Ehhhhh! You've come!" said his friend, who fitted him out with a uniform and a machine gun. The men showed him how to load and unload the gun and that was his training. Abou was a hunter and claims he could shoot pretty straight. When his friend finished his guard duty, he took Abou to join his battalion, and after that they worked together at the checkpoint. Sometimes one of the rebels recognized a man in ordinary clothing as a policeman or gendarme he knew. They sent those to the chief for interrogation. If the chief was satisfied with the men's answers and they wanted to stay, they gave them a uniform. Some were former soldiers and could train the others.

Abou was taught to fire heavy arms. After learning how to load and line up the target, he shot only a few times at a palm tree, watching to see if his charge hit the fronds. They couldn't waste ammunition on target practice.

He and eight others took over the empty house of a gendarme. They knew this because they found a pile of uniforms as well as photos of the man wearing them. Perhaps the gendarme was lucky enough to get away quickly, dressed in ordinary clothing. But if he didn't leave quickly enough, he might have been one of the gendarmes who were rounded up on October 6, 2002, before Abou arrived. "Remember Yopougon?" the rebels asked them. An investigation had placed the blame for the mass grave discovered in Yopougon on the gendarmes stationed at Abobo, but the government ignored the report and no one was punished. "Now it's your turn!" That day and in the days following, sixty gendarmes were murdered in Bouaké. Some of their family members were also murdered. It was one of the cruel reprisals northern soldiers exacted for the years of harassment, terror, and impunity.

Bouaké was the military and political capital of the rebel enterprise. Each morning, Abou turned up for assembly, and if there were new recruits, he helped train them. His commander never hid his objective—Abidjan. "How could we split the country in two?" Abou asked rhetorically. "We would have what? Nothing. We wanted to take Abidjan and everyone would be on the same footing—equal. Then there wouldn't be Koukou, no Kwadjoe, no Kassoum, no Jula, no Christian. Everyone the same, no matter whether you have a Baule name or a Jula name. Everyone would have his papers. Our commander always said we are waiting for the day when God helps us and we will take Abidjan. When he said it, everyone clapped and cheered."

After the cease-fire, when Bouaké was calm, they started "working" so commercial activities could resume, people could shop, and they could profit. The New Forces organized the Centrale, a treasury with a system of customs and tolls on all people and products. Just as the government gendarmes had done, the New Forces set up roadblocks at intervals on every road in the North. At the entry to each town, there was a barricade, supposedly for security but in fact to raise money. At every roadblock, the soldiers collected tolls, sometimes handing out little receipts torn from preprinted booklets.

Each vehicle had to purchase a permit to travel through New Forces territory and display it on the windshield. For a car, you paid $10 or $20. There was no longer much trade with the South, but the merchants in Bouaké and

Korhogo had quickly reorganized their routes and were bringing in truckloads of merchandise from the port of Lomé in Togo and from Guinea, Ghana, Burkina, and Mali. For a truck, the price of a laissez-passer varied between $200 and $500, depending on the value of the cargo. Abou was assigned to work as a liaison between the rebellion's treasury and the merchants. How he got this plum job I don't know. "People got to know me and saw I was straight" is his explanation. Although his ability to read and write was basic after three years of school, he was literate and spoke some French, and that made him more capable than many young rebels.

"We are going to create a structure to work with the merchants," his officer told him. "You must be polite with them, not violent." When they were expecting a delivery, the merchants called to let him know. They had already paid at the border, but now they paid again. "I have two semis coming in from Lomé," one would say. "One cooking oil and one tomato paste." Abou made out the customs form for each truck—$300—and they paid him. At the end of every week, he turned in the money and the receipts. He examined each truck because the duty he charged depended on the size of the load and the value of the merchandise. "If he says candy, well, that's not very valuable, so for a load of candy he would pay at most two hundred dollars. But cooking oil—one container sells for twenty-four dollars and there are thousands of them in a truck. And then medicines—some brought truckloads of medicines from Ghana and Guinea to sell—now that! They are going to pay more than five hundred dollars because pills—a truckload of pills—it's worth a lot!"

Abou says that he was told to look at the bills of lading, but he soon realized they were meaningless. He had to open the truck and examine the goods. "A merchant will never show you a bill of lading that is straight, exactly regular. Never! Never! Trafficking—if he's doing it, he will never say it!" The irony of this situation, the representative of the rebels, who have taken over half the country and are running it as their private fiefdom, trying to make sure local merchants pay the proper customs fees—Abou doesn't comment on that. He just shrugs his big shoulders.

He worked Monday to Saturday and then turned in his receipts and the money. His boss gave him back something—usually about $30 for the week, and sometimes he received small gifts from the merchants—$20 for gas or $10 for cell phone units. But if a lot of trucks arrived and he brought in a big sum that week—say $2,000—then his boss might hand him back a substantial bonus, $200, for his week's work. Business was best right before the month-long Muslim festival of Ramadan, when truckloads of clothes, sugar, and cooking oil were coming in from Lomé, Togo, Ghana, Burkina, and Mali. Then, he might turn in $10,000 in a week.

Abou admits you could work the system—you could put down candy on the receipt when it was really cooking oil and put something aside. They worked on trust. He says the Centrale used the money to buy food and uniforms. At the beginning, he saw pickups filled with arms arrive at the camp, but he didn't know who bought them or where they came from. "That was not at our level!" He didn't eat at the camp. Only the soldiers who didn't have jobs ate there. After he started working at the Centrale, he was able to bring his wife and children to Bouaké to live with him in the house of the absent gendarme.

"Once you started working at the Centrale, war—we forgot all about that. You were just there, earning your little-little coin." If you talk plainly about war, he explains, then you admit that war turns out to be a business like any other. "Once things were working, everyone earned a little, a little—the merchants, everyone did their little business—and those that didn't have jobs, they ate at the camp, they ate well." With what he earned, he helped a partner go into the cement business in Abidjan. He also bought a large lot and gradually built a spacious residential compound for his family and a store to rent out.

Nawa and the Old Healer

One Thursday night, finally pregnant for the first time since her husband's terrible bus accident, large and unable to sleep, Nawa's friend Assiata went outside to sit in the courtyard in the fresh air. She was surprised to find Nawa's husband, Gozana, awake, too, pacing quietly back and forth. He couldn't sleep either, he said. She wondered if he were anxious about the next day, when he would attend Friday midday prayers at the mosque for the first time.

The next morning, Nawa was at her table at the market when someone brought her a message that her husband needed her at home. They had invited friends and family to join them after the prayers for a celebratory meal, but Gozana needn't worry, she thought. She and Assiata would have everything ready by the time the men returned from the mosque and the guests arrived.

"It's serious," the messenger told her. "You need to come now!"

She entrusted her vegetables to her friends and left. In preparation for this day, Gozana had bought a boubou, the long robe that Islamic men wear, a little white hat, and a prayer mat. His head had been shaved. He had also bought fish and meat and rice, so Nawa and Assiata could prepare a special meal.

When she arrived home, she found him very ill. That morning, he felt so thirsty he bought eight of the little baggies of water the vendors sell, he told her. Then his heart began to pound very fast, so he came home. He vomited up the water along with blood. Gozana begged Nawa to go to the market, find his sister's husband, and ask him to come and take him to the hospital. "I don't want to leave you like this!" she said, starting to cry. In tears, she ran to the market. When she returned with the brother-in-law, her husband was dead.

When the guests arrived for the celebration that afternoon, they heard the wailing. The imam declared that Gozana should have a Muslim funeral, even though he hadn't yet prayed at the mosque, because he had dedicated himself to Allah in his heart.

"Mama," their little son Yardjuma said, "someone is sleeping in our house and he has covered himself with a white sheet. Who is it?" She told him not to go in. Her family was divided about showing Yardjuma his father's body; some felt he should see it, others said he was too young. She wasn't sure what was best, and she couldn't think clearly. She decided against it; he had been especially close to his father and she didn't want to frighten him. The women tearfully cooked the food Gozana had bought for the celebration and served it at his funeral. The story of his death traveled all across Korhogo, and even in other neighborhoods, people heard about the man who died before he could pray at the mosque for the first time. This was someone who loved God in his heart, people said.

Shortly after Gozana's death, one of his nephews arrived, sold his inventory of used clothes, and took everything from the house, including a wooden chest a friend had made for Nawa and the mattress she was sleeping on. The landlord told her to stay even if she couldn't pay the rent, and Assiata looked after her and tried to comfort her. Yardjuma often asked when his father was coming back, and a man who lived in their courtyard always responded that his father would return soon, which didn't help. One evening Yardjuma patted the mat he was sitting on and told the other children to come sit next to him. "Wait here with me. My Papa will be home soon!" Nawa gently explained to him that his father had died and gone to live at the cemetery.

When the rains started, Yardjuma asked if his papa had a house at the cemetery. At night, he sometimes woke her. "Mama, open the door so Papa can come in. Papa is outside and he says to open the door for him." She would get up, open the door, and show him no one was there. Each time, she lay awake afterward until dawn. Once, when Yardjuma disobeyed her, she gave him a spanking. That night she dreamed of her husband. He just stood there looking at her, his arms crossed. He had never liked her to lay a hand on Yardjuma. One rainy night, Yardjuma again insisted that she open the door because Papa wanted to come in. She opened the door and looked out. No one was there and she told him so. "He has already come in. Lie down, Mama, so he can lie down, too." His assurance made her so uneasy that she put the little boy on her back and went outside. She would rather be walking in the wet dark night than stay inside with her husband's ghost.

When the hunters guarding the intersection heard her story, they accompanied her to her parents' house. In the morning, her mother urged her to move back in and she did, bringing her two boys. Her sadness and lethargy stayed with her until one night when Gozana came to her in a dream. Don't be sad, he told her. Think of our son. After that night, Nawa roused herself and tried to go on with her life.

After she completed the Muslim period of mourning for a widow, four months and ten days, she went back to work at the market, selling her mother's produce as well as vegetables she bought from other market gardeners. One day, her mother came to the market and encountered a woman selling lengths of printed cotton from a basin on her head. A woman with means will buy a set of three matching lengths; she wraps one around her hips like a skirt, the second is tailored into a matching blouse, often with elaborate detailing, and she wears the third loosely around her waist or, if she has a baby, as a matching sling to carry her baby on her back. The printed cotton cloths range in price, depending on the quality of the fabric and printing, and the most popular designs are given nicknames. Nafini admired a print on a green background. Its nickname among the women meant, in Ivorian street slang, "Give me a fist bump!" but she didn't know that; she simply liked the color and design. Six thousand CFA francs, the woman told her. Nafini didn't have the money with her, but she took the fabric to Nawa's table, hoping Nawa would be able to pay for it.

"But, Mama, that is too much. You should have come and asked me. These sell for five thousand." Nawa advised her mother that when the woman came to collect, she should apologize and explain that she didn't know the price. But by the time the woman arrived, her mother had gone home, leaving the cloth with Nawa. "The cloth you sold to my mother, really it's expensive. Those normally go for five thousand. But since my mother already took it, I am willing to give you five thousand five hundred," Nawa said. She wished her mother had done as she usually did and let her navigate the world of commerce for them both.

The woman said Nawa had to pay the price that her mother had agreed to. "It's too expensive. I can't pay six thousand." Nawa held out the folded cloth. But the woman refused to take it.

"You," the woman announced loudly, "are a troublemaker—you always get into arguments over prices!" She was a *jeli*, and when it comes to making scenes in public, *jeli* are professionals. Around them, the market was suddenly quiet. Then one woman spoke up. "Listen, madame, except for today with you,

Nawa has never gotten into a fight with anyone. It's you who came and started this argument." The other women chimed in, "That's true! Nawa doesn't start arguments. She doesn't cause trouble!"

The woman drew herself up and gave Nawa a scathing look. "Well, it's true that this is the first time you have gotten in an argument with me. But this is the last time you will ever cause a problem like this. You will never speak badly to anyone at the market ever again!"

Nawa paid her the six thousand CFA francs, although she could ill afford it. One morning after that, a morning that Nawa remembered as the very next day but her mother recalled as a month later, Nawa woke up with her mouth stretched tightly to one side. When she spoke, her family could barely understand her. When she tried to drink, the water dribbled out, and her eye on that side watered and stung because she couldn't close it. Her father said he thought high blood pressure could cause this and took her to the hospital. At the hospital, Nawa's blood pressure wasn't elevated, but they kept her all day and monitored her, just in case. She didn't have any other symptoms, and finally they gave her some blood pressure medication, told her not to eat salt, and sent her home.

Every week after that, Nawa went to have her blood pressure checked. The tightness in her cheek and jaw gradually softened a little. She could eat, drink, and speak, although with some difficulty, because her mouth still drooped. Her eye still watered; she could feel the wind blowing in it, and because it didn't close completely, specks of dust frequently irritated it. Nawa's friend Minata did not believe Nawa's illness could be treated at the hospital. She believed it was a supernatural illness and required an African cure. "Someone has wounded you," Minata said. She used the Senufo word for a supernatural curse: literally it meant a hidden wound, an invisible wound. That was when Nawa remembered the cloth vendor and her final words.

Nawa visited a healer in her neighborhood, and he gave her a pottery jar filled with medicine and told her to rub the medicine on her mouth and pull on her skin to stretch it back into place. But this hurt and didn't seem to be helping. As payment, the herbalist asked for four chickens, which Nawa gave to him. Then, although she wasn't any better, he demanded a goat. "You are a know-nothing and a thief!" she told him. She never went back.

Once a week, she made the trip to the hospital on the other side of town. One day when she was sitting in the waiting room, an old man looked at her carefully. "What is wrong with you, mama?" he asked kindly.

She told him she had problems because of high blood pressure.

"That's not high blood pressure. That's a supernatural illness. That is something Africans did to you."

Nawa thanked the old man and resolved to take her friend Minata's advice to see a diviner. Minata had heard of a powerful elderly diviner and healer who lived in a little town nearby, and she arranged for a man she knew to take the two of them there on his motorycle. Nawa paid for the gas. When they arrived, instead of throwing the cowries, the old man examined Nawa's right palm. After looking at it for a long time, he finally spoke softly. "I can help you."

Minata asked what he would charge for the treatment.

He said he knew Nawa didn't have much money and if he charged a large fee, she might steal to pay it, or she might go into debt. He didn't want to encourage either. He would treat her, and afterward, if she had something and wanted to give him a gift, fine. The old man filled a pottery jar with medicine and taught her how to prepare it. Twice a day, morning and evening, she boiled water with the leaves. With her right hand, she drank four handfuls, and with her left hand, she drank three handfuls. Then she bathed with the rest. She stayed with the old man and his family, following the treatment daily for a short time, then moved to the house of an aunt in a nearby village. She could barely eat, and some days, when she woke up she felt as if her limbs were tied to her mat and it took all her strength just to get up. Her aunt cooked for her and washed her clothes. If her cousin, a traveling photographer, was there, he took Nawa on his moped to get more medicine. Nawa was always welcome to spend the night with the old healer's family and sometimes she did. Very gradually, the lopsidedness of her face improved, but she remained weak and suffered from frequent diarrhea. After a year, she returned to Korhogo.

When she arrived at her parents' house, her mother was upset to see Nawa so thin and weak. "If you were still this sick, you should have come home and gone to the clinic!" Nawa went back to the old man once for medicine, but before she visited him again, she received a message that he had died. She made the trip to give her condolences to his wife and children, but she regretted she never had the chance to thank him properly or give him a gift. "He was so kind to me," she said. "So very, very kind."

Chékun in Abobo

Chékun's new home, Abobo, was a crowded, fast-growing neighborhood north of downtown Abidjan, nicknamed "Abobo-the-war," after a popular song about how you had to battle to get a place on a bus.

She was taken aback when her old boyfriend called one day and said, "Chékun, you need to give me my daughter."

"*Your* daughter!"

"Yes, send her here to live with me so I can send her to school."

A street in Abobo, a commune of Abidjan (photo by Tom Bassett)

"*Your* daughter? When I was pregnant, you said she wasn't yours!" She hung up on him. He was still living with the same woman, but they had no children and he kept calling. "I want my daughter to come and live with me."

"Now you say she's your daughter! What if I had been angry that day and gone and had an abortion?"

"But you didn't. Let her come here so I can send her to school."

"I can perfectly well send her to school myself. And just as soon as she is old enough, I will!"

When his phone calls got him nowhere, he sent his friends to plead his case. These emissaries sat in her living room, drank the water she politely offered, and told Chékun they knew their friend hadn't been the father he should have been. They apologized for his lapses and asked her forgiveness; they stressed that now he was ready to take responsibility for his child and begged her to reconsider. They had local custom on their side because if parents separate, children belong to the father, and once they are old enough, they are sent to live with him. But in this case, the father had renounced his claim and now wanted the luxury of changing his mind. Chékun had a feeling that what he really wanted was revenge on her for marrying someone else.

The school year started, and she was teaching in a large urban school and coming home to take care of Desirée and her little boy. The phone calls, the visits, and the badgering were stressful. Ngolo, although he treated Desirée like his own daughter, said nothing, acknowledging that it was her decision. Finally she called the magistrate who had taken her in when she gave birth and asked his advice.

"Your daughter will eventually hear from people that your husband is not her real father and she will want to know her father," he said, "so since he wants her, you should give her to him. He's in Abidjan, you are in Abidjan, so you can still see her from time to time. It's not like you are losing your daughter altogether."

Chékun said she understood, and since he had been like a father to her, she would follow his advice. But she couldn't bring herself to do it. Desirée was only four. "Her father kept telling me his wife wanted to raise her as her own. But I didn't know his wife, I didn't know if she was kind or not. I didn't know how they would treat her there and I worried and worried about it."

It's not uncommon for Ivorian children to be raised in other households. Some parents give a child to their mother to raise, as Yaya did. Sometimes girls, like Nawa's friend Assiata, are sent to live with an aunt or great-aunt who doesn't have daughters. Village parents send their children to stay with a *jatigi* who lives in town near schools, and city parents sometimes send young children to live with family members who farm. Parents who grew up farming see rural life as the way to learn discipline and a good work ethic. Chékun herself had lived in her uncle's household from the age of thirteen. She felt the expectations of her world pressing on her from all sides, and finally she gave in and named the day she would bring Desirée to her father's house to stay.

She had one bit of reassurance. The magistrate's wife was visiting Desirée's father and his wife at their house in Abidjan, and Chékun knew she planned to stay for an extended visit. The magistrate's wife had been there when Desirée was born, and Chékun trusted that she would look out for the little girl and also that she would be her eyes and ears and let her know if things weren't going well. Chékun and Desirée came into the house and settled in the living room, as if the visit were just a social call. After a short time, Chékun managed to make herself get up, open the door, and walk away. She was trying hard not to feel anything; she felt numb. But in one corner of her heart, which she was trying so hard to harden, she did register the tiniest thud of relief—the mistake of her youth was resolved. That night she called the magistrate's wife, who assured her Desirée hadn't even cried. Chékun knew Desirée had no idea what was happening and assumed her mother would soon return for her. She felt she should let her daughter bond with her new mother and not confuse her by coming to visit too soon, so she made herself stay away for five months, contenting herself with phone calls.

On September 19, when the rebels attempted to take Abidjan, Chékun was at home on maternity leave. She had had a scare with this pregnancy, and it seemed she might go into early labor, so her midwife had placed her on bed rest. A neighbor stopped in and told her there was a curfew. *Couvre-feu.* The French word means literally "cover the fire." Fire cover? Cover fire? The word made no sense to her. Although she had lived in the South for some years, she had been largely protected from harassment because she lived in a village of many northern immigrants and because schoolteachers were valued community members. She didn't pay much attention to politics. She focused on her work in the classroom, her church, and her family. Having never been in Abidjan during a crisis, she had never experienced a curfew and she didn't understand until, as evening approached, the street filled with rushing people, frantic to get home.

Her father had sent one of her younger brothers to school, but after the rebellion, the little elementary school in Kalikaha was understaffed and barely functioning. When it was safe, Chékun arranged for him to come to Abidjan and live with her. To her surprise, although he had gone to school for three years, he couldn't read, so Chékun hired a tutor. The availability of tutors was the sole advantage of the huge surplus of educated unemployed young men; they formed an informal private army of educators, a parallel educational system.

After that, she asked her parents to send her youngest sister, Zele, to live with her and babysit her two little boys while she taught school. "If Zele goes to Abidjan, she will never come back and I will lose her," said their mother. But Chékun insisted she needed help, and finally her parents agreed to let Zele come. When her chores were done, Zele paid close attention to her brother's tutoring sessions, and soon she knew the alphabet and was trying to write. "If you buy your sister the first-grade workbook, I'll work with her, too," the tutor offered. Zele zipped through first grade and Chékun bought the workbook for second. She completed that, too. "I want to go to school," she told Chékun.

She would have to ask their father, Chékun told her, as that had not been part of their agreement. He refused, but Zele continued to study with the tutor at the family table, and the next year, having completed three years of schoolwork at home, she said again, "I want to go to school."

Finally their parents agreed that if Chékun assumed the expense, Zele had their permission to go. To register she needed a birth certificate, but their father had never made the trip to the administrative office in the nearest town to register her birth. Zele was twelve, too old to enter third grade, so when Chékun filled out the forms, she did what everyone does for children who start school late—she lopped three years off Zele's age. Fortunately, Zele was small for her age because officially she was now nine. Chékun signed her up for fourth grade, hoping she could keep up. When the year ended, she was first in her class.

Chékun and Ngolo were also *jatigis* for two young men who had been accepted to the university. They had not an inch of extra space in their apartment, and crossing the city by bus over dilapidated roads jammed with traffic was an expensive and time-consuming ordeal, so Ngolo decided to see if he could get them a dorm room on campus. The dormitories were controlled by a student union closely allied with Gbagbo. Through his job, Ngolo met men across the political spectrum, and one of his contacts acted as a go-between and arranged a meeting. Although this union had been created to promote students' rights, it had become a violent militia that targeted northerners and terrorized professors, as well as a mafia-style business empire that sold pirated movies, rented dormitory rooms, and extorted money from small business owners near the university. Most of the younger politicians on every side had cut their teeth in the student union.

They met in the afternoon at a nightclub the man owned. Ngolo explained that he wanted to rent a dorm room for two young brothers who were starting classes soon.

"What's their political party?" the man asked.

"I haven't asked them," he replied carefully. "I'm not political, and I don't discuss politics with people."

"Well, if they are willing to swear allegiance to the Popular Front, we can talk," the man said. "Otherwise . . ."

Ngolo politely asked for the road and left. He rented another small apartment down the street from theirs, and eventually six young men were living there, either studying or looking for work. Ngolo paid the rent and bought their rice, but the rest of their expenses, including transportation every day across town to the university, they had to manage themselves. In Gbagbo's Abidjan, dorm rooms were for his supporters.

One Sunday in August 2006, just before school started, Chékun and the children came out of church. "What's that smell?" she heard people saying. The moment the rotten egg smell entered her nostrils, her head ached and her nostrils and throat burned.

"Toxic waste! Haven't you heard? Someone dumped toxic waste!"

It was the first time Chékun heard that two-word phrase. Her husband was away. Now that his internship had finally turned into a regular job for a large French company, he was sometimes sent to other countries to repair machinery. She hurried the children home and herded them inside. The littlest boy was vomiting, the older boy was coughing, and a little boy Chékun was caring for because his father had died broke out all over in an itchy red rash. Chékun closed the windows but that trapped the noxious air inside the apartment, so she reopened them.

The television news announced that the toxic waste had been taken off a ship and dumped in numerous locations around Abidjan. They warned people to stay away from the dump sites and if they were suffering from a reaction, to go to the nearest hospital. Treatment would be provided free, the announcer said reassuringly. That evening Chékun and Zele, their heads splitting and their sinuses stinging, took the children to the hospital. They were given aspirin as well as prescriptions, but only the aspirin was free. Chékun took the prescriptions to the pharmacy and paid to have them filled.

More than one hundred thousand people sought medical help for symptoms brought on by the waste. The toxic sludge arrived in the port of Abidjan in a tanker chartered by Trafiguera, an international oil trading company. Although Ivory Coast had no facilities for processing this waste, Trafiguera contracted with Compagnie Tommy, an Ivorian firm that had recently been licensed, to dispose of it. Tommy's quote was handwritten and the price per cubic meter was remarkably reasonable compared to what had been quoted in The Netherlands. After night fell, Tommy's trucks drove around the city, emptying their tanks in empty ravines, vegetable fields, waterways, and outside a baby food factory. Although the dumping was illegal, the port director allowed the tanker to depart. Pregnant women were advised to stay away from the waste, and some people left their homes and went to live with relatives in less polluted neighborhoods.

Classes were starting soon, Chékun had to work, and she didn't want the children to miss school, so they stayed put, although the smell lingered in their neighborhood. A French worker for the remediation company told a journalist he had never dealt with anything remotely like it—so much chemical waste dumped in the middle of such a densely populated city.

The television news reported that two children had died, then four, then ten. There were also reports of miscarriages, and anger in the city mounted. The transportation minister was dragged out of his car, beaten, and thrown into one of the toxic ponds, and a furious mob set the port director's house on fire. Gbagbo's government collapsed and his entire cabinet was forced to resign, which was unprecedented. They were reappointed, except the ministers for transportation and energy.

When the government newspaper published a list of victims eligible for compensation because they had sought treatment at the hospital, Chékun combed the columns. But she found only one name—that of the child she was babysitting. When she heard about an Ivorian association representing victims, Chékun went to their office and registered her family.

The following February, in a British court, Trafiguera settled with the Ivorian government and paid $198 million to clean up the waste. The company denied liability and sued news outlets for reports linking them to the deaths.

After that, Chékun occasionally received phone calls from the victims' association. They needed $10 for each person to set up the case files, then $4 to prepare the information for the lawyers, and $2 to make cards for each person in the case. Another time, they were drawing up a new list and if she didn't pay $21 each, they would be dropped from the lawsuit. Each time they called, Chékun made the trek to the office, where people sat behind computers at desks piled with papers, and paid. But in her neighborhood and at church, other people dropped out because they couldn't afford to keep paying the fees. Chékun wanted the lawsuit to go forward, for the wrongdoers to face real consequences this time. She knew government officials did illegal things all the time, took payoff money and got away with it, but this time the political big men who profited off everyone else had gone too far. This time they had poisoned an entire city! Besides, she had invested too much to drop out. So each time they called, she made the trip after school to the office and paid the fees so they could stay in the case.

The lawsuits continued, including a case in Ivorian court against Ivorians who created an organization, claimed to represent victims, and embezzled some of the settlement money. They received twenty years in prison. The child she was babysitting eventually received about $400, but Chékun and her family never received any compensation.

Yaya

Your Nationality Is Questionable

The gendarmes and police strutted through Yaya's Abidjan neighborhood demanding little payments. His partner in the scrap iron business was from Burkina Faso, and Yaya saw the way the police preyed on immigrants, but northern Ivorians were also harassed. One day, officers from CECOS, a paramilitary unit supposedly created to fight crime but known for harassing northerners, stopped Yaya and asked for his identification papers. The officer took the photocopy and scrutinized it.

"What's the problem?" Yaya asked him.

"Well, there is some doubt," the officer replied.

"Doubt about what?"

"About your nationality. It's questionable."

"Since I was born I have never even been to Burkina or Mali. I don't know Benin. I don't know Guinea! It's only Ivory Coast I know, and it's here in Ivory Coast I got my papers," he retorted. "Me, I was born in the department of Korhogo, the village of Kalikaha."

"There is some doubt" was the official phrase the government used about Alassane Ouattara's citizenship and the connection wasn't lost on Yaya. But he paid for speaking up—they made him go with them and wouldn't give his papers back until he handed over $3.

Another day, Djeneba went to the nearby woodworking workshops with a group of women to collect sawdust, which they used to start their cooking fires. A few of the women were from Burkina or Mali, but most were Ivorian. The police rounded them all up. When he heard, Yaya got on his motorcycle and went to the police station. The police chief told Yaya he would have to pay $6 to get his wife released.

"But why?"

Yaya

The police chief didn't bother to answer. He looked away.

Yaya paid the money and got Djeneba out the door. Then he turned back. "One day . . ." He raised his long thin finger. "One day, all this, *all* this . . ." He circled his finger in the air. "One day all this will end!"

Harassment of northerners had been government policy ever since the 1990s era of *ivoirité*, but with the country divided, it became even tougher to be a northerner in government-controlled Abidjan. Policemen or soldiers who spotted someone wearing a boubou or read a Jula name on an ID card were likely to call the person a rebel, insult them, demand money, or throw them off the bus, although they had a ticket. Sometimes police and gendarmes came to the scrapyards and demanded two thousand francs, about $4, from every man there. Yaya paid and was left alone, but others didn't have the cash in their pockets. They rounded up the ones who couldn't pay and tied them together, the front of one man's shirt to the back of another. They went through the men's pants pockets and took whatever little bits of cash they had, then marched them around the neighborhood most of the day. When they wanted to head back to their barracks for dinner, they untied the men and let them go. The police paid a visit to their mosque and informed the imam that if the neighborhood wanted the harassment to stop, they needed to pay $300 a week. If they didn't pay, there would be even more problems. The imam asked Yaya if he could help come up with the money.

"I'm not paying twenty cents!" burst out Yaya. "Here, we are in Ivory Coast. I was born here, I am Ivorian, and there is no law here that says you have to pay the police so they will leave you alone. If they want to round us up, they will just have to round us *all* up." The policemen came to the mosque twice more, then gave up. But in another part of the neighborhood, the extortion scheme worked. "Here almost everyone is Ivorian," Yaya explained, "but over there, they were afraid because they are from Burkina. They didn't have a choice. They paid six hundred dollars every week until the end of Gbagbo's time."

One night Yaya went out after curfew. He didn't like being cooped up with the women and children and felt it was nobody's business if he went down the street to chat with a friend. He wasn't wearing the pants and short-sleeved shirts he wore to the scrapyard; he was wearing his at-home clothes, a long boubou. Wearing a boubou marked you as Jula and made you a target for Gbagbo's security forces. As the two men sat outside brewing sweet gunpowder tea, a dark truck pulled up with five ominous letters printed large on one side: CECOS.

"Don't you know there's a curfew?" the CECOS officer demanded and ordered the two men onto the bench in the back of the truck. They had no idea where they were being taken or what would be done to them, and as the truck bumped through the streets, his friend leaned over and said they should offer the soldiers some money to let them out.

"How much do you have?" Yaya whispered back.

"Three thousand." That was equivalent to $7, enough for a respectable bribe.

Under his breath, Yaya chuckled. In his pocket, he had one hundred thousand CFA francs, a king's ransom, more than $200. The CECOS officers would be delighted to relieve him of it. Yaya didn't tell his friend about the money. Instead, he leaned over holding his stomach, squeezed his legs together tightly, and groaned.

One of the officers looked back. "What's wrong with you?"

"I'm sick. I was going out to get some medicine when you picked me up."

The truck stopped. "Get out! Get out! Get down right now!"

Yaya climbed out and speed-walked away, as if he were making for the nearest latrine. A bit later, his friend offered the soldiers the three thousand CFA francs and was let out, too.

"Imagine," Yaya said, slapping his palm on his thigh and chuckling, "imagine sitting in a CECOS truck with one hundred thousand in your pocket and getting out for free!"

North and South

In March 2004, the opposition political parties organized a peaceful march to the center of Abidjan to pressure President Gbagbo to institute the peace agreement he had signed. Once again the security forces blocked the roads from Abobo and other opposition neighborhoods. One hundred and twenty demonstrators were killed, nearly three hundred were wounded, and others went missing.

In November 2004, Gbagbo broke the cease-fire and tried to retake the North. Abou the rebel was asleep at his house in Bouaké when the other soldiers woke him to say a fighter jet was headed their way. "We don't have any planes!" he exclaimed, throwing on his uniform and running to his truck. They could hear the thud of bombs falling nearby. The planes circled low again and again. Abou figured they were looking for their hidden ammunition depots.

The planes didn't find the camouflaged ammunition, but they bombed the French military base, killing nine French soldiers and an American consultant who had taken refuge there. Gbagbo's government said they bombed the French camp by mistake, but the French didn't believe it, and neither does Abou. "Flying right over so low like that—how can you make a mistake? The French camp was big!" He thinks Gbagbo bombed the French because the French soldiers were stationed between the two sides. They blocked the rebels from moving south to Abidjan, but they also prevented the government troops from moving north. Gbagbo's fighter planes also bombed Korhogo; fortunately no one was killed.

Within hours, the French military retaliated, destroying the small Ivorian air force and taking over the airport. Gbagbo's militias, the so-called Young Patriots, were exhorted by their leader, Charles Blé Goudé, to defend Ivorian honor by attacking French citizens and French businesses, and for three days they rampaged through the streets of Abidjan, burning and looting French homes, businesses, and schools. Ten thousand French citizens and other expatriates were evacuated.

In 2005 Gbagbo's five-year term expired, and Ivory Coast should have held elections for president, but the United Nations and the international community, including the African regional organizations, conceded that organizing an election was impossible and gave Gbagbo an additional year in office. In order to draw up the list of eligible voters, the country had to resolve the question of citizenship and figure out how to register all the people who were Ivorian citizens but had no papers and had been left off previous lists. When the extra year was up in the fall of 2006, the election was still not feasible and was postponed again. Gbagbo was a master at stalling, and as long as the two sides continued to negotiate the details, he remained in the presidential armchair.

Return to Divided Ivory Coast

Tom and I had left Ivory Coast in 2002, six weeks before the rebellion. We finally returned in the spring of 2008, nearly six years after our last visit. Exactly one year had passed since the most recent peace accord had been signed, and the Ivorian newspapers were filled with upbeat stories about reunification. But despite all the talk, the North was still under the control of the New Forces, and we needed a laissez-passer, purchased for $10, to cross the line. Our friend Lazeni, a professional chauffeur, was driving us. He had the phone numbers of a few old friends who had joined the New Forces. "But you have to know people on both sides," he said. "If you don't know anyone and you don't have money, they'll just tell you 'tomorrow, tomorrow.'"

We drove north out of the government zone and entered the narrow trust zone controlled by the United Nations. Rows of sandbags surrounded the UN peacekeepers' camp and a sentry in a lookout tower watched the road from behind a mounted gun. It was hard for me to believe that this UN camp, which looked like ones I had seen in photos of war-torn places, was on the south-north road I traveled every time I came to Ivory Coast.

The North was divided into zones, and each zone had a New Forces commander called a com-zone. The roadblocks dividing their fiefdoms were welded together out of old bicycle parts and metal pipes and rolled back and forth across the road on small metal wheels. At each barricade, the soldiers barely bothered to check our New Forces laissez-passer. They were more interested in begging for spare change. "Just a little something! Just the price of tea!" they wheedled, looking tough in their camouflage but sounding pitiful.

It's hard to say no to beggars with machine guns, so we handed over a coin worth about a quarter at each barricade. "Don't buy cigarettes," Tom lectured them. "They kill, you know."

"No, no! No cigarettes! We are going to buy meat for our stew and tea to share!" They rolled the barricade open and let us pass.

"It's a racket," said Lazeni. "But honestly I prefer this, when they ask straight out for money, over the old way when the gendarmes pretended something was wrong with your license or your insurance."

We were fortunate to be riding in a car. It was far worse to be a passenger in a bus. At each barricade every passenger had to get off, line up, file into the little office, and pay a fee to the New Forces before the bus could go on. "Did you hear the one about the rebel who hitched a ride in a truck going south and fell asleep?" Lazeni asked, smiling. "Well, when they got to the line, he was sound asleep. And the truck driver didn't say a word, he just let him sleep, and by the time the rebel woke up, they were deep in government territory! He had to take off his uniform and sneak back across. It was the driver's revenge for all those times he had been stopped and made to pay!"

For the past six years, the New Forces had been occupying the spacious old hotel in the center of Korhogo, but two months before our arrival they had moved out, and the wall around the flower bed in the front drive had just been repainted with the hopeful slogan "Reconciliation, Reintegration, Reconstruction in Peace." The cold running water worked most of the time. A New Forces commander was staying down the hall. Polished black boots sat outside his door and a pickup truck of soldiers guarded the parking lot.

On the main street of Korhogo, the banks and stores were boarded up and the sidewalks had been taken over by vendors selling used clothing—a used T-shirt printed with "Fourth Grade is Fun!" went for fifty cents and a pair of jeans cost between $2 and $4. Even the grocery store where we used to buy supplies was closed, so Kass, from whom we were renting a 1985 diesel Mercedes, showed us a couple of small shops that catered to the United Nations personnel and postconflict NGO workers who had moved into Korhogo. In preparation for going to Kalikaha, we loaded up with bottled water, canned sardines, rough pink toilet paper folded in a stack, and powdered milk. Korhogo bustled with people and mopeds. With commerce reoriented to the north, the agricultural market town had become a busy commercial crossroads, but only a few people seemed to be profiting. The New Forces had built a small covered market for the women who sold vegetables and an open-air stage for concerts for young people. But the dirt roads had crevasses big enough to swallow a car, making them nearly impassable, and it was the UN and NGOs that collected the garbage. In the dusty run-down city, several new four-story buildings with shiny facades stood out, built by rebels enriched by the years of not-peace.

When Adama pulled up on his motorcycle the next day, we had an emotional reunion. He looked thinner and older, with more than six years of lines added to his face. "You have to come to the house tonight for dinner," he told us. "The family will be so glad to see you. They're all well, and they send you greetings." Then his face clouded and he departed from the formula. "There is one thing I have to tell you," he said quietly. "It's about Nawa. She isn't well. She has been sick for three years." The light went out of his eyes, replaced by worry and sadness.

Even with this preparation, it was a shock to see her. She had always been slender but now she was stick-thin. She pressed up against me and I pulled her close, something I had never done when she was a little girl because she had never stayed still long enough. When I learned that her second husband had died, I wondered if she had been tested for AIDS. But when we quizzed Adama about her illness, he described what sounded like a stroke. Three years later, one side of her mouth still drooped, and she, who used to beam at everyone, rarely smiled. As we said good night after dinner, Nafini and I stood next to the car holding hands; her fingers were calloused from hard work. "We have to go and greet the people of Kalikaha," I said.

The main street of Korhogo

She nodded in agreement, and responded softly, "Greet them for me."

"But we will be back in a week and we'll find out what's wrong. We'll make sure she gets treatment." I wasn't sure how I would keep this promise, but I was determined to try.

When we reached Kalikaha, the road was blocked by a barricade of three large oil cans painted the Ivorian national colors—green, orange, and white—with wooden poles laid across the flat tops. A young soldier came out of a thatched enclosure and asked what we were doing there.

"We live here." We pointed up the road.

"You live *here*?" Before he could recover enough to ask for money, we drove around the barricade and up the rutted dirt path. We knew that during the six years we had stayed away, no one had replaced the thatch of our house, and once the roof was gone, the earthen walls had collapsed. Our *jatigi*, Donni, had moved the metal trunks in which we stored our folding cots, mosquito nets, sheets, and enamel metal dishes into his storage room. But once again we needed a place to stay, and once again it was just the two of us, as it had been the first time. Chékun's brother Tenena was a little boy shadowing his father on our first stay, and over the years we had watched him grow up into a capable farmer. In the six years we had been away, he had acquired two wives and two little sons. This time it was Tenena rather than his father who moved in with one of his wives and offered us his comfortable three-room cement house. It had a corrugated tin roof, a front porch, electricity, and a built-in shower (a room with a drain where you could take sponge baths). A walled open-to-the-sky latrine was shared by everyone.

"The war is not really over and yet you've come back," the land priest and head of the *poro* said to us. His eyes glowed in his long, lined face as he asked about our children and gave us blessings for their long life. There was no good news to share with us, he said, only bad. Nothing but difficulties had come of the war. "We are like one of the little millet pancakes that a woman grills. When it's burned on one side, she turns it over and burns it on the other."

In a place where life was already difficult, the war made everything harder. The nurse at the clinic was a southerner, so when the rebels arrived, they came looking for him; the villagers hid him in the fields that night and the next day spirited him away to safety on the back of a moped over back-country trails. After that, the small clinic stood empty. One of the most useful innovations in Kalikaha had been an ancient ambulance donated by a French church.

Every neighborhood contributed to a fund for gasoline and when someone was seriously ill, the nurse drove them to the hospital in Korhogo. But the rebels seized anything with wheels, including the ambulance. When the schoolteachers at the elementary school no longer received their government salaries, they stayed on, living on handouts from the villagers, but when Gbagbo threatened to fire all civil servants who didn't return to the South, the teachers left. The students who had managed to finish high school and qualify for the university couldn't go south to study, so a generation of future leaders was blocked. The farmers couldn't get their cotton and cashews to market, so they had to accept low prices; some years the payment for their cotton never arrived at all. Meanwhile, in the wartime economy, the prices of batteries, medicine, fertilizer, and pesticides rose. On top of everything else, the village had to supply the rebel soldiers with sheep and sacks of rice. "They are our own children," said the elder, "but they take from us, too. They failed to push out Gbagbo, but instead of farming so we can all eat, they demand to be fed from our fields!" He leaned toward us. "I want to make sure you understand one thing." He waited until he was sure he had our attention. "Not one person was killed here. In Kalikaha, no one was killed because of the war."

We said we understood and were grateful.

He nodded sadly. "All these things lost from this war, and nothing gained. Nothing gained. But," he added, raising a thin finger, "we can't blame Gbagbo because it was our young men who started it." Northerners supported the rebellion because the rebels promised to end *ivoirité* and the policies of exclusion, but it cost them dearly. The rebel commanders put up roadblocks on every road and taxed every single thing that moved. The International Crisis Group estimated the ten com-zones shared among themselves $65 million a year by taxing the impoverished North.

"It's no wonder you didn't come all these years," a neighbor said. "You can't visit a place where there is a war. War," he added, "it's just a word you hear on the radio. You don't think it will happen where you live. And then it does."

An educated northerner confided that he worried about the North because the war had changed the young men, especially in the towns. "They see rebels doing as they please, beating people, and that changes them. Their families can't offer them anything, can't provide for them or send them to school, so how can they respect their elders?" In Abidjan, the young desired cars, fancy cell phones, and watches, and in towns, northern young men wanted those things, too. But young men from rural villages dreamed of jobs that earned a little more than subsistence farming, something that would enable them to marry and supply their families with food—not necessarily put food *on* the table, because a dining table was a luxury in northern villages and people sat on stools to eat from bowls on the ground. What the young men in the rural North wanted was a job that would put food in bowls day after day and send children to school. To join the army and receive a monthly salary, to have a little store with a few shelves of canned tomato paste, sugar, and salt, or to be a farmer who got a decent price for his cotton and owned a few cattle to fall back on in a bad year—these were the dreams young men in the North talked about. In most cases, their elders could not help them achieve them.

The rebels taxed everything that moved on the roads, even cattle. Every herd had to have a laissez-passer, and if your cattle were caught crossing the road without one, the fine was $30. Chékun's uncle had given up on the Twenty-Two Places and rented a big truck instead, loading the back with cargo and piling the passengers on top. He said it was the only way he could come out ahead after he paid the tolls. As touchy as ever, he kept up a running battle of insults with the young rebels at the roadblocks. Once, despite his age, they ordered him to get down and do push-ups in the road. "If you keep me from working, you'll have nothing!" he reminded them, and drove away.

The rebels even taxed the vendors at the weekly Kalikaha market. Twenty-five CFA francs, the equivalent of a nickel. It was the same fee whether you were an old woman with one plastic basin of peanuts or a vendor from Korhogo with fifty plastic basins for sale. Adama was one of those who spoke up at a community meeting. "It's like we live in a hole in the ground here. Our produce can't get out to market—and now you want us to pay more? Our mothers come to market with a few red peppers to sell in order to buy bouillon cubes. Sometimes they make fifty CFA or seventy-five CFA francs and now you want to take twenty-five? You're going to kill us!" The market fee was dropped.

We helped Donni harvest his cashew orchard, admiring the fat comma-shaped nuts hanging from the bottoms of the red fruits and stooping to gather fallen nuts carefully because snakes loved to lie under the crisp leaves. Ivory Coast had quietly become an important cashew producer. No development organization or government extension agency had come to the villages in the North and suggested the farmers plant cashews or enlarge their orchards. They had done it on their own as a way to diversify their incomes and depend less on cotton, which was risky and paid so little for so much work.

That evening as we sat on the porch sharing beers with our neighbors, Tom brought out a little bag of roasted cashews he had bought in Abidjan. "Do you know what these are?" Tom asked the farmers, who all had orchards. "Cashews. You might have grown these. And do you know how much I paid for this little sack in Abidjan?"

They shook their heads.

The little bag had cost nearly $2. Tom worked out the price in Julakan.

Their mouths dropped open. They had no idea the nuts they grew were so valuable. They were lucky to get thirty cents a kilo for them in the hull. Their cashews were shipped to India and Vietnam and processed in factories there. Shelling cashews is difficult because of their irregular shape and because they are related to poison ivy and contain a caustic fluid that burns the skin. Our neighbors immediately grasped Tom's point: someone was making big profits from cashews and it wasn't them, the farmers. We passed the bowl of cashews around and they were surprised at how good they tasted. It was the first time they had eaten the nuts. One said he thought people bought them to make medicine.

Tom, Adama, and I were sitting on the porch one afternoon waiting for a late rain to stop when two women from the neighborhood joined us. Tom was wondering if household economies had changed while we had been away and asked them. The women listed the things they bought for the household—the ingredients to cook the sauce every night, the children's clothes, the children's medicine. "Unless a child is about to die," one added. "Then a husband will usually step in and pay for medicine." Wives were supplied with corn or rice for the days they worked in their husbands' fields but not for the other days. So on those other days they had to provide food for themselves and their children.

"What about your clothes?" Tom asked.

"Heeey, we buy our own clothes!"

"So," Tom asked, "just what do husbands do?"

"Only one thing!" They doubled over with laughter. "They call us to come in the night, they do their night work, and then we separate! That's all they do!"

Some women had tried growing cotton and a few had been successful, but the men refused to load their bales onto the market truck, so women were turning to cashews to make ends meet. They didn't plant the trees openly because planting trees required permanent rights to land, which women didn't have. Instead, they planted a few trees in their peanut fields and sold the nuts quietly. "But eventually," Tom asked, "won't your husbands see the trees and take the fields for themselves?"

"Yes, they will see them eventually. They won't like it, but these are our peanut fields and they will leave them alone."

Another woman who had been in Tom's original farm study twenty-seven years earlier told us she had made ends meet that year by selling a few cashews. "So you have a little orchard, then?" Tom asked.

"No." She leaned toward us and lowered her voice. "I stole them from my husband's orchard." Her husband was sitting on the other side of the courtyard stripping palm fronds to repair a roof. She was slightly gleeful as she recounted the small sums she had gotten each time.

One night a tall thin man who lived in Abidjan called on us. I didn't care for this man, I never had. He joined the circle sitting outside our house, and after greetings, he announced that thanks to his indefatigable efforts and close connections with First Lady Simone Gbagbo, Kalikaha would soon be accorded the status of a commune. It would have its own town hall, mayor, and town council, and receive funding from the national government, and this was all due to his influence. I wasn't as naive as I had once been, and I was pretty sure he was opening his campaign for mayor and feeling us out as potential backers. Tom and I would not have gotten involved in local elections, but he didn't know us well enough to know that.

"In the United States," I said, "you have to live in a place to run for mayor, and so I am not used to this idea you have here—a person lives in Abidjan and holds two or three elected posts in the North. I think it's important for whoever is mayor to live in the community."

This wasn't what he was hoping for, but he pretended to agree. Ivory Coast's structure of government administration is based on the French model—commune, subprefecture, prefecture, region, republic. I was unclear about how a commune worked. How many people would be on the town council, I asked, and what authority would it have? Would it work with the traditional chiefs and land priest? The group of ten or twelve men sitting with us leaned forward, and those who understood French translated for the others. The council, they thought, would be large—perhaps about thirty members.

It would of course work with the traditional leaders. As for what issues it would decide, that was a question no one could answer.

"Well," I said slowly, "if there are thirty council members and half the people of Kalikaha are women, here is the question I would like to ask . . . how many of those thirty do you think should be women?"

The circle fell silent. Perhaps they felt a question so bizarre didn't require a response. Several friends smiled affectionately—in embarrassment, for me, I suspected; others gave me glances that bordered on pity, as if I were mentally deficient to ask such a foolish question. Everyone knew that council members were elder men.

Weeks later in Abidjan, I was going to visit Chékun's school and the tall thin man had offered to be my guide. We were side by side, crammed into tiny folding seats in a *gbaka*. "You know," he said to me, "it isn't that I am opposed to women being on the town council." This came out of the blue, and I was surprised he had been thinking about my question. "It is just that there are no women who are literate. There are no women qualified—that's the problem."

I retorted that you didn't have to be literate to be wise, what mattered was to know the concerns of the women and to speak for them. He agreed, but I could tell I hadn't persuaded him.

Abou the Rebel

Demobilization

In 2008 Abou the rebel's father fell ill, and he received leave to visit him in Kalikaha. When his father died three weeks later, Abou asked to go back for the funeral, but he had just taken a leave, so it took two days of making the rounds with forms in search of signatures before he received permission. "What about my mother? She may die, too, and I can't go see her? When I was a *gbaka* driver, you go see your boss and you say, 'Boss, my elder is ill' or 'My elder passed away.' He's going to say, 'Park the car and go. You should go.' But in the army, it's not like that. First you go to see your section commander. Then he will go see someone else. You will have four papers and they all have to be signed—really!"

Some of his friends dreamed, if the country was reunited, of being inducted into the army and making it their career. Not Abou. "I told them I didn't want to be in the army anymore. I wanted to work for myself or have some other work where you can leave the same day." He went to the demobilization office and signed the papers. He received an official card of demobilization but no money for turning in his arms.

Demobilization, disarmament, and reintegration of ex-combatants, or DDR in international policy speak, was a major issue in the peace process. After the conflicts in neighboring Liberia and Sierra Leone, there were already too many armed young men floating around West Africa with no skills but the ability to wage war. Former fighters from those wars had played a big part in the Ivorian conflict, especially near the western border with Liberia. Until it split apart, Ivory Coast had been a stabilizing influence in the region, and if it was to be one again, the young men on both sides who had taken up arms must give them up. DDR was part of the United Nations mandate for the peacekeeping mission in Ivory Coast and the peace accords signed by both sides. But neither side wanted to take the first steps to disarm.

Abou was one of an estimated thirty-five thousand young men who had fought for the New Forces. Five thousand of the ex-rebels could be absorbed into the army and another four thousand into the gendarmes and police. That left twenty-six thousand. They needed work in a civic rebuilding program or help to start a business or an incentive to return to their villages to farm. But in a divided country with a stalled economy, where unemployment and underemployment seemed to be the norm rather than the exception, it wasn't easy to create jobs for so many unskilled young men.

At the DDR office, they wrote down Abou's work history, his three years of schooling, his skills and interests. He wanted to raise chickens and sell the eggs, he told them. The DDR staff urged him to form a cooperative with three other former fighters and submit an application. They would evaluate it and probably fund the project. But Abou was wary. "The others will take out money for their family problems, weddings, funerals, all that, and it won't work. Or if I don't come with a group, they will just put me in with any three or four ex-soldiers that I don't even know and I don't want that because they might smoke or drink." He knew plenty of former fighters who had formed cooperatives for one project or another, but he hadn't seen a single one that worked. Abou claimed the mechanics made out the best because the DDR program gave each of them a complete toolbox for repairing either motorcycles or cars, depending on their expertise. "No one said they had to work together! All they had to do was find a place to set up and they were in business!"

Since he had driven a *gbaka*, he tried to get a job as a driver, but employers were leery of former soldiers. "They don't believe we can just put down our weapons and take up life peacefully again. They think we are violent people now." Despite all the talk around international conference tables about the importance of DDR to the long-term stability of the region, in the towns and cities of northern Ivory Coast where the young soldiers still begged at the roadblocks, not much was happening.

Abou was in a much better position financially than most former rebels, thanks to his job at the New Forces treasury, so he financed his own reintegration project by building two long chicken houses and investing in a thousand chicks. Six months passed before they started to lay, but when they did, he was making about $30 a day. The chickens produced for a year or so, and after eighteen months, he sold them and started over. He also tried raising chickens for meat. Every forty-five days, a company called Hot Chicken bought his chickens. If not too many died and the price of chickens stayed stable, he made about $200 each time. Abou took a second wife, a young student who had been his girlfriend for the past two years. "The Koran says if there is a woman outside the house, you should bring her into the house," he said in a serious voice. She was studying for her bac exam and hoped to be a teacher. The next time I visited, there was a large blackboard on the courtyard wall filled with the children's arithmetic and grammar homework, written neatly in multicolored chalk.

Nawa's Terrible Secret

I had promised Nawa's mother I would help find a treatment for Nawa's illness, and when we returned to town, Nawa's youngest brother, Djak, short for Djakaridja, a high school student, told us Nawa had been given a blood test and they were waiting for the results. I made him promise that when they went back to the clinic, he would ask detailed questions about her diagnosis and write down the answers. "You have the right to ask about whatever you or Nawa doesn't understand," I drilled into him before we returned to Kalikaha.

When we returned to town again, Djak showed us three written prescriptions: a vitamin supplement, an antibiotic, and a third drug I didn't recognize. "Did you ask questions and write down the answers?" I asked.

He pulled out a slip of paper. "She has the white *pette*." He sounded nervous, and I assumed he hadn't asked questions as rigorously as I had demanded. It would be rude for him, a young man, to question a nurse who was his elder. Tom and I tried to look up *la pette blanche*, but it wasn't in our dictionary. At the slow-drip internet café on the main street, we googled it. And we asked people we knew. No one had heard of the disease.

The next day, Djak came to our hotel room and in a trembling voice said he needed to speak with us. We already had one visitor from Kalikaha, and we invited him to join the conversation, but he said it was a private matter, so he and Tom walked off together. He wouldn't say a word until they reached the far end of the garden. "I wasn't telling the truth last night," he admitted haltingly. "We were afraid to tell you the truth because you might be angry or you might think badly of our family. The test was for AIDS. It was positive."

"You did the right thing to tell us the truth," Tom replied. "Now that we understand the problem, we can make sure she gets treatment."

He and Nawa had been sent to a small nonprofit clinic where they had given her three prescriptions, but she had barely slept since.

"Do your parents know?" Tom asked.

His mother did but not his father. Adama was in Kalikaha, overseeing the large field of corn that would provide the bulk of their food for the coming year and guarding their cashew orchard to make sure thieves didn't make off with the nuts before he could harvest them. "We have talked it over and we would like you to tell him when you go back to Kalikaha," Djak said. We agreed to do this.

I wanted to make sure the clinic was dispensing antiretroviral medication, and when I said I intended to visit it, Djak said he would like to come along. It was a Sunday afternoon and the clinic was closed, but the guard opened the gate and let us in. The only person there was the director, who welcomed us into his office. I explained that a young woman in our family had been sent there for treatment, and we were coming to find out what sort of care they could offer.

He didn't take offense at this or at being interrupted. He was a northerner in his forties wearing an African printed shirt over tailored pants. He explained how he had started the organization with very little. Now they had funding for a doctor to be there most afternoons, and several other health workers. They were dispensing antiretrovirals, which cost about $6 for a three-month supply, but before starting Nawa on the drugs, they had given her a two-week course of antibiotics to clear up infections and vitamin supplements to build up her strength.

She was so anxious she wasn't sleeping, I told him, and he urged us to bring her back and make an appointment with the counselors. There were women counselors with whom she would feel comfortable, he said reassuringly. We went away from the conversation impressed by his professionalism and sensitivity and hopeful the clinic could help Nawa manage her illness. When I saw her, I held her close, and she pressed against me for comfort. Her face was pinched, and she was so thin it was like holding a tall child; I could have circled her upper arm with my fingers.

After we returned to Kalikaha, we waited for a time when none of our neighbors were around to tell Adama about Nawa's diagnosis. We thought after dinner would be best, but as soon as we had eaten, Adama left, saying he was tired. Djak, who was worried about his father's response, called a short time later. The cell phone network worked better at night. "Have you told him?"

"Not yet."

He sighed and wished us a polite good night. The next day, there were always people with us, so we put it off again. The third day, we went back to our house at lunch, closed the door, and told Adama that Nawa had been tested for AIDS and the test was positive. We explained about the antiretroviral drugs that couldn't cure the disease but would keep her alive and healthy.

He was silent for a long time. "Is it contagious?" he finally asked. "Because Nawa plays with the neighborhood children and I wouldn't want them to catch it from her."

It was hard to believe that in 2008 he didn't know the most basic facts about how AIDS was transmitted. We had given him our old shortwave radio and I knew he listened to the United Nations station. But I hid my surprise and answered matter-of-factly that he didn't need to worry about the children because AIDS could only be contracted through blood or sexual contact.

"Do you have other questions?" Tom asked.

"Not now," he answered. He put his head in his hands.

When we returned to Korhogo the following week, Nawa asked me to go with her to her appointment. I thought it was a good idea. Djak or Old Man sometimes went with her because it never hurt for someone like Nawa to have an educated person who spoke French with them, and an educated white American was a triple bonus that would ensure no one would try to take advantage of her. As we sat in the waiting room, a friendly older woman came in, sat down, and greeted us. Nawa responded politely but cautiously. The woman's voluminous boubou and matching headwrap were printed with giant green leaves on brilliant orange, and at a time when most people's clothes were faded, the bright colors marked her as someone with a job. My Julakan was rusty after six years away, but my attempts had her in chuckles and she chatted and joked with us until even Nawa relaxed a little.

A young man opened the door from the examining rooms. "We will take everyone in the order they arrived . . . won't we?" he asked, looking at me.

Well, of course, I thought, nodding. A long moment passed while the gears in my brain turned. Thirty years ago, the white person in the room always went to the head of the line. In those days, I was always, against my will, a representative of lingering colonial power. The fact that I was American rather than French didn't matter. Thirty years later, Ivorians knew the difference between America and France, knew about dollars and basketball. I wasn't their former colonizer, but I was powerful because I came from the developed, industrialized, educated world—the Global North, as Tom taught his students to call our part of the planet. That was obvious because I was white. At this clinic, I was expected to wait my turn, a good sign, I thought, but they were checking to make sure I would not take offense.

When Nawa was called in and we entered together, the doctor looked at me pointedly. It was obvious I wasn't a member of her immediate family, and he wanted to respect her privacy. I liked him immediately for this, for not giving in to the white American power I was trying to wield on her behalf. After several general comments about working with her family to improve her health, he asked me, "Do you know her diagnosis?"

"I know she's HIV positive."

As soon as I said the words, he relaxed. "The main reason for this appointment is to determine how her family is accepting the diagnosis." While the social worker talked to Nawa in Julakan, Dr. Tanoh told me horror stories about families that thought their HIV-positive relatives were inhabited by evil spirits, made them sleep apart, refused to touch them or eat with them, and subjected them to painful and sometimes dangerous "cures."

"This family's not like that! They would never reject her. They're a loving, close family."

He nodded but said the social worker would visit just to make sure, and Nawa described how to find her house. In Julakan she and the social worker used the word *sidabana*. SIDA is the acronym for AIDS in French and *bana* is Julakan for disease. Later I would realize that what I told the doctor was only partially right. Adama and Nafini's family was close and loving, but not all would support Nawa once they knew she had *sidabana*. Naively, I had underestimated the power of the stigma and how it was wielded against women.

The doctor explained that it would take about three months before her body stabilized and her health began to improve. Of course, a few people didn't respond to the treatment, but it was a small percentage, and there was every reason to be hopeful.

I mentioned how anxious she was and that she wasn't sleeping. The cheerful woman in the bright boubou was one of the counselors, and he made an appointment for Nawa to see her another day. "She will know how to talk with Nawa about her situation," he told me reassuringly.

Afterward, I explained to Adama that we had to be patient because it could take three months for the medicines to improve her health. I also told him about the upcoming visit.

"Someone from the clinic will come to the house?" he asked. "Is that absolutely necessary? It would be better if they didn't come."

I told him Nawa had already agreed, and although he didn't object, he looked uneasy. A few weeks later, he told me the caseworker from the clinic was someone he knew and the man hadn't said anything about illness or the clinic, so in the eyes of the neighbors, it had simply been a social call. He was obviously relieved. "People think all sorts of things if you have AIDS. I wouldn't want them to think those things of Nawa."

"You know, this isn't Nawa's fault," Tom told him firmly for the tenth time. "She was infected by her husband. What could she have done? You have to remember that."

Although he did not do it within my hearing, Adama criticized his eldest daughter, saying she must have been chasing men. It was painful to hear Nawa tell me this. I had been friends with Adama for thirty years and expected better from him. Her two youngest brothers, Old Man and Djak, both high school students, risked their relationship with their father by interceding on her behalf. Young men were not supposed to talk to their elders about sex or relationships, nor were they supposed to give their opinions without being asked, so speaking up took courage. They weren't sure if their intervention helped or not.

When Nawa lay awake at night, it wasn't death she feared, she told me. It was the rest of her life. If you were a woman who lived alone, even a widow with two children, men talked, made up stories, accused you, insulted you—said you were out chasing men left and right. And if she were sick, finding a third husband would be impossible; she would have to spend the rest of her life living with her parents like a child. This wasn't an easy future for her to contemplate. She was thirty-five and used to running her own household. She and her mother were close, but they had their own ideas and ways of doing things, and when her parents argued, she hated being a witness. Nawa had been thrown out by one husband and widowed by a second, but she had been hoping to marry again so that at the very least, her two sons would have someone they could count on. Learning she had *sidabana* and would have it for the rest of her life devastated her, for now this hope would never come true. It was her younger brother Old Man, tall and thin like the grandfather he was named for, thoughtful and serious for his age, who comforted her. Gently, he urged her to take heart and go on with her life, and gradually she accepted his words.

A year later we returned for a month, and Becca, a senior in college, came with us. Nawa was especially delighted to see her again. After a year on antiretrovirals, Nawa's health had improved and she was selling fried yams every evening by the road. When she held up the blouse I had brought her as a gift, it was obviously too small, and her younger sister happily claimed it for herself, which made all of us laugh with pleasure.

Becca had been warmly welcomed by the elders and our neighbors, and at the end of the trip, she said she was glad she had come back to Kalikaha. Her time there had reminded her why she had become the person she was and why she cared so much about certain things, especially education.

Election 2010

The First Round

Fifty years had passed since Ivory Coast became an independent country in 1960, and whether it would survive for another fifty was an open question. The only hope was to hold a successful election and reunite under a single president, and after six postponements, Election Day was finally set for October 31, 2010. More than five million Ivorians were registered to vote, fourteen candidates were running, and I was determined to be there, in Kalikaha with my neighbors.

A little more than a week before the election, I landed in Abidjan. Night was falling as I walked out of the airport, and above me the bats clinked and chinked as I sat down in the first red taxi in line. Its engine turned over but wouldn't catch, so the other drivers gathered behind and pushed, and the little red car wheezed into the traffic heading across the bridge. Smoke, humidity, exhaust—Abidjan smelled the same as ever, but the roadsides were dominated by brand-new election billboards.

The campaign, limited by law to two weeks, opened on the fifteenth of October. Although there were fourteen candidates, it was a three-way race. The three front-runners were the dubiously elected incumbent, Laurent Gbagbo of the Popular Front; the former president and architect of *ivoirité*, Henri Konan Bédié of the old ruling party, the Democratic Party of Ivory Coast; and the former prime minister, the heretofore excluded Alassane Ouattara of the Rally of Republicans.

In the battle of the billboards, Gbagbo was the victor. "We've won the peace. Now for development," they read. At some intersections, three or four of his blue billboards jostled for attention: "Gbagbo—The Man of the Hour." And his broad smile against a background of bright blue covered the soccer stadium. Of course, the history professor turned politician had been in office since 2000, ten years of hours, the equivalent of two terms, but he wanted one more in the presidential armchair.

Bédié's billboards touted his experience with education and with agriculture. They didn't mention his experience with exclusion or corruption. On the agriculture billboard, Bédié shook hands with a man wearing overalls and the conical hat of a Fulani cattle herder—an outfit that made no sense in Ivory Coast. Herders and farmers were often in conflict, and there, American denim overalls did not signify farming. When I asked what it meant, friends shrugged.

Alassane Ouattara's orange billboards were crammed with policy promises—development projects, regional universities, free maternity care. They made no reference to the long-running controversy over his citizenship, which made him the personification of the volatile North-South divide.

Each candidate had a symbol for nonliterate voters. Bédié, the candidate of le Vieux's old ruling party, had a map of Ivory Coast. After running it for so long, they felt the country was theirs. Alassane Ouattara had a round hut with a pointed thatched roof, the kind of home poor people in villages lived in, which pointed to his interest in development. If you knew the North, you knew a round house was a woman's house, so it was possible to interpret this as a message of inclusion to his base. Gbagbo planned to win, and his symbol was two fingers forming a *V* for victory.

All elections matter, but this one mattered more than most. To turn the page on civil war and a stagnant economy, to elect one president and reunite the country was what Ivorians desperately wanted. Remarkably, the special representative of the secretary general of the United Nations who headed the UN mission to Ivory Coast had been invited to certify the election. Certification involved more than just the vote count. There were five criteria: that the election had taken place peacefully, that it had been equitable, that all candidates had had equal access to state media, that the electoral list was inclusive and nondiscriminatory, and that the results could be independently verified. If certified, this would be the first democratic presidential election in Ivory Coast, the first UN-certified election in Africa, and there would be no ambiguity about the outcome.

As part of the peace accords, any Ivorian citizen could run, but the election was between the big three, with their long history of feuds and alliances and so much unfinished business between them. Here they were, the ones who had ripped the country apart after le Vieux's death, enthusiastically campaigning for the job of stitching the shreds back together.

In Abidjan, a buzz of hopeful excitement permeated the streets and there was only one topic of conversation. This time is for real, people said. It's really going to happen! But there was also a current of nervous fear in the air because so many things could go wrong. "Billy Billy has it right," a music vendor in the market called out to me, waving the Ivorian rapper's latest CD aloft. "You know what he says about African politicians . . ."

"Tell me," I said, giving him the opening he wanted.

"A snake is a snake," he rapped softly. "There's no big or little . . . African politics are like Brazilian soap operas . . . they start different, but they all have the same ending."

He had lost me. "Brazilian soap operas? How do they all end?"

"Oh, you know, in the beginning there are problems between the lovers, but in the end, they always get together." He laughed. "African politicians—each one starts differently, but they all end the same—violence and dictatorship."

Their stories do start differently—Gbagbo, a history professor, a Bété from the cocoa-growing region, a plain talker with a round face and a big grin who wore African print shirts and could get down and dance to his campaign song. Sixty-five years old, he had served time in jail for his political activism and lived in exile in France, where he had formed alliances with French socialists. But when he became president, he reassured French businessmen by joking that yes, he was a socialist, but not practicing. His second wife, Simone, was also a political powerbroker. The couple had been Catholic, but after surviving a serious automobile accident, they became devout evangelical Christians. They were surrounded by preacher-advisors and maintained connections with American evangelicals.

Alassane Dramane Ouattara, or ADO, had a PhD in economics from the University of Pennsylvania, and to get through grad school, he drove a taxi. He worked as a technocrat in the upper echelons of international development finance and in middle-age married a French widow, a wealthy Abidjan businesswoman. He was Jula, a northerner, and ostensibly Muslim, although not practicing—never seen at a mosque or wearing a boubou. Sixty-eight years old, cosmopolitan, sophisticated, reserved in his suit and tie, he was a policy wonk—even his nickname, ADO, sounded like a development-speak acronym. When he campaigned, he tried to look casual by sporting an orange baseball cap. The cap symbolized two things Ivorians associated with the United States and wanted: hard work and meritocracy.

Bédié, the oldest at seventy-eight, had been le Vieux's successor; he was Baule, from the center of the country, a stalwart of the old single party and Catholic like his political mentor. He had served out the last two years of le Vieux's term and been reelected in 1995 by a huge majority but a very small percentage of the population because the opposition boycotted. His presidency was characterized by economic crisis, the creation of *ivoirité,* rising ethnic and regional tensions, and large-scale corruption. Deposed in a military coup in 1999, he fled to France. Short and stout, he reminded me of an aged elephant, no longer agile but unwilling to step aside, determined to lock tusks with his old adversaries one more time.

The Cliffs Notes version of their ancient scores and shifting alliances: the two who were out of power allied against the one who was in, and Ouattara was always one of the two who was out. At the moment, with Gbagbo in the presidential palace, Bédié and Ouattara, old enemies, had formed a coalition and signed an agreement: whoever made it to the second round would be supported by all.

"So goes Abidjan, so goes the election," said observers, because 30 percent of registered voters lived in the densely populated port city. Half of those urban voters were under thirty-five, and half of those under-thirty-fives were unemployed. All the candidates were promising jobs for young people, but who could deliver?

On Sunday, Nawa's brothers Old Man and Djak came to my upscale neighborhood in Abidjan for lunch. Old Man wore his school uniform—black pants too short for his long legs, white shirt, and bright-red tie. Tom and I were paying his tuition and he had completed one year of a two-year computer science program. Djak had passed his bac that summer. We had agreed to help him, too, and he had just arrived in Abidjan. As we sat on the terrace of a restaurant and worked our way through a platter of roasted chicken, we talked about their plans. In just one more year, Old Man would have his diploma, and if the election went well, he felt confident there would be jobs for young people with computer skills. Once he was working, he could send money back to their family in Korhogo, who needed it so badly.

Schools were closed until after the election, but when classes were in session, Old Man left his *jatigi*'s house in Abobo at five thirty in the morning and didn't return until six or seven at night. It was exhausting but he didn't mind; he was excited about the year ahead when he would no longer just learn from a textbook but actually get to work on a computer. When he could afford to, he went to a cyber café. His face, usually so serious, lit up as he talked about exploring the internet.

It was clear his school didn't have enough computers, and I worried whether he could learn enough from a textbook to get a job. Old Man's *jatigi* was the tall man I distrusted, and that also made me uneasy. The platter of chicken slowly disappeared as Old Man talked and his younger brother, Djak, listened, his eyes bright with excitement. Djak's *jatigi* was Yaya, whom he met for the first time when he arrived to join the cluster of young men living with Yaya's family.

Horns honked and we heard the catchy notes of Gbagbo's campaign song. A *gbaka* passed by with Gbagbo's supporters hanging off the sides and out the windows, singing, "Easy as eating corn on the cob! Vic-tor-y!" I asked Djak and Old Man if they planned to campaign, but both looked uneasy and Djak changed the subject back to school. He had decided to go to a professional school like Old Man's rather than the university. "At a professional school," he said, leaning forward and lowering his voice, "there isn't anything like the student union." With his northern name, he didn't feel safe at the university. Before we parted, I took a photo of the two brothers standing side by side against a bright blue door, handsome and filled with youthful hopes.

That afternoon, I strolled through Abobo soaking up the election fever with Chékun. On the traffic circle where we met, a chorus of chink-chink, chink-chinks filled the air. Young men wandered the neighborhood, offering to trim fingernails for a few cents; the chink of scissors opening and closing was their advertising cry. The manicure guys weren't unemployed, but they were underemployed, trying to earn enough in the informal economy for a meal. During the years of crisis, Ivorians flowed into Abidjan from the impoverished North and the unstable, violent West. No one knew how many people were living in Abidjan, but rents kept rising and schools were overcrowded. Chékun's class had been put in the teachers' lounge, but since the lounge was smaller than the other classrooms, they had divided the fifth graders, and Chékun taught half of them—seventy-eight—every morning. After lunch, the other half took over the narrow room and their teacher also tried to compress the day's lessons into four hours.

On the Sunday of Election Day, the schools would be turned into polling places, and like all the teachers, Chékun had been drafted to help. The country needed sixty thousand literate trained poll workers, three at each polling place. "I would really prefer to vote first thing in the morning and then stay home with the children," she said. "Just in case . . ."

"But this time the United Nations will be here."

"I hope so. I hope they will be *here* in Abobo." She glanced around her and I knew she was thinking about her husband's close escape during the 2000 election. Abobo was Rally of Republicans territory, so if the pro-Gbagbo militias went on another rampage against Ouattara supporters, they would come to Abobo. Massive white United Nations vehicles filled with blue-helmeted peacekeepers cruised the main boulevards of Abidjan, but it was impossible to picture one of the slow-moving behemoths turning into this labyrinth of narrow, unpaved, unmarked streets.

Ahead of us we saw a mass of bright orange shirts—a rally for Ouattara. "We are worn out!" cried the young speaker in French and Julakan. "We are exhausted, we have nothing, nothing!" The crowd murmured and nodded in agreement. "It's time for change!"

At a nearby school, people pored over voter lists stapled to a plywood board and pointed out their names with satisfaction and relief. This voter list had been so contentious, had taken so many years to compile, and had cost a king's ransom, and yet here it was, in a school on a back street of Abobo. It was a remarkable achievement, made possible by the United Nations and international donors. In one of the classrooms, Rally of Republicans supporters from the neighborhood packed the worn wooden benches and sat on the floor in the aisles. The campaigners, all young men, held up a sample ballot horizontally. It was long, with fourteen vertical columns. You could mark the ballot either with the ballpoint pen in the voting booth or by touching your fingertip to an inkpad and then to the box of your choice, they explained loudly, miming the actions. If you couldn't read, how should you find ADO's column among the fourteen? "Look for the little round hut! Remember—the little round hut! And if you can write your name, *don't! do not* write your name! If you sign your name," they warned, punctuating each word with emphatic finger pointing, "*your—ballot—will—not—be—counted!*"

The following morning, I headed north. Kass pulled up in a boxy white Mercedes with a blue interior and proudly demonstrated its power windows.

Completely legal, with all the papers, he assured me, and only twenty-one years old. Like all the cars we had rented from him over the years, it was a France Au Revoir, an old French car—they came into the ports of West Africa by the shipload. When Kass was laid off from his job, he couldn't make the remaining payments on his own ancient Mercedes and lost it, so he had rented this one to drive me around in. It was a considerable upgrade. The air-conditioning didn't work, but the cassette player did, and Kass proudly inserted a cassette of his favorite music, old American R&B. As we headed north, he hummed along to the songs and I provided a running translation. "In this one, he is sitting by the water, like at the port of Abidjan. He is far from his family and he watches the ships come and go." Kass nodded with satisfaction and said he could feel that loneliness in the music.

"In this song, he says he loves her so much that he's going to come right home and give her all his money."

Kass grinned. "He didn't really say that, did he?"

Every time I came, I brought Kass one thousand condoms, donated by a clinic. They took up a lot of space in my suitcase but weighed nothing. Kass didn't understand why his friends weren't terrified about AIDS. He was. Before he was laid off, he had worked as a driver for an international nonprofit that rebuilt medical clinics destroyed in conflicts or natural disasters. My condoms were his own little public health project. "When I talk about Prudence condoms, they ignore me, but when I say I have American condoms, the young men come running to get them! And I tell them, when these run out, you have to promise me you'll buy Prudence."

"Do you think they do?"

"I try to persuade them. I am not very educated, but this is what I can do. I am a young man, too, so I know how to talk to them. As long as you keep bringing the condoms, I will keep talking to them about AIDS."

"Now this song—we danced to this when I was in high school. He tells her she is like sunshine on a cloudy day." Kass nodded along, smiling. "And this one is about women and how their lives are hard. Even young girls get worn out. They need a little tenderness."

Kass glanced at the cassette player with new respect. "That, that is true."

When we reached the city of Bouaké, the road was blocked by the crowd at a campaign rally for one of the minor candidates, an independent whose symbol was a blue rooster. I asked one of his organizers if he had a chance without a party behind him.

"Better an independent!" the young man said, adding proudly, "My candidate has not played *any* part in Ivorian politics!"

Bouaké was the New Forces capital, and on the main street the businesses were still boarded up and every one of Gbagbo's bright blue billboards had been defaced. Long black oily lines dripped from his wide smile. "We are all tired of this!" cried the blue rooster candidate. "We are worn out!" It was the dominant refrain of the election. We are worn out. Worn out with political conflict, worn out with partition, worn out with corruption, worn out with an economy stuck at a standstill. Worn out with government politicians and New Forces commanders who think only of themselves. But not with the election itself! Ivorians flocked to rallies and gathered around flickering television sets to hear the candidates speak. Although they didn't stand a chance of winning, the eleven minor candidates, including one woman, who was a former minister of justice (her symbol was clasped hands), and a popular comedian (a smiling mouth), were campaigning hard. For an hour and a half every night, one candidate stood at a podium and answered questions from journalists. The program, *Face the Voters,* ended at eleven and it felt as if the entire country stayed up to watch, although it was in French, which only educated Ivorians could understand. The questions were not pushover questions. "What will you do if someone in your administration is caught doing something corrupt?" "How will you create jobs?" "Where will the money for that program come from?"

The eleven minor candidates went first and spoke frankly. "Tourism? Low on my list. Our people need to eat." "Foreign investment? Investors won't come until we have a transparent judicial system." "Social security accounts. Education accounts. Railroads." "Taxes—for education. Lower taxes for youth and women." "Regional universities." "More women in government." Ideas soared out of color televisions in urban apartments, out of grainy black-and-white televisions in rural villages, and to attentive crowds in bars and open air cafés. No matter what happened on Election Day, these proposals had been released into the hopeful sky and they floated there, waiting to see if the country could hold a successful election and survive.

The fourteen candidates had all signed an oath in the presence of Ban Ki-moon, secretary-general of the United Nations, in which they promised to accept the results of the Independent Electoral Commission. No state funds could be diverted for campaigning and all the candidates were promised equal access to the media. They also pledged not to attack another candidate's personal life, ethnicity, gender, or religion. Used to the incessant hammering of negative campaign ads and the evasive, polarized rhetoric of American elections, I had the chance, for the first time, to experience an election in which government policy was the topic of every debate and every response was delivered respectfully. Candidates sometimes agreed with their opponents! Entrenched interest groups, like those in the United States organized for and against gun control, abortion, and taxation, don't exist in Ivory Coast, so voters coalesce around ethnic and regional alliances. But since all the candidates had signed the oath not to talk about the religion, ethnicity, or gender of their opponents, they talked about the future of Ivory Coast. The political euphoria was contagious, and I felt like I had died and gone to African election heaven.

On television, public service announcements played over and over: In an animated one, two young men walked down a street in campaign T-shirts. A sneaky-looking man with a briefcase appeared and, after a brief discussion we couldn't hear, handed them a wad of bills. They quickly pulled off their T-shirts and put on the ones he gave them. A big red X appeared across the screen. Taking money to support a candidate was wrong.

Another featured four stars of the Elephants, the national soccer team, who ran out one by one. "I'm Yaya Touré and I'm from the North." "I'm from the South." "I'm from the East." "I'm from the West." Over the stirring music of the national anthem, they linked arms and urged their fellow Ivorians to unite for democracy the way they united on the soccer field. "To violence and exclusion, we say, *red card*!" As they shouted the last two words, they whipped out red cards and held them up. It played constantly, and the hope rising off their graceful young bodies got to me and a lump rose in my throat every time. The biggest star, Didier Drogba, had his own public service announcement. As the national anthem played, he urged his fellow citizens to turn out and vote peacefully.

From Bouaké north, Kass and I were in New Forces territory and the road was the livelihood of the rebels. When the young soldiers begged, I found it easiest to pay up; one hundred CFA francs, about a quarter, handed out the window, satisfied them. Kass didn't fault me for it. "You have to, you're white." On principle, he refused to pay a single franc. "It's my country. I don't pay to drive on the road." But to my surprise, this time the machine guns had been put away for the election and the welded barricades were open. Instead of putting their hands out, the soldiers waved at us as we drove by!

Late in the afternoon, we arrived in Korhogo. On the main street, the banks had been rebuilt and the grocery store had reopened. The morning newspapers from Abidjan arrive in Korhogo in the early evening, and the newspaper vendors tack them up on plywood boards; only their front pages show. In the falling light of dusk, crowds gathered, not to buy papers, which cost about fifty cents, but to read the headlines. A few of the papers were independent, but most were affiliated with a political party. This was a press that understood perfectly the potential of a misleading or sensationalized headline and had perfected the genre. Many headlines dwelt on the new national identity cards. The papers sympathetic to Gbagbo claimed distribution was proceeding smoothly and on schedule. The opposition papers claimed the cards had not been delivered to some areas.

When northerners didn't receive their identity cards in time to vote in the summer of 2002, it was the last straw. This time, citizens had to return to the center where they registered to pick up two new cards—a national ID and, if they were eighteen or older, their voter registration card. In Korhogo I visited two centers in two different neighborhoods. One had registered 2,647 voters, and all but 144 of the cards had been picked up. In the other, of 2,955 cards, all but 108 had been claimed. If these centers were representative, the registration was remarkably successful. President Gbagbo announced the process would be extended an extra day and all government workers would have a paid holiday to make sure they had time to pick up their cards.

The national identification process was the key to a fair election and had taken years of work. It was sensitive because it brought up all the old tensions. Who could register? If you received a card, you were an Ivorian citizen, with all rights and privileges. Southerners didn't want immigrants from Burkina Faso and Mali on the voter list. Northerners didn't want to be excluded because they shared last names and ethnic ties with the immigrants. Unspoken in every negotiation was Alassane Ouattara. Each time southerners tried to exclude him, northerners, whether they lived in the North or South, became more determined to elect him.

One enormous complication had been the many citizens who had no papers. In Kalikaha, only a few people traveled thirty kilometers to the government office to obtain birth certificates for their children. In order not to exclude citizens like these, mobile hearings were held all over the country between 2006 and 2008. When the judges arrived in a village, people without papers could appear before them, and through the testimony of witnesses, they could establish their identity and citizenship. The mobile hearings succeeded in providing legal documents to more than seven hundred thousand undocumented citizens.

From the crowded dirt streets of Korhogo, I headed to Kalikaha. When I called on the old chief and asked for the news, he informed me sadly that his brother had died. Although three months had passed, he hadn't become accustomed to life without his brother by his side. I responded with condolences and blessings and a contribution to the funeral I had missed. "We have some other important news to share with you," he told me, "and it concerns you, too, because a person belongs to a place when they share its sorrows and joys, and so you and your family belong to Kalikaha." A list of towns had just been published that would become communes and subprefectures at the same time—and Kalikaha was on the list. Every town on the list would receive an ambulance and perhaps even a water tower!

This was big news, but some villagers were cynical about the timing. "Gbagbo must have run out of money, so he is carving up the country and giving it away for votes," one of Ouattara's supporters said drily. If the election was fair, he thought ADO would win, but he was afraid of what Gbagbo might do to stay in power. Gbagbo was nicknamed the Baker. It didn't sound dangerous—who didn't like baguettes? But in French, to roll someone in flour meant to come out on top through trickery. That Gbagbo was a master was widely acknowledged. While you were listening to just what you wanted to hear, he was heating up the oven.

Nine hundred and seven people were registered to vote in Kalikaha, but most were illiterate, and I hadn't seen any training sessions like the one in Abobo. Two days before the election, I asked my acerbic friend Natagoura, a diehard Rally of Republicans supporter, whether anyone from her party had showed women how to vote. "No, the men are too busy with the campaign," she said. "So I decided to call a meeting myself. The women from my neighborhood are gathering at my house tonight to learn."

Natagoura wasn't literate, but someone had given her a black-and-white photocopy of the ballot and showed her how to mark it correctly. She also had a brochure that explained the rules for voting. A nongovernmental organization (NGO) had distributed the brochures to encourage women to vote, but they bewildered women more than they helped them. The women couldn't read the text and the sample ballot was an invented one, so when they looked for the symbol of their candidate, it wasn't there. This made everyone who saw the brochure nervous. In their opinion, a ballot with ADO's symbol deleted was just the sort of flour Gbagbo used for his baking.

When I reached Natagoura's earthen house that night, about forty women, dressed up for the occasion, were sitting on mats under the long fluorescent lightbulb on the outside wall. Natagoura held up the photocopy of the ballot and shined a flashlight on it. The women passed the ballot and flashlight around and repeated her explanation of how to vote Rally of Republicans. "Find the little house and then go straight down, and in the box under it, make an X with a pen or touch your finger to the ink and put it carefully *there*."

Two of the women told me they couldn't vote because their ID photos came out too dark; they could have their cards remade, but not until after the election. But the others had all received their cards without any problems. While the ballot and flashlight slowly passed from one huddle of women to the next, Natagoura surprised me by changing the subject to something far more controversial than voting for the opposition candidate.

"We want to marry this young girl to that young man and we, the parents, we start playing the drums and singing even if the couple is unhappy. Whether they are happy or not, the parents dance. All that—the old forcing the young to marry—that is going to change soon. It's going to be over. We need to let it go." It was a radical statement. A few women agreed or disagreed, but with the election looming, most stayed focused on why they had come—getting a look at the sample ballot so they would know what to do in the voting booth.

The next day, Chékun's mother asked me to show her how to vote. She can clear land and harvest rice with ease, but she is not used to holding a piece of paper and she looked at the fourteen portraits with dismay. Over and over, she and two friends practiced laying out the sample ballot the correct way, with the symbols on top. Once she had that down, she found the symbol she wanted, the little house, and slid her index finger to the box below. She touched the tip of her finger lightly to the paper, as if marking it with ink. "Voting is difficult!" she said, smiling with excitement.

A neighbor who is president of the cotton farmers' cooperative supported Bédié because when he was president, the price of cotton was higher. In his emphatic bass voice, he boomed, "If we get a decent price for our cotton, we can buy what we need. We can send our children to school! Ethnic group, region, that doesn't matter to me. I'm a farmer!" What mattered to him was the price of cotton. The farmers would harvest the crop shortly after the election, and it promised to be a good year. But even so, if the price was low, they could end up in debt. The other thing that mattered to him was to get rid of corruption. "Now, nothing works here. I want my children to be president." He gestured to the sky, as if to acknowledge the vastness of the hope. "Why not? But now, it doesn't do any good to send them to school because you have to pay to pass the tests. You go to an office and the people can't do their job. They paid to get it. The people who are *not* good at papers are in the offices and the people who *can* do papers are unemployed. Nothing works!"

On Saturday, the day before the election, I went to see my neighbor, a fervent Rally of Republicans activist. To differentiate him from all the other Ngolos, everyone calls him Ngolo Politique. He and Yaya's older brother Abou-lonala, holding ADO T-shirts, were about to leave for a nearby town for training as party pollwatchers. A group of friends had gathered to see them off. Their eyes were shining with excitement. All three major parties had local chairmen, they explained to me, and since no one wanted to be the chairman of Gbagbo's party, the elders drafted Dinaba; they knew he was too shy to argue.

"Your candidate's too old," someone teased the two Democratic Party of Ivory Coast chairmen. "He didn't go on television because he can't stand up for an hour and a half!" In a little tantrum over the ground rules, Bédié had opted out of his interview on *Face the Voters*, a major tactical mistake because it reinforced the impression that he was decrepit and that the old ruling party couldn't adapt to a world in which it didn't make the rules.

"Every party must be represented here," countered Dinaba quietly, "or it's not a good election."

"Who do you support, Carol?" someone asked.

"I can't vote in an Ivorian election. You know that."

"Yes, but who do you *support*? ADO went to school in America."

"True. Well, I've been listening to all of them and there is one candidate who keeps saying something I really agree with."

"Who? Who?"

"Jacqueline. She says Ivory Coast needs more women in its government. I totally agree!"

They laughed at my predictability. This argument over women's roles had been going on as long as they could remember. I had started it with their fathers.

"May the creator of the sacred grove give victory to the one who can put the country in order and reestablish peace," said someone wisely.

"Amina," we all chorused softly. Amen.

I went back to Korhogo to send a radio commentary over the internet. I wanted Ivorian voices, but it was nearly impossible to find anyone who spoke enough English. One schoolteacher managed to say haltingly into my microphone that he feared what Gbagbo would do if he lost because he was a bad man, a very bad man.

The night before the election, it felt as if the entire country were holding its breath. The electricity went off, plunging us into darkness. Then on again. Light! Then off. Dark! I finally slept. Sunday morning, Election Day, I stepped outside the wall of the hotel to find the streets of Korhogo empty and the town silent, the metal grilles of the stores all closed and locked. The market was deserted. A convoy of massive United Nations armored personnel carriers and trucks drove by slowly, stark white against the orange dirt road. Where was everyone?

When I arrived at the high school where I had arranged to meet Adama, I found the people of Korhogo—they were already in line to vote. Hundreds stood waiting outside the eight classrooms being used as polling places at that school, and more continued to arrive. The day before, many people had been wearing campaign T-shirts, but today, as instructed, they had left them at home. Some women carried stools on their heads and many held worn wrinkled plastic bags used for peanuts or powdered red peppers but that now, carefully washed and dried, safeguarded new voter registration cards. Adama was twenty-fifth in line. His election day had started at two in the morning when a neighbor knocked on his door with a message he had received on his cell phone. "You need to get everyone in your family up, and every person must take a bath in cold water. Then you can go back to bed. If we don't all do this, the war will start again!" With the future of their country at stake, Adama and his family were afraid not to comply. The women drew water from the well and each person bathed. They woke their neighbors and passed on the instructions.

Adama got up again at first light, dressed, and set off, determined to be first in line. "Why are you going to the polling place now?" a neighbor asked. "It's too early. You should go home and come back later." By the time he politely extricated himself, a line had formed. "This neighbor, he is for Gbagbo. That is why he discourages people from going to vote."

"Did you get up in the night and bathe in cold water?" someone asked. Everyone in the line said they had. Later, when I asked educated people in a middle-class neighborhood the same question, they looked at me oddly. They hadn't received any middle-of-the-night messages. Someone had started this curious cellular chain letter in a poor neighborhood to play on people's fears and ruin their night's sleep.

The polling place opened forty-five minutes late, and Adama was making no progress because as elderly women arrived, they were escorted to the front. Men in uniform are infamous for *le racket*—setting up a roadblock and then shaking down whoever passes for a little cash. Ivorians refer to this with a pun that plays on two identical-sounding French phrases—men in uniform (*les hommes habillés*) and men with bills (*les hommes à billets*). But here were those same racketeers, their uniforms neatly pressed, and instead of demanding thousand-franc bills, they were gallantly offering their arms and ushering grandmothers to the front of the correct line. It seemed, after the night of electric outages, as if I had woken in an alternative Ivory Coast where all seemed possible: a reunified country, a single functioning government, even an end to corruption! Every face in every line had the same focused expression: something I would call civic determination. We have this one chance to save our country and ourselves, their expressions said. We won't let it slip away.

It was a foregone conclusion that Ouattara would win Korhogo in a landslide. A vote for Ouattara was a vote for the reinclusion of northerners in the political process and a vote against the past ten years of division, instability, grinding poverty, and impunity. This was not an election that favored the incumbent.

At midday I drove to Kalikaha. Adama, his index finger stained dark red to show he had voted, rode with me. In every village we passed through, outside the schools, voters were lined up in the hot sun. In Kalikaha, three classrooms were in use, and the lines were filled with women. Most of the men had already voted. When I asked why the men voted first, the men said, "Oh, you know, the women are busy in the morning with household chores. It's easier for them to come later." The women weren't complaining, though. They were all smiles. Chékun's sisters posed for a portrait, proudly pointing their ink-stained fingers to the sky.

Two women who had walked eleven kilometers from a smaller village were shown to the head of the line. Another woman joined them; she had walked even farther. Each classroom had a folded cardboard voting booth and a transparent plastic ballot box, its lid attached with plastic ties. A young New Forces soldier drove up on his moped. "Everything fine here?" he asked the poll workers. He proudly showed me a stamped paper authorizing him to ensure security. Again I had that feeling that I had entered the looking-glass Ivory Coast, the one where everything was official, where administrators collaborated rather than obscuring the rules in order to collect bribes. I offered a silent salute to the electoral team from the United Nations who had spent years in the country to help set this up.

When the polls closed, more than 80 percent of the registered voters had voted. The teachers working a very long day as election officials had been told that someone from the electoral commission would arrive to help with the

Natagoura (*far right*) and friends proudly show off their national identification cards and voter registration cards in October 2010

vote count, and they watched the dirt road anxiously, but no vehicle appeared. Night was approaching quickly and the school had no electricity. Each polling place had a president, a secretary, and a poll worker. They took out two very small battery lanterns included in their supplies. "We only received a short training," one of the young teachers confessed to me nervously as he studied the instruction booklet. But they were determined to do this exactly right. The president read out the steps for counting the votes and asked for six voters who could write their names. They, along with the party representatives, would sign the affidavit as witnesses. The six took their places at the old wooden desks.

The president cut the plastic ties with the scissors provided and dumped the folded ballots on the floor. The secretary, a young woman, drew fourteen columns on the blackboard. Dusk was falling and bats flew in and out, letting out small metallic cries, like a squeaky gate swinging open and closed. Everyone was hot and tired. All afternoon, people had been smiling and holding up their index fingers, ink-stained to show they had voted. I had snapped photo after smiling photo. But now that it was time to count the votes, everyone fell silent and an ominous tension filled the classroom.

The president unfolded the first ballot and called out the result. "Look," he insisted nervously, holding the ballot up, facing out. "Does everyone see? Does everyone agree?" The room murmured yes. The secretary balanced her baby on her hip as she marked each vote on the blackboard, counting fives the French way: for each vote, she drew one side of a square and for the fifth, she crossed the inside with a diagonal. One by one, the ballots were unfolded and displayed. Six ballots were not filled out correctly and couldn't be counted. The popular comedian who promised to lower the price of beer got one vote and the room let out a chuckle, easing the tension. The first woman to run for president had one supporter. President Laurent Gbagbo received five votes. Former president Bédié six. The vast majority went to Alassane Ouattara. The six voter-witnesses checked the numbers and signed the affidavit and everyone moved to the next room, polling place number 2. They had to read these ballots by flashlight. It was late by the time they completed counting the votes in the third polling place, and later still by the time a pickup truck arrived to pick up the ballot boxes and take them to the regional collection center.

The older people had voted when Ivory Coast was a one-party state. They reelected le Vieux as president every five years, although he promised only stability. But this time, the United Nations and the international community had their backs, and the farmers, although they could not read or write, touched their fingers to an inkpad and voted their choices. The incumbent president received only 17 votes out of 734. Bédié had 37, Ouattara had 655. Another 25 ballots were incorrectly filled out and void. By law, the Independent Electoral Commission was required to announce the results within three days. But the mud-brick grain silos were empty and the rice was waiting to be harvested, so the next morning the farmers were back at work in their fields.

On Monday, the day after the election, everyone was elated. They had done it—turned out and voted peacefully! Tuesday, people began to look anxious. I returned to Korhogo. The results from the Department of Korhogo were handwritten on sheets attached to a plywood board outside the electoral commission office. The turnout was extraordinary, more than 90 percent in some places. Ouattara had received 86 percent of the vote, and Bédié had come in a distant second. Gbagbo had received 6.5 percent of the vote, roughly the same percentage as incorrectly filled-out ballots. In front of the board, cell phones to their ears, people passed on the results to friends in other towns. Maybe ADO will win in the first round, people said, but with a field of fourteen candidates, that was impossible, the United Nations election experts had told me. There would have to be a second round, a runoff between the top two.

Tuesday midday, the Korhogo office of the Independent Electoral Commission was besieged by several hundred young people who had worked the polls. "Where's our money?" they cried. "We worked! Now we need to eat!" The prefect and the political head of the New Forces were both there trying to defuse the situation. The New Forces civil leader promised the money would be distributed just as soon as they sorted out which substitutes had actually worked and the paperwork for the payments was complete. At noon, I walked to the edge of the crowd, found Kass, and hopped on the back of his motorcycle. Nawa was cooking lunch for me. As we were about to drive away, a man in uniform stepped out of a black SUV. He strode in his black boots across the orange dirt street as if he owned it. I knew instantly who he must be. Only one man in Korhogo could have that assurance—Martin Kwakou Fofié, the New Forces commander or com-zone of Korhogo. Just as he shook hands with UN peacekeepers, I snapped his picture, an ironic moment because he was under UN sanctions for war crimes and could not leave the country. Fofié, the most powerful man in Korhogo, rarely appeared in public. That he came to calm the situation showed just how much the election mattered. Despite all the talk about reunification and despite the redeployment of the government administrators, the New Forces still ran the North and Fofié ran Korhogo. The young poll workers knew Fofié had the money to pay them, so his appearance reassured them, but that evening, they were still waiting impatiently for their day's pay. "The election went so well," one young man said. "We spilled blood here, we don't want to go backward. But we need our money. We need it to eat!"

On Tuesday night, a few provisional results were finally read out. But the numbers were small and gave no indication of which two candidates would face off in the second round. It was the results from the heavily populated neighborhoods of Abidjan everyone was waiting for. Since the handwritten results were posted in each department, text messages and phone calls zipped around the country, passing them along. By Wednesday, Ivorians were worn out with the wait, and the longer it took, the more suspicious they grew. "If the party in power had won, we would have known by now. They are trying to block the announcement!" Even the favorite Ivorian pastime of sharing conspiracy theories and rumors had lost its appeal.

Nawa again cooked lunch for me—rice and my favorite peanut sauce with smoked fish and vegetables. "Gbagbo," she said softly, her head propped on her hand. "I could never vote for him. I don't like the way he uses his *fanga*." We were having this conversation in Julakan; the word *fanga* means "strength" or "power." "Remember the people found buried in Yopougon? Over fifty of them. And the people killed in the streets . . . over a hundred." She shook her head gently. "Gbagbo, he has too much *fanga*."

Shortly after midnight, the head of the Independent Electoral Commission finally announced what everyone had figured out already by cell phone. The runoff would be between President Laurent Gbagbo and Alassane Ouattara. Gbagbo came in first with 38 percent of the vote. Ouattara was second with 33 percent. Former president Bédié received 25 percent. Would Bédié honor his promise to support Ouattara in the second round? And if he tried to persuade his voters to vote for ADO, would they listen? Many of them thought of Ouattara as the man behind the rebellion and they could decide to stay home.

Election observers from the Carter Center and the European Union noted only minor infractions. Even the slow announcement of results, they remarked, was the result of disorganization rather than fraud. More than 80 percent of

Ivorians voted, and in the North the turnout was even higher. "You have surprised the world," announced the United Nations special envoy Young-jin Choi of South Korea, beaming. Choi had his own independent system to tabulate votes for the certification process, and after the international observers turned in their reports, he certified the first round.

I returned home a few days later, in early November. The runoff between Gbagbo and Ouattara was scheduled for November 28, so I would have to follow it from a distance. The International Crisis Group warned that of all the possible matchups, this was the riskiest. Gbagbo, a powerful entrenched southerner, pitted against a northerner who had come to personify both the political exclusion northerners felt and the inclusion they sought. Everyone wanted peace and an end to division; everyone identified as Ivorian. But northerners and southerners still distrusted each other.

The candidate who came in fourth with 2 percent of the vote quickly gave his support to Ouattara, as promised in the coalition agreement. Bédié, with his 25 percent, held the trump card. He prevaricated, and I pictured him again as an old elephant, giving a little stomp and refusing to budge until he was courted. Finally, after Ouattara called on him at his home, he kept his promise and urged his supporters to vote for ADO. But many said they were under no obligation to comply.

"I'm here and I'm staying," said Gbagbo, confident as ever. "Easy as eating corn on the cob," sang his supporters. "Victory!"

Ouattara's coalition had one fear and it loomed over every conversation: if Gbagbo lost, which he surely would if Bédié's supporters turned out, would he concede? Or would he somehow find a way to roll them in flour and hang on to his power?

The Second Round

Many observers said the election would turn out to be, per capita, the most expensive election ever held. But without a peaceful runoff, the years of work and the millions spent would count for nothing. Neither the New Forces in the North nor the pro-Gbagbo militias in the South had disarmed, and some experts even warned that if the runoff went awry, Ivory Coast could stumble over the brink to become the next Rwanda.

On television, a new series of public service announcements featured cute kids. "I'm eight," announced one little boy, "and in ten years I'll be able to vote like you. Guard the democracy for me!" In another, a little girl tossed her arms into the air and exclaimed, "Maman says that whoever wins is the president of everyone!" In the streets, the tension rose; the campaign rhetoric grew more inflammatory; in Abidjan, students clashed; and, in the town of Daloa, in the turbulent cocoa-growing region, two people died in election-related violence. Thursday evening before Sunday's runoff, Gbagbo and Ouattara debated live on national television, a first for West Africa. Gbagbo began his opening statement by announcing a curfew for the weekend of the election. Ouattara said he wished his brother Laurent had talked to him before taking this step because a curfew was unnecessary. But his tone remained fraternal and professional, Gbagbo replied in kind, and the debate continued. The sight of the two candidates calmly debating the best way to restart the economy reassured Ivorians. At the end, Ouattara urged his fellow "Ivoriens et Ivoriennes" to vote peacefully. He always used this particular construction; it explicitly included women. Then he looked Gbagbo in the eye and asked him to pledge once again to accept the results of the election. Gbagbo agreed and they shared a gentleman's handshake. The country breathed a sigh of relief.

If things did go wrong, they would go wrong in the streets of Abidjan. Gbagbo's curfew would make it easier to control his Young Patriot militias, but with only journalists, poll workers, and the security forces allowed out after dark, it would also be very easy to declare yourself the winner on the government television station. Ivorians had seen Gbagbo do this in 2000. They remembered the street demonstrations that resulted . . . and the violent repression of those demonstrations. Ten years later, some things were the same: a curfew would go into effect at dusk and Gbagbo controlled the security forces. But in other ways, this election was very different: the system of counting the votes and signing the affidavits in front of the party representatives and witnesses made it nearly impossible to manipulate the results. The United Nations team had its own method to tabulate the votes independently and verify the results, and the presence of international observers made it difficult to intimidate voters without everyone knowing. And finally, cell phones were everywhere.

As Chékun walked out of school one day, the school director came up to the teacher she was chatting with and reminded her about a meeting that afternoon for teachers. Chékun hadn't heard about a meeting and asked if she could come. "We didn't think you would be interested," he replied, "but you are welcome to come with us." Chékun hadn't wanted to miss out on a professional opportunity, but the meeting turned out to be a rally for Gbagbo. "There are elections and then there are elections!" said the speaker, the wife of a prominent businessman. "And we are counting on you, the intellectuals, the teachers, because you will be in the polling places. But there are some things we can't say here because there are too many people, so we will call another meeting." Another speaker urged everyone to chip in five cents and they would buy a bicycle for Ouattara so he could ride back home to Burkina. "We will chase him out of here!" The crowd cheered and pumped their fists. Chékun told the other teacher that she had to leave to pick up her children, and looking straight ahead, she walked out quickly.

In Korhogo, Kass was hired by Gbagbo's campaign as a driver. He got the job through a relative who supported Gbagbo and the campaign organizers assumed he shared their politics and talked freely in front of him. The day before the election, he drove a group to a meeting where the leader laid out their strategies. First, buying votes. "If that doesn't work," the organizer explained, "you have to incite people to violence. Then, we'll pull our people out of the polls. Our reps will say they didn't feel safe and leave, and they won't sign the affidavits." This worried Kass. It seemed they had found a weak point, the affidavits in each polling place. What if they simply refused to sign the affidavits in the northern polls where most of the votes would go to Ouattara?

On Election Day, Kass drove the group from one small town to another. In every place, voters were lined up outside the polling places, and each time they stopped, the leader, a woman with a hard expression, tried to provoke the voters. "You can vote for Gbagbo or not vote for Gbagbo, but either way, it will be Gbagbo who will stay in power! We're going to annul your votes!"

He wasn't sure how far she was willing to go, but the cold look in her eyes made him nervous. Once they were back in the car, before he turned the key, Kass asked quietly if he might say something. Without waiting for their assent, he went on. "Pardon me, but as President Gbagbo himself has told us, 'If someone sends you on a mission, you have to figure out yourself how to manage it.'" Gbagbo had said this on television not long before when a colonel he sent to the United States got caught trying to circumvent the UN arms embargo and buy arms illegally. The implication was that the colonel should have managed his mission better and shouldn't expect help now. Kass continued, "We are out here in the countryside and we don't have anyone to protect us. In Korhogo, there is the police, there is the United Nations. But here, they could kill us, they could destroy this car which I don't own, and so I would appreciate it if you would calm your tone a little." No one replied and they drove to the next town in silence.

"This time everyone didn't go first thing in the morning," Adama reported when I reached him in Korhogo that evening, "so there weren't such long lines. People understand now, that they can go in the afternoon and still have plenty of time to vote." Just as many people voted as in the first round, but it went much more quickly because voters and poll workers knew what to do. There *had* been some incidents in the streets in Korhogo. Several campaign workers for Gbagbo had been chased and beaten, and one of their cars had been burned. Ouattara supporters claimed they caught them with a stuffed ballot box and cash for bribes. They also claimed the Gbagbo activists had been handing out cash for votes outside the polling places. But these incidents had happened in the streets, both Adama and Kass repeated reassuringly, not inside the polling places, so they shouldn't affect the vote or the affidavits. The New Forces soldiers had showed up quickly each time and urged people to ignore the provocations, stay calm, and vote peacefully.

In Abobo, Chékun received a call at the poll that one of her children was sick and she was replaced by the substitute on call. "This time people were anxious," she said. "They voted and went directly home." In her polling place, 67 percent of voters had voted for ADO and 33 percent for Gbagbo. This was no surprise. Abobo was an ADO stronghold. But what would Bédié's supporters do? Their votes would decide the election. Would they listen to him and vote Ouattara? Go over to Gbagbo? Or avoid the issue by staying home?

The two camps staked out positions—Gbagbo's camp claimed violence against its voters in the North; Ouattara's camp accused Gbagbo of trying to prevent the publication of the results. Meanwhile, Ivorians did their own tabulations, based on the local results they traded by cell phone. According to the cell phone grapevine, ADO had done well in the center, the home territory of Bédié's Democratic Party of Ivory Coast. On Monday, the day after the election, UN special representative Choi announced that except for some violent incidents in the West, the election had taken place in a democratic environment with a participation rate of 81 percent.

The Gbagbo people hired Kass to drive some of their injured campaigners from Korhogo back to Abidjan the following day. They rented an ambulance, which carried eleven people, and in his car Kass took four more. When they stopped for a rest, everyone got down and walked around. Some had been roughed up, but none were seriously injured and others had no injuries at all. In the car, they made small talk amiably. When they reached the clinic in Abidjan, an older man called his wife, and when she arrived, the couple sat and chatted, but others lay down while their fellow activists wrapped them in large bandages and covered them with sheets. Kass wondered what was going on. Suddenly Charles Blé Goudé, Gbagbo's general of the streets, strode in wearing jeans, a T-shirt, and a baseball cap. He was surrounded by about fifteen bodyguards—army soldiers, police, and gendarmes in uniform, armed to the teeth—and a cameraman from the government television station. "We are going to film the wounded of Korhogo," he announced. "These people were harassed and attacked in Korhogo!"

Kass slipped away out of sight. As the camera rolled, the older man came from behind a door, his wife appeared from the other direction, and they flew into each other's arms. "Oh, thank God you are alive!" she cried.

"Oh, in the North they tried to kill us, they beat us! They nearly killed us!"

"Oh, they have nearly killed my husband in Korhogo!"

Once the filming was over, Kass came out and Blé Goudé paid him. When he arrived at the small hotel in Abobo where he always stayed, Kass told the manager, "You are going to see some real theater on the television news tonight!" But the hospital soap opera was not the only drama on the news. That evening the spokesman for the Independent Electoral Commission took his place behind a forest of microphones to announce the election results. The printed results were stacked in front of him and he opened his mouth to speak. The two pro-Gbagbo members of the commission, sitting on each side of him, suddenly stood up. "These results have not been through the proper procedure!" one said, grabbing the papers and walking away, crumpling them in front of the cameras as the spokesman stared in disbelief.

That night, a truckload of soldiers armed with machine guns drove by the hotel where Kass was staying. Strangely, two of them were hooded, so you couldn't see their faces. He had never seen soldiers patrol there before, nor had he ever seen Ivorian soldiers wear black hoods.

The next morning, Kass got up and left for Korhogo. North of the city, he was stopped at a barricade. Two gendarmes looked at his ID card. "You are from Korhogo, eh? You're one of those who beat up Gbagbo's representatives!"

"No. I passed here yesterday. I was with the ambulance taking the injured people to the clinic," Kass said carefully. "If I beat them up, why would I take them to the hospital?"

"It's true," the other gendarme said. "I remember his car. He was with the ambulance." They waved him on.

The United Nations special representative, Y. J. Choi, knew from his own tabulations who won and who lost by midnight on election day. He recounts that Wednesday night, the first of December, he went to see President Gbagbo. Gbagbo greeted him even more warmly than usual and brought up the massive fraud in the North, stating emphatically that something had to be done about it. Choi asked what options the constitutional court, the highest Ivorian court, which had jurisdiction over elections, had at its disposal. Gbagbo said the court could invalidate part of the vote and only count the results from the rest of the country. That was the most likely course.

Choi urged Gbagbo to carefully consider the consequences and his place in history. He stressed the danger of violence, the possibility of a large number of deaths in the streets of Abidjan, and the potential intervention of the International Criminal Court. He told Gbagbo frankly that if the constitutional court invalidated votes without cause, he would tell the truth, that their decision was not based on the facts. Gbagbo looked somber. Choi explained, "The action of the constitutional court risks provoking a blood bath on a large scale."

"The blood bath is not an option for me," Gbagbo replied. "But at the same time, I would not want to abdicate because of a possible blood bath."

"Abdication, Mr. President?" Choi asked. It was a telling choice of words, and ended the conversation.

On Thursday, December 2, the chamber of the constitutional court charged with adjudicating election results declared it was now in charge. It claimed the Independent Electoral Commission had missed its deadline and was incapable of tabulating the results, thus the constitutional court would evaluate the sworn affidavits and declare the winner. The members of the court were all close to Gbagbo, so everyone knew how this would turn out. The Independent Electoral Commission office, where the results were supposed to be announced, was surrounded by a threatening blockade of uniformed security forces.

But the head of the Independent Electoral Commission managed to slip away to the Golf Hotel, and protected by United Nations peacekeepers, he announced the provisional results to the journalists assembled there. Fifty-four percent of Ivorians had voted for Alassane Ouattara. Forty-six percent had voted for Laurent Gbagbo. Ouattara was the new president. These results were provisional and would be final once they were verified by the constitutional court. Ouattara's supporters danced in the streets.

The following day, Friday, December 3, the head of the constitutional court went on Ivorian television. Rather than verifying them, he declared the results invalid. The new election results? Laurent Gbagbo 51.5 percent. Alassane Dramane Ouattara 48.5 percent. The court achieved these numbers by annulling the votes from seven departments in the North, including Korhogo, where the court claimed there had been massive fraud. In those departments, Ouattara won 93 percent of the vote. When you subtracted those votes, Gbagbo won. There was no legal recourse to appeal a decision of the highest court. No credible evidence supported Gbagbo's claims of intimidation in the North. There were, in fact, more irregularities and more violent incidents in the western part of the country, which Gbagbo carried. But the court hadn't thrown out those votes.

In Abobo, when Chékun heard the court had declared Gbagbo president, she ran straight to the walled courtyard of their church, where the boys were playing soccer, and took them home. The armed forces closed the borders and the airport. Foreign radio and television broadcasts were banned. Chékun and her family heard shots Friday night and Saturday morning. Demonstrators had marched against the curfew in Abobo, the antiriot brigade responded with live ammunition, and three people were killed.

United Nations special representative Choi countered by certifying the original results. Ivory Coast's election was the third in the world to be certified by the United Nations, after East Timor and Nepal. The turnout of 81 percent was believed to be the highest on record. Choi's team had tabulated the results independently by three different methods, so there was no ambiguity about who won. By certifying the election, Choi made clear to the world that Gbagbo's claims of fraud in the North were not credible and that the Ivorian people had elected Alassane Ouattara as their next president.

There had been problems, certainly, including deaths. And there had been no concession speech. In the North, the government prefects investigated each allegation of intimidation or violence, but they did not find any incidents in which Gbagbo supporters were prevented from voting. They published the investigation results on the internet, but a short time later, these government reports disappeared.

Saturday, December 4, in a ceremony at the presidential palace, Gbagbo was inaugurated. His wife Simone wore white lace, like a bride. His usual smile was missing, and when they heard a noise outside, the audience members looked nervously over their shoulders. On the road Gbagbo had taken, he would always have to watch the door, wondering who might burst in, how it might end. When the presidential necklace of gold medallions was placed around his neck, he finally smiled and gave his supporters two thumbs up. In his inaugural speech, Gbagbo railed against foreign interference in Ivorian affairs. The former history professor reminded his listeners that Napoleon had crowned himself. Although he summoned the pope for his coronation, during the ceremony in Notre Dame, Napoleon took the crown from the pope's hands and placed it on his own head. Gbagbo held this up as a heroic act, a stand for French nationalism against the domination of the Vatican. For a former prodemocracy activist who claimed to have won an election, it was an odd parable. If Gbagbo was now the Emperor Napoleon, who was playing the pope? Perhaps he wanted us to think it was the French whose neocolonial interference he often railed against. Or was he talking about the international community and the United Nations team that certified the results as they had been invited to do? Or the Ivorian people themselves who had dared to vote independently? Like the pope, Ivorians were forced to watch as Gbagbo crowned himself, but the pope only had to watch Napoleon once. The investiture of Gbagbo played over and over on state television. Every time Ivorians turned on the only channel they could get, hoping for news, there he was, starring in his own reality soap opera. But they were trapped in it, too, and it wasn't a comedy. Living in the Golf Hotel, protected by United Nations peacekeepers, Alassane Ouattara also took the oath of office as president and sent his sworn oath to the constitutional court.

The next time I reached Chékun in Abobo, she told me they had not gone out since she rounded up the children. I pictured the small apartment and the eight people trapped inside, including three active little boys. "How can the children stay inside all the time?" I asked her.

"They'll get used to it!" she responded instantly. The fierceness in her tone reverberated across my internet connection. "We have no news," she said. "We have only the government television channel and they play the same speeches over and over." I told her that the United Nations, the African Union, France, and the United States had all recognized Ouattara as the legitimate president, that Prime Minister Soro had resigned from Gbagbo's government and been reappointed by Ouattara, and that the International Monetary Fund refused to work with Gbagbo's government.

"We didn't know any of that," she replied soberly. Text messages were blocked. The United Nations radio station was blocked, and it was too dangerous to go down the street to an internet café. Rumors passed from person to person by cell phone. "How could they annul all those votes?" she demanded. "Korhogo, Bouaké, Ferké—it's like we're not part of the country!" Her brother called every day from Kalikaha. "They are furious," she said. Although they voted peacefully and the representatives of Gbagbo's party signed the affidavits, their votes had been thrown out. Northern votes invalidated—the same political exclusion that brought on the rebellion was being enacted again.

It was hard to phone the North, but eventually I got through to Korhogo. Adama didn't think Gbagbo would back down. "Even if the country is ripped apart, even if the people are dying of hunger, even if they die of poverty, it's not his problem." Every person he talked to was sad—Natagoura, Ngolo Politique, the elderly head of the *poro*. More than anything, they wanted their country reunited under one president. But they had two. It was bizarre.

When I reached Old Man in Abobo, he spoke softly into his cell phone because his *jatigi* was one of the rare Northerners who supported Gbagbo. They were eating only two small meals a day. At night, Gbagbo's Young Patriots came into their pro-Ouattara neighborhood with sticks. "If they catch you, they beat you, and at the end of the street, the security forces are waiting, ready to chase you back to the house."

On the opposite side of Abidjan, his brother Djak, who lived with Yaya, was also in a pro-Ouattara neighborhood, but adjacent was a public apartment complex filled with Gbagbo partisans and Young Patriots. Also nearby stood the imposing walled headquarters and barracks for a unit of gendarmes, and when Djak and his friends went into the street, even during the daytime, the gendarmes chased them back to their houses. "The streets are filled with tear gas," he said quietly. "We can't go out." This was part of Gbagbo's strategy, to contain the resistance by bottling up the young men from pro-Ouattara neighborhoods so they couldn't reach a central location to join a popular uprising. Gbagbo was counting on the peaceable nature of most Ivorians, their ability to adapt to difficult circumstances, and the insistent demands of making a living and feeding their families. He seems to have believed that if he could contain the resistance for several days, Ivorians would resign themselves to the outcome and accept him as inevitable.

Chékun's husband, Ngolo, told me he worried about what was happening on the back streets of Abobo at night. The electricity went off, the curfew kept ordinary citizens inside, and Gbagbo's militias had free rein.

"But the world is with you," I responded. "The international community recognizes Ouattara. The former president of South Africa is coming to mediate."

"No president can convince Gbagbo to step down," said Ngolo sadly. "We who live here understand this." Former South African president Thabo Mbeki arrived to mediate and spoke to Ouattara and Gbagbo but then reboarded his plane having achieved nothing. US president Barack Obama called the presidential palace twice, but Gbagbo refused to come to the phone, so Obama sent a letter urging Gbagbo to respect the vote and step down, and he invited him to the United States, where a position as a distinguished professor awaited him. But that skinny carrot didn't interest Gbagbo; his days as a history professor were in the distant past.

On the government television, officials and Gbagbo-allied pundits made legalistic arguments: *The nation's highest court ruled. The United Nations should remember its mandate and not interfere in internal affairs. The electoral commission announced the provisional results in a hotel of all places, where people hold assignations—how could those results possibly be valid? The electoral commission is an administrative body, but the constitutional court is a judicial body so it has the final say. The Independent Electoral Commission had allowed politics to taint its actions. The French, the United Nations, the Americans—these foreign powers were trying to interfere, as they had so many times before, to deprive Africans, who had suffered so long under colonialism, of their right to democracy and elections.* No opposing views were presented. Meanwhile, the chess game was on. Both governments tried to gain control of the treasury and both wanted the queen—the cocoa money.

"We are so worried," Chékun told me the next time I called. Her voice dropped to a whisper. "The military comes into the neighborhood at night. We don't sleep. It's very dangerous here." She paused and lowered her voice again. "We think people are getting killed. Not just anyone—they don't go to just any door. They go to the houses of people who are known, known for working for Ouattara."

I wanted to pass on something hopeful, so I told her women had demonstrated in the streets of Bouaké in support of the United Nations mission and special representative Choi. "We could never do that here," she replied quickly. "They would shoot us."

Since Ngolo could no longer go out at night to meet his friends at his little open-air bar, he sat outside on the roof of their building. From there, the things he saw disturbed him. "You know, the men of the North dress in boubous, so these soldiers dressed in boubous, like the people here in Abobo. The electricity was off in that area so it was dark. They knocked at a door. The other soldiers were hidden behind, the SUVs were hidden behind. Seeing someone in a boubou, the family opened the door. Then the armed men went in." He heard shots. "They come and knock at the doors of certain families. These last days, they choose someone who . . . who opposes the power here. At night, under cover of the curfew, they come, and they . . . they . . ." His voice dropped. "They do whatever they want."

To find these houses in Abobo, where there are neither street names nor addresses, they had to have informers. He thought the informers must be hiding inside the black vehicles without license plates. Perhaps that was why, if they saw people watching them, the black SUVs did U-turns and drove away. He had also seen that happen. "My country doesn't deserve this," Ngolo said softly. "But we who are here, we know that no negotiation will work with him. No president can convince him. Nothing but force."

I called a Gbagbo supporter, who explained briskly, "The problem is election fraud—they cheated in the North. They intimidated the observers from Gbagbo's party and in some cases they even beat them up. In three hundred polling places, there were no votes for Gbagbo, even though he had two observers in every polling place! That's fraud! And that is why the results from those departments had to be annulled."

I knew perfectly well why there could be two observers but zero votes for Gbagbo in a polling place. As shy Dinaba, in one of his rare remarks, had said, "Every party must be represented or it isn't a good election." He had represented Gbagbo's party, but that didn't mean he had voted for Gbagbo.

With rare solidarity, almost the entire international community supported the people of Ivory Coast. But how much good did our support do? We were far away in our comfortable houses; the conflict in Libya dominated our news; and they were trapped there, with only the state channel on television, with food prices rising, with violent militias in the streets at night, held hostage by a president who would not give up power.

In Bouaké, Abou the rebel was taken aback by this strange turn of events. The idea of war starting again frightened him. He and his friends called each other constantly. "What is it like where you are?" "Are we going to have to go down there and dislodge him?" "It's a fight, it's force he wants, so let's give it to him!" But since their president wanted to try diplomacy and spoke out against violence between Ivorians, they decided to be patient. If he doesn't leave, we will take up arms again, they promised each other. When the Rally of Republicans announced a march to Abidjan to demand Gbagbo's departure, Abou the rebel joined. "I was there! Because I am 100 percent Rally of Republicans!" The marchers chanted, "Gbagbo, Leave! Gbagbo, Leave! We don't want Gbagbo! He has to go!" Busloads of men and women from the North joined them, but they hadn't gone far when, at a little bridge south of Bouaké, they encountered an armed blockade. As soon as he saw the soldiers,

Abou knew they weren't going any further. The soldiers, Liberian mercenaries in his opinion, started shooting, and the marchers turned and ran. He reached his motorcycle, hopped on, and didn't stop until he was back in Bouaké. Whenever he went to the New Forces camp, his friends were sitting around depressed. They were willing to give the negotiations a chance, but if the negotiations didn't work, they said they would have to go and give Gbagbo a whipping.

In Abobo, where Chékun and her family and Old Man lived, people suspected that the night raiders were Liberian mercenaries rather than Ivorians. Surely Ivorians wouldn't do this to other Ivorians. The only haven in the night was the safety of the crowd. When the curfew went into effect and the electricity was turned off, young men took up posts on the corners, and when they saw the black SUVs, they called up to the apartment windows and balconies, "Come out, come out, they're coming in!" People left the safety of their houses and gathered at the nearest intersection or stood on their balconies banging pots and pans with spoons. The young men picked up their cell phones and alerted neighborhood watch outposts farther away. They called it Operation Cooking Pot. "Let's get a good look at them! Let them know we see them! Come out! Come out!" When the black vehicles arrived at a street filled with people, they made a slow U-turn and drove away.

The next time Chékun and I talked, I could hear someone crying. It was her young sister Zele. Several days before, she left the apartment in the morning for middle school and was making her way through the crowded *gbaka* station near the market when someone started shooting. Chékun heard the firing and knew it was coming from just where Zele must be passing, but there was nothing she could do but wait. Hours passed with interminable slowness. When the firing started, Zele ran, and when she stopped, she was lost. Circling through unfamiliar streets, she walked for hours before she reached home. She hadn't been to school since and she cried frequently. "We are here-*dé*," Chékun said bleakly. The *dé* adds emphasis. "No one will come to help us. We are in God's hands."

I tried to reach Old Man. "Number not available," said the recorded voice.

By the end of January, the United Nations estimated that since mid-December, more than 270 people had been killed and more than 50,000 people had been displaced from their homes, notably in Abidjan and in the West. By late February, four hundred people had been killed. Many more had been beaten or had disappeared. Some imams had been targeted, and a few had even been murdered. Religion had never been a cause of the conflict between North and South, but southerners conflated northerners and Muslims and drew religious differences into the hostilities.

In Yaya's neighborhood, the trouble started with a fire. Two of the metal workshops burned down in the night. Yaya felt sure he knew who had set the fire, because not far from the scrapyards was a neighborhood of hardcore Gbagbo supporters, young men who belonged to the Young Patriot militias and lived together in government housing. They had barricaded the main street and threatened the metalworkers, who were mostly Jula from the North or immigrants from Burkina Faso, and the two workshops that burned were the ones closest to their barricade. Yaya was for confronting them directly. Taking two younger men with him, he went to their barricade and told the young men on guard duty he wanted to speak to their leader.

Eventually they were escorted to the leader, whom Yaya knew by name and sight. "If you burn our workshops, we can't work," Yaya said. "How can we support our families?" And then he added, "But here is the real problem, and you need to think about this very carefully. You don't know where we live, you only know where we work. We live in lots of places. Some of us live nearby here in Koumassi, some of us live in Abobo or Yopougon. You don't know our homes, but we know yours. If you burn our workshops again, we will come here, to your homes, and we will burn them. So if you want to do politics, do it on the road, and leave the places where we work and where we sleep alone."

The threat worked and there were no other fires, but pairs of young men slept at the scrapyard and in the workshops every night in case the arsonists came back. The Young Patriots controlled the main road with their barricade. Young men like Djak in school uniforms were allowed through, although they sometimes confiscated their cell phones. Yaya still went to the scrapyard every day, but he no longer took the main road because he would have to pass too many dangerous places—the gendarme headquarters, the housing where the Young Patriots lived, and their barricade. The back way, a wide dirt path, passed through friendly territory.

On February 23, Yaya's childhood friend Draman called him. Draman was now the imam of a small mosque nearby. Two policemen had just come, he told Yaya, and accused him of holding political meetings. Draman thought someone had misinterpreted a ceremony at the mosque, but the police dismissed his explanations and served him with a written summons. This was serious—a person could go to the police station and never be seen again, especially a Jula northerner in a boubou. Draman immediately moved his family into a friend's house, in case the police found out where he lived and went there to look for him. His friends urged him not to obey the summons—it was too dangerous—and Yaya helped him disappear into another neighborhood, where he lived with friends, waiting for the conflict to end.

Saturday night, February 26, 2011, explosions kept Chékun and her neighbors awake most of the night. "From ten until four in the morning they were shooting at us! It was the worst we have experienced!" Gbagbo's security forces were shelling Abobo. "It sounds like they are right outside the door," she told me on the phone the next day, "although they are over on the paved road. The noise alone could give you a heart attack! The building shakes and feels like it is going to fall any minute. It's so frightening-*dé*!" The children were terrified, and she wanted to leave, but some people said the road north was blocked. She had relatives in safer neighborhoods of Abidjan, but it was dangerous to cross the city because the main roads were barricaded by pro-Gbagbo militias who were on the lookout for strangers arriving in their neighborhoods. "If they see them, they are supposed to kill them," she reminded me. "They have their orders."

Meanwhile, small units of armed men had slipped into the city to fight back against Gbagbo's attacks. People called them the invisible commandos. They were invisible in multiple ways, which enhanced the fearsomeness of their reputation. The way they had arrived and taken up their positions without being seen meant they must have the kind of supernatural powers the most powerful northern hunters had—invisibility and invulnerability. Some of them wore the handwoven shirts covered with amulets that hunters wear, and stories traveled around the city about invisible commandos walking through showers of bullets without getting hit. Grainy cell phone videos claiming to show these feats passed from phone to phone. These commandos were also invisible in a pragmatic way. In the light of day, one could hide his weapons, put on a T-shirt and jeans, and melt into the sympathetic population of certain neighborhoods. The invisible commandos retaliated for the dark-of-night raids, launching their own nighttime attacks on pro-Gbagbo militias, which made the situation even more dangerous for the people living around their camps, who were trapped in a combat zone. About forty members of Chékun's church walked all day through back streets to seek refuge at the church and escape the fighting between the invisible commandos and Gbagbo's troops. When the streets were calm, Chékun cooked and carried food to them, but she was on her last bottle of propane. She had a little charcoal and she still had rice and peanuts, but prices had doubled and there was no way to get more cash. The banks were closed and Western Union and Moneygram worked through the banking system, so it was nearly impossible to send money. Everyone was making do by eating less.

In Treichville, another city within Abidjan, women demonstrated for peace and against the high price of food, Chékun told me proudly. Now that Ouattara's government, with the help of the United Nations, had set up a new government television station, Chékun received more news than I did. Rumors reported that the Ouattara government station broadcast from mobile vans so Gbagbo's forces couldn't bomb them into silence.

In Kalikaha, Chékun's sister Bara went to the weekly market and saw a haggard family get off the truck. They had come all the way from Abobo, they said, and were lucky to have escaped alive. They described mortar shells destroying houses and killing everyone inside and stray bullets that struck people as they ventured out to buy food. Everyone was out of cooking gas and charcoal, there was almost nothing to eat, and families spent days cowering in their apartments. Bara ran home, lay down on her mat, and curled into a ball. When she woke, she remembered the frightening words but couldn't recall how she came to be back at her house on her mat. Her hand, curled next to her face, was empty, and she remembered she had been holding a thousand-franc note, the equivalent of $2, the money for the week's groceries for her and her children. She got up and retraced her steps, knowing the bill had surely been pocketed by someone. How she would make sauce for her husband this week she had no idea. When she reached the place where she had stood and listened, she found a broken flip-flop lying on the ground. She turned it over and there, underneath, was her thousand francs. She ran straight to the cell phone booth and paid to call Chékun, but the call didn't go through. Later that night, she tried again, and Chékun answered. "We are still here. We are hanging on. That is all we can do," she told Bara.

Gbagbo continued to insist he had won. He accused the French and the United Nations of overthrowing a democratically elected African government to install their choice for president. Gbagbo's anticolonial, anti-Western rhetoric played well with many Ivorians. For every incident in the streets of Abidjan, there were two opposite explanations, and websites for both sides sprang up with "proof" in the form of blurry cell phone videos and photos. The pro-Gbagbo websites published long diatribes about the UN overstepping its role and French neocolonial interference.

When I talked to Djak on the first of March, he said there had been shooting near their house that day. "People marched to protest the high price of food. Everything is expensive now. Everything!" He had talked to Old Man. They had neither water nor electricity, so Old Man couldn't charge his cell phone and he couldn't leave the house, but he was safe.

Gbagbo declared the Canadian and British ambassadors personae non gratae and they left the country. The French ambassador was also ordered to leave but stayed, despite the risks. When a pro-Gbagbo journalist asked the American ambassador, Philip Carter III, what he would do if the president asked him to leave, he responded, "If the president asks me to leave, I will. But President Ouattara has not asked me." This reply delighted many Ivorians. Gbagbo also ordered the United Nations out, but Choi, repeating a phrase of Gbagbo's, said, "I'm here and I'm staying." Young Patriots surrounded UN vehicles and camped outside the UN radio station, demanding that the UN depart. "But we are angry at the UN, too," Djak said. "They come the day after something happens. They have every resource possible, so why don't they act?"

When I called again the next day, Djak said they heard firing all night, and at ten in the morning the firing started up again. The women were afraid to go to the market. "Rice is very expensive now," he said. "It's difficult. We manage to survive but we don't eat much." He had heard on the news that the African Union had given its mediators a month to negotiate. "A month is very long," he said slowly.

The Women of Abobo

On Thursday, March 3, three months after the second round, early in the morning, a woman marched through Chékun's street blowing a whistle and calling women to come out and march. The women of Abobo were going to march peacefully to demand Gbagbo's departure. After three months of waiting, Chékun desperately wanted to go, to do something, but her husband was at work and she knew he would say not to demonstrate unless the white United Nations trucks were there. As women walked past her apartment toward the traffic circle, they called out, "Come and join us! Come and march! Enough is enough! We are worn out! Too much is too much!"

"Do you think it's safe?" her neighbor asked.

"I don't know. I want to go, but what if they shoot at us?" she answered. Another neighbor joined their huddle. It's something we have to do, they told each other. We can't just keep waiting like this. Chékun called Ngolo at work and told him the women of Abobo were going to march, her neighbors had decided to go, and she was going with them.

"I'm not there, I am here at work and you are going to leave the children alone to go march? You think that's a good idea?" The connection went dead. "Fine, go!" he yelled into the dead phone.

Women were singing and blowing whistles just a short distance away on the paved road. As she and her neighbors walked toward the sound, they heard a loud explosion. Then another! A terrible cry went up, wails of shock and grief. They turned and ran home.

"They say one woman has died," she said when I called to say good morning. "And I saw them carry two others into the clinic on my street. Why?" she asked. "Why didn't the United Nations protect them?"

As we talked, I searched the internet: "Abobo demonstration women." "It says here six are dead," I told her sadly. Witnesses said the women marched toward the intersection, waving leafy branches and singing. Gbagbo's security forces, in military vehicles, passed the women, then turned around and shot into the crowd.

"They say the blood is still on the pavement," Chékun told me the next day. "But I'm not going up there. I don't want to see that. If I see something like that, I will never be able to get it out of my mind."

Seven women died that day, at the place Chékun met me every time I came to visit. "Gbagbo is worse than the French colonial army. Even they didn't shoot women," an Ivorian friend said bitterly, referring to an anticolonial women's march in 1949. The United Nations said two hundred thousand people had fled Abobo, but on Chékun's street only one family had left. The rest had no money for gas or bus tickets, or they had no safe place to go.

The War in Abidjan

Every morning I opened Skype and dialed my friends' cell phones in Abidjan. I was especially worried about Nawa's brothers, Djak and Old Man. They were young, the same ages as my own children, caught in a precarious situation far from their families and separated from each other by an urban war zone. Life was calm again in Koumassi, Djak reassured me, although they were eating less and less, he admitted. When I tried to call Old Man, I always got the same message: "This number is not available."

But the next time I called, Old Man answered softly.

"Everyone has been worried about you," I told him.

"I know," he answered. "We didn't have any electricity here, so I couldn't charge my phone. Today it came on for an hour." I pictured him on the other end, the way he thought his words through before speaking.

"It is really difficult here," he told me. His voice trailed off. "So difficult." Half the houses around his were empty and all the businesses were closed. He hadn't gone to school for two weeks. There was shooting every night and sometimes even during the day; you never knew when it would start. The people who got shot were trapped in the street when the shooting started, so he stayed inside. The women in the family still went to the little market nearby to sell yams and condiments. "But it is very difficult. We can't keep on like this . . ." He had talked to Djak a few days earlier. "He went to school—they are holding classes." His voice was wistful.

I asked him if it was true that the invisible commandos controlled Abobo.

"It's true!"

"Then why is there still shooting?"

"The security forces are trying to take back the neighborhood," he explained, "but at every corner there are groups of young men armed with grenades and small arms." He didn't know who was shooting. When it started, he went into his room. But later, if he looked out into the street, he saw bodies. Sometimes people piled tires next to the bodies and burned them. The United Nations helicopters circled above, but he wasn't sure how much they could see. "I can't go to school. It is too dangerous."

There would be time for school later, I assured him. "You are witnessing the history of your country as it happens." It was the sort of serious idea he liked, and he promised to tell me everything in detail the next time I visited.

On March 17, I called Chékun, and when she answered, she sounded like her old self. Abobo was calm. No gun shots. No mortar fire. They had slept all night. She had even ventured to the market early that morning and returned with onions, salt, and ground hot pepper. "The onions that are usually one hundred francs were two hundred and the pile that is two hundred francs cost four hundred!" What a relief to hear her outraged about something as ordinary as the price of onions.

I asked her about propane gas bottles for cooking. "None in Abobo," she answered. "The trucks can't get through the barricades. Gbagbo's soldiers have cut us off." She had a little charcoal left, she still had rice, and she had peanuts grown by her mother for sauce. The big sack of peanuts, a gift from her mother the last time she visited, was seeing them through the crisis.

"Your husband will be pleased with your sauce tonight!" We laughed about how much better her sauce would taste with the onions and salt and a pinch of cayenne pepper. Obviously, a good night's sleep and the ordinariness of the trip to the market had done her good, and I hung up relieved. But the calm interlude was already over; we just didn't know it. Shortly after she bought her onions and left, Gbagbo's security forces fired mortar rounds into the marketplace, killing thirty-five people. Witnesses said they were mostly women and children; at least another forty were wounded.

Two days later, we revisited that conversation. "I was so lucky," Chékun said. "Right where I was earlier that morning!" We lingered over prayers of thankfulness for her close escape, but when we thought about Gbagbo, our feelings darkened and turned bitter. How could he be so determined to hold onto power that he murdered his own citizens? Hundreds of Ouattara's political activists had already died. They had received the fatal knock on the door, the deadly visit in the night. I thought about the young men I had seen campaigning, how enthusiastically they waved the sample ballots aloft and explained how to vote for ADO. I hoped they had somehow gotten away.

On March 19, Charles Blé Goudé, Gbagbo's general of the streets, called on the Young Patriots to step up and enlist in the army. For the past four months, these young men had inhaled an inflammatory plume of xenophobic exhaust. State television told them their country had been taken over by the United Nations and foreigners and they needed to act courageously and patriotically to liberate it. In Abidjan's poor neighborhoods, thousands of unemployed young men volunteered to join Gbagbo's brutal security forces. They turned out by the hundreds at open-air recruitment events, gave the military their phone numbers, and waited for the call to arms. If the calls went through, it would be civil war by cell phone.

The other side was also recruiting in Abidjan secretly. Yaya saw retired soldiers and veterans coming through his neighborhood and talking quietly to young men. They would have to dislodge Gbagbo by force, and they needed troops.

Chékun was desperate. "They come in day and night now . . . shooting! The children are frightened. We can't stay here any longer!" From her balcony, she had seen a man shot as he ran down her street. But a bus ticket to Bouaké, on the other side of the line, cost about $30. Her husband, Ngolo, intended to stay, but they needed tickets for her, the children, her brother and sister, and the housegirl. The banks, Western Union, and Moneygram were all closed. Chékun heard you had to wait two days at the station for a seat to Bouaké, and that was only halfway to her family. They would arrive penniless in Bouaké and where would they stay? All sorts of rumors circulated—one was about buses stopped by soldiers outside town. The people on them were never heard from again. For the moment, Chékun and Ngolo decided it was safest to stay put.

A rocket landed in the courtyard of her church. It didn't explode, but it made a clear point—the refugees living in the church needed to move on. The church was too close to the paved road where the shelling came from. The church members had hired vehicles and were leaving in a convoy for Korhogo, but Chékun and Ngolo couldn't afford enough seats. Instead, they decided that she and the children would try to reach a town about fifty miles away, where they could stay with Ngolo's aunt and uncle. They had enough money for the tickets there, and because it was so close, the buses were not likely to be filled.

I called Lazeni, a chauffeur with his own luxury SUV whose clients were often diplomats. Usually he liked to turn over the latest political news and tell me what he had observed as he drove them to meetings, but this time when he answered, his voice was strained.

"What's wrong?"

The week before, he told me, someone tapped on his door at one in the morning. When he asked who was there, he heard, "It's Yapo."

"Is there a problem?"

"No problem. I just want to talk to you."

"At this hour?"

"Yes." Yapo was a man from the neighborhood, a ne'er-do-well who liked his moonshine. Since it was him, Lazeni opened the door. Thirty men were standing there, staring at him. Recounting the moment, he exhaled in fear and despair. He lived near the lagoon and the men were Ebrié, the ethnic group that controlled the neighborhood; the Ebrié were fiercely pro-Gbagbo. He tried to remain calm and put on a brave front. "What is happening?"

"We have come to see you about the nighttime meetings you are holding."

"Meetings? What meetings?"

"You know what I am talking about."

"No, I have no idea. Where are these meetings you say I am holding?"

"Somewhere over there."

"Over where?" Lazeni was surprised to find himself asking the questions.

"No, no, no. You know what happened to the others and we are going to do the same thing to you."

Lazeni turned to Yapo. "What is going on?"

Yapo made a gesture to say, no, no, later, later . . .

"Tell me what is going on here," Lazeni insisted.

"You have been warned," the spokesman said. "What was done to those others, that is what will happen to you." Lazeni thought he might be referring to Abobo and the violent confrontations between Ebrié who lived along the lagoon there and invisible commandos. But he wasn't sure. The men left, but Lazeni couldn't go back to sleep. They are going to kill me, he thought. He called one of his friends who was active with the Rally of Republicans and lived nearby. "Exactly the same thing happened to me," he said. "They came to my place, too."

"They know my last name," Lazeni said, his voice trailing off. His last name marked him as a Jula Muslim from the North, although he had never lived in the North and was a practicing Catholic.

"If they have come once, they'll come back," I said. "You should leave." He was thinking about it, but he didn't have enough gas money to get to Korhogo, and if he ran out along the way, anyone with a weapon could steal his luxury SUV, which was his livelihood.

When I called back a few days later, he sounded exhausted and had decided to leave. He and a cousin planned to spend every franc they had on gas and to try to make it to Korhogo. Since the night visit, he was afraid to trust anyone. Every time he saw soldiers drive into the neighborhood, he thought, here they are, they have come to take us away and kill us. "Have you seen the pictures of the young men burned alive?" Lazeni asked me in a flat, sad voice. I hadn't. "The videos are on the internet. One tries to escape and they push him back into the fire. In another, they hit him on the head. It's horrible. One hundred twenty-five, they call it. One hundred francs for the gasoline and twenty-five for the box of matches. You'll be sorry if you look—but you're like me—you want to know."

I didn't look for the 125 videos, but I came on them as I searched for information. Just as Lazeni had said, they were horrible moments of torture and murder in the road. While someone was being killed in an Abidjan street, someone else had held up their phone to film, then uploaded the murder on the internet. Was this person a cell phone terrorist or a cell phone witness? Or both?

Koumassi was relatively calm, and some people from Abobo had taken refuge there. "Even if we don't have much to eat, at least we are not in danger here," Djak said when I reached him. But he worried about Old Man. "Why doesn't the United Nations act?" Djak asked me again. I didn't know what to say.

"Gbagbo," said their father ruefully. Two of his sons were trapped in Abidjan. "If he kills all the people, he will be president of what? The animals?"

While the world watched Libya, the Security Council debated whether to ban heavy arms in Abidjan, and Gbagbo continued to fire them at civilians. Meanwhile, a newly constituted army called the Republican Forces of Ivory Coast was moving south toward Abidjan. The Republican Forces included former rebels like Abou's friends, defectors from Gbagbo's armed forces who recognized Ouattara as president, and any other young men they could recruit. They hoped to defeat Gbagbo's forces, capture Gbagbo, and end the stalemate. Although the Republican Forces was led by professional soldiers, many young recruits had no military training.

Ngolo drove Chékun and the children to the bus station on the morning of March 23. She didn't think the children, jammed into the backseat, could see out the car windows, for which she was grateful because there were bodies on the ground beside the road. The bus station, always crowded, was crammed with people who had already waited two days for a seat to Korhogo. Their tickets cost nearly twice the normal fare, but they got seats because their destination was so close. Most people wanted to get to the North.

When the bus was stopped at the first barricade, Chékun started praying. They were in Yopougon, a divided part of Abidjan. If the barricade was manned by Gbagbo's militias and they saw their northern names, anything could happen. Children were allowed to stay on the bus; the house girl, who had no papers, squeezed under the seat and hid, and Chékun climbed down with her ID card. The soldiers at the barricade were Republican Forces, the new army of Ouattara's government, and she breathed a sigh of relief. She showed her ID, paid $2, and they passed her through. Every few miles, they were stopped at barricades, and at each, she had to pay. When they arrived, her aunt asked if her ID card said "teacher" on it. It did. "You were lucky! I heard the Republican Forces are stopping everyone whose card says 'teacher' or 'student' because they say they are pro-Gbagbos!"

Chékun didn't know if this was true, and if it was, what saved her—maybe her Senufo name. "In any case, God protected me that day!"

When I reached her a few days later, she sounded like her old self. "I got the little children into school!" she told me excitedly. "I'd like to go home. But we'll stay here for now and see what happens." I reached her husband in Abobo the next night. Gbagbo's forces were firing mortars into the neighborhood; I could hear them popping in the background. I asked him how he managed to get out of Abobo, to his job, and back again. "I used to pray to God every time I left the house," he said. "As I drove, I would pray not to cross the tanks. Now we have to pray all the time, wherever we are." The city was dead, he added, businesses were closed, the port was empty. Too many mortars were landing in their neighborhood, so he was moving in with a nephew in a more remote part of Abobo. It wasn't only the mortars, he admitted. He had been warned that a man had come around asking about him and he was afraid to sleep at home. What if someone knocked at his door in the night? Ever since the march of 2000, he had been careful not to be seen at any public political meetings, but now he was living all the time with a knot of fear in his stomach.

I called and called Old Man. According to the internet, a mortar had landed in his area of Abobo. Old Man's cell phone rang and rang. "Network error," said the message.

As pro-Ouattara invisible commandos emerged from their hiding places in Abidjan and the head of Gbagbo's armed forces abandoned him, RTI, the television station of Gbagbo's government, broadcast a story about bread. Trays of crusty baguettes were pulled out of large ovens. What could be more appropriate for Gbagbo the Baker? But the city was encircled by the newly constituted Republican Forces, loyal to Ouattara, and Gbagbo's own soldiers were shedding their uniforms and disappearing. It wasn't a great day for baking. After baguettes, RTI moved on to an interview with a socioeconomist who said all Ivory Coast's problems were caused by the West, which wanted to control Ivorian wealth for its own profit. "We need two things—an independent economy and leaders who work for Ivory Coast and not for themselves." The economist disappeared in a not-so-subtle edit. He reappeared a moment later praising the president, who on RTI was Laurent Gbagbo. A statue of the Virgin Mary in a traffic circle appeared on the screen. The statue was delicate and white and wore a blue sash. A young Muslim girl had seen the statue move its folded hands. "A manifestation of the Virgin," said a priest softly. "The Virgin chose this Muslim girl."

I skyped Djak. The sound of machine-gun fire was so loud it was difficult to talk. He said four invisible commandos armed with machine guns walked down their street earlier, reassuring residents they meant them no harm and urging them to stay inside. He and his neighbors had gone out to see the smoke, which seemed to be coming from the gendarme headquarters nearby. The shooting sounded like it was near the airport. Huddled inside, they weren't sure whether to be hopeful or terrified.

Next on RTI was an Ivorian soap opera. One of the characters was offered a post as minister and asked his wife if he should accept. "I just don't want any bad things to come into our life because of this," she demurred. A reasonable concern—two of Gbagbo's ministers trying to flee to Dubai had just been stopped at the airport. After the soap opera, finally, the news. President Gbagbo was closely following the situation, but because it was evolving so quickly, he had postponed his planned address to the nation. A music video called "Let's Respect the Constitution" came on. Snippets of the constitution appeared on the screen as singers rapped and dancers danced. After the musical interlude, a panel of journalists and academics expounded on RTI's version of Ivorian history: Westerners sent their agents and puppets, in particular Alassane Ouattara, to carry out their programs and serve their interests so that all the riches of Ivory Coast would go to the West. Laurent Gbagbo, like Nelson Mandela and Patrice Lumumba, was a hero who fought for democracy in Africa. RTI's sound turned scratchy. On the internet, witnesses said there was shooting near the station.

In the real world outside RTI, the people of Abidjan were fearful, exhausted, and hungry. They huddled in their houses, hoping to survive the night. Four months had passed since Gbagbo refused to step down in early December, and during those four months, the suspicions and resentments between political parties, between northerners and southerners, and between ethnic groups had deepened and darkened. The civic unity I witnessed during the first round was long gone. Ouattara's undisciplined young fighters wanted revenge for the murders of their friends and relatives. Gbagbo's young partisans had nothing to lose. And in Abidjan, darkness fell every night on millions of frightened people.

Old Man

The next time I called, Old Man answered. The fighting had moved to other areas of Abidjan, Abobo was finally calm, and the electricity was back on. Now that the invisible commandos and pro-Ouattara soldiers ruled Abobo, and an army supporting Ouattara was rapidly heading south, his *jatigi* had seen the writing on the bullet-pocked wall and switched sides. We chuckled about that, remembering how his *jatigi* had bragged about his connections to Simone Gbagbo. Old Man had been sick but was feeling better. He was worn out with war and being sick, he told me, and he just wanted to be at home in Korhogo with his family.

In one more week, I reassured him, there should be peace. Then we can get money to you and it will be safe for you to travel. Once he was home and eating well again, I felt sure he would recover quickly. But on Saturday, Old Man got much worse and was having trouble breathing. His *jatigi* took him to the Red Cross clinic. The Red Cross said he needed to go to the hospital across town. But with the battle for Abidjan raging, it was too dangerous. Saturday night, Old Man died.

"Everyone is crying here," his father said as the two of us cried across the scratchy phone line. "Not only the family but also all the neighborhood children that he tutored over the years." His father was not able to go south for his son's funeral. Even Djak could not cross Abidjan to attend. Old Man's *jatigi* notified the pro-Ouattara soldiers that controlled Abobo, and four soldiers came with a flatbed truck. The soldiers took them to a cemetery on the northern edge of Abidjan, along with another family burying an old woman. In their beaten earth courtyard in Korhogo, Old Man's family gathered to say the prayers.

The official number of people killed by the violence was terribly high, but the actual number of people who died was probably much higher. One of those was a young man I have known his entire life, a young man who was bright, hard-working, and full of sweetness and promise. He was only twenty-six, the same age as my own son. The last time I saw Old Man was our Sunday lunch together in late October, and he was hopeful that when he graduated, he would find work and be able to send money to help his family.

"Ala i den balo," his mother and I say to each other each time we part. May God nourish your children and keep them alive. "Amina," we both reply. Amen. Now across the cell phone network, I had to offer the blessing you never want to say about your friends' child: "Ala ka hinara." May he go to heaven. His father, the person who thirty years earlier had taught me to say this, replied in a broken voice, *Amina*.

The Mad Baker in the Bunker

Hidden in the bunker below his residence, Gbagbo the Mad Baker told the world in sincere tones that it needed to respect the Ivorian constitution; urged people to pray for Ivory Coast; and turned his eyes on the African presidents, United Nations envoys, and international diplomats who came to mediate and explained that Ivorians needed to resolve this among themselves. He was shocked that the world was trying to decide his country's fate with a game of poker, and he needed, he said, a cease-fire in order to have a frank dialogue with his opponent.

All along, Gbagbo had used his African-liberation anti-imperialist rhetoric to adroitly maneuver Ouattara into a corner. If Ouattara turned to France and the United Nations, the most reliable sources of help and the ones that would demand the least destructive things in return, he proved Gbagbo right: he was a puppet of the West. So Ouattara, the democratically elected president, was forced to turn to the New Forces commanders, the com-zones. They had been sidelined by the election process and the impending reunification, but as they moved toward Abidjan to help Ouattara take his rightful place in the presidential armchair, they were marching right back into the center of the story, and afterward, Ouattara would owe them, big-time. Ouattara and his minister of defense asked their troops to refrain from acts of vengeance and promised to return the cars and money their troops looted as they entered the city. But words only go so far when people are desperate, and a fast-moving, untrained army of poor, angry young men is difficult to control.

Was Gbagbo crazy? Like a fox. Using his false outrage, his strategy was to play for time. If he could stay in, he might get dealt a better card—someone might loan him some cash for more mercenaries or his few remaining loyal troops might gain some ground. His opponents might quarrel among themselves or make tactical errors. It didn't seem to bother him that his best cards were ethnic massacres, food shortages, death squads, and urban civil war. What was he thinking then as the Republican Forces army encountered little resistance and moved quickly toward Abidjan, as his soldiers shed their uniforms and vanished? Gbagbo was surrounded by a closed circle of evangelical preacher-advisors who seem to have assured him that God had chosen him and only God could remove him. Perhaps he truly believed that he would, with divine assistance, triumph over his enemies. On March 30, as the Republican Forces army moved closer to Abidjan and the rest of the world tried to convince Gbagbo to negotiate a surrender to avoid further bloodshed, as the United Nations passed sanctions against the Gbagbos and three associates and invoked the possibility of crimes against humanity, a US senator, James Inhofe of Oklahoma, defended his evangelical friends, Laurent and Simone Gbagbo, on the Senate floor. He insisted the election had been unconstitutional and fraudulent and that Ouattara's troops were the ones terrorizing the population and committing atrocities. He supported Gbagbo's call for a cease-fire. Religion had not caused the conflict in Ivory Coast, because Ivorians are, as a society, tolerant, but it had played a role, and it certainly blinded some people, especially evangelicals both within Ivory Coast and without.

In Koumassi, there was no water for three days. Women spent hours going from house to house with their basins, asking their neighbors to share what they had. Yaya's family drank from the well they normally used only for washing and bathing. When a French television station announced that Gbagbo had surrendered, they and their neighbors went out into the streets, thinking the four-month ordeal was over. But when the news turned out to be false, they were doubly disheartened. Armed young men prowled the streets. "The pro-Gbagbos have killed one young man near us and badly wounded another. He will die, too. There is no medical care." Djak's voice drooped. "If only he could have gone to the hospital . . ." But he wasn't speaking of the wounded neighbor; he was talking about his brother Old Man.

When Gbagbo negotiated a cease-fire, the banner on his website changed: URGENT! PRESIDENT GBAGBO IS NOT IN A BUNKER IN HIS PALACE AND HAS NOT SENT HIS GENERALS NOR ALCIDE DJEDJE TO ASK FOR ANY KIND OF SURRENDER.

His message made no sense. Had he gone mad? Chékun said they had stopped speculating about Gbagbo. "We don't even know what to say anymore. But this has to end soon. We can't hold on much longer. Even here, an hour from Abidjan, food is scarce and prices are rising." She had talked to her husband in Abobo; he said people left their houses that morning to find food. But with all the shops closed and no trucks moving, there was very little to be had—a few pitiful tomatoes that normally cost a few pennies were selling for $2. "When people finish the last food they have stored, what will they do? There will be a famine." Where she was, they were pounding manioc leaves and mixing them with powdered hot pepper to make sauce. The one thing they did have was bananas. Since the trucks couldn't take them into Abidjan and they wouldn't keep, the farmers were practically giving bananas away. The little boys had eaten so many they were sick.

In a wealthier neighborhood of Abidjan, a flat of eggs, which usually cost about $3, was going for $12 and the small plastic bags of *attieké*, ready-to-eat manioc that women usually sell on the street for $1, were selling for $6. The big stores near Yaya's house had been locked and guarded since the crisis began, but when crowds of local people stormed them and demanded food, the pro-Ouattara soldiers broke open the doors and people helped themselves. "I don't think it's stealing," Djak said. "The rice is labeled World Food Program, but Monsieur Gbagbo's government made deals with the merchants and sold it to them instead. It was sent here for us and now we need it to survive." His voice turned urgent. "People keep talking about how Ouattara is supported by the international community. But what about the *national* community? A majority of us voted for Ouattara, but we have been taken hostage by Gbagbo and his minority. We need help. We are worn out. People are dying. We just want peace."

"As soon as possible I'm going back to Abobo," Chékun told me.

"But it's calm where you are and the children are in school."

"There is no one else here right now, so I can talk frankly. Here's the thing—this area is *very* pro-Gbagbo. If Gbagbo is killed and there is some kind of retaliation . . . well . . . here we are." She made a little clicking sound with her teeth, the sound of finality. "You should hear what they say about the women—the ones who were killed in Abobo. They say the videos were staged, that the blood was red *bissap* juice, and the woman who starts to get up and lies back down—do you remember that?" In the grainy cell phone video, one of the women pushed herself up and looked around, for help, or one last look at life. Then she sank back down. "They say she was acting and she realized she had gotten up too soon, that the film wasn't finished. They say that proves it was staged." Chékun's voice turned tight. "I was there that day! I heard the crowd wailing, I talked to the nurses in the clinic who treated the wounded." She sighed. "How can they say it? That it was staged!"

"What do you say when they talk like that?"

"Nothing! I'm a guest here. Well, at first, when some women asked me about what happened, I did say that I came from Abobo, that I was there that day and I am absolutely certain the shooting was real and seven women were killed. I told them I saw two wounded women carried to the clinic. I wanted them to hear the truth. But I don't say anything anymore. Everyone, even here, feels this is about to end and Gbagbo will lose, and I am afraid of what these people will do then. They say Gbagbo won the election, but the French and the United Nations want Ouattara, so they are trying to assassinate him. As soon as it's safe, we will take the bus back to Abobo."

I asked her how the fractures could be repaired when the groups didn't believe the same history.

"It's too soon to think about that. First we need peace. Then we can figure out how to rebuild."

From his bunker, Gbagbo told a French television station, "I am not a kamikaze. I don't want to die." Psalms appeared on his presidential website. They were all the same genre, Old Testament calls for God to come down and smite the living daylights out of his enemies.

"May burning coals fall on them; may they be thrown into the fire, into miry pits, never to rise. May those who seek my life be disgraced and put to shame; may those who plot my ruin be turned back in dismay. May they be like chaff before the wind, with the angel of the Lord driving them away."

In the middle of the nights, I woke up in a fury and lay awake composing my own letters to Gbagbo. Having experienced the high-flying hopes of the first round and felt how close the country came to resolving its crisis peacefully, I felt a terrible, vast sense of loss. I felt betrayed and angry. His apocalyptic biblical language was strangely appropriate, and I found myself borrowing it, calling down plagues and storms on Gbagbo and the death squads. So much had been gained and then all of it—and more—had been lost again. That the hard-earned reconciliation could come undone in four short months was shocking. Gbagbo had not pushed the country back to where it was in October before the election; he had pushed it much further. The old recriminations and prejudices had returned, but now there were new mass graves dug by both sides, new deaths and disappearances to turn families on both sides bitter and mistrustful, new narratives to justify each side's actions.

Chékun's husband, Ngolo, was coming home to Abobo from work when he was stopped at a Republican Forces barricade. The young soldier who looked at his ID was Senufo like him. "You," he said roughly to Ngolo, "you're military! You're hiding!"

A second Senufo came over. "What's the problem here?"

"He's military. He's one of our brothers but he's in the military, so I am going to take his car and turn him in."

Ngolo knew what the young soldier wanted out of the last days of chaos—a France Au Revoir—and he had decided Ngolo's old car was his best chance.

But the other Senufo spoke up. "You aren't ashamed? Even if he *is* in the military, he is your real brother and you are going to sell him out? What if the boss kills him, what then? If he is really in the military and he drove up to our barricade, he's with us."

That the danger came from one of his own, a hotheaded young Senufo parched with car thirst, made the moment even more frightening. The young man couldn't steal, for if he stole, his amulets and power medicines would no longer protect him, but if Ngolo was using the car for enemy business, it wasn't theft. Ngolo prayed silently.

"You and me," the second soldier said to the first, "we may have to kill each other today. If you send his ID over to the boss, you are going to find out what I will do to you!" He took Ngolo's ID and passed it back to him. After that day, Ngolo parked the car and didn't go to work again. He had coped with everything else, but that a fellow Senufo was willing to see him as an enemy in order to steal his old car—that rattled him. Next time he might not be so lucky.

On April 11, 2011, Gbagbo was arrested and taken out of his bunker. As with so many other episodes in this story, we saw only the cell phone videos posted on the internet. The filmmakers of this docudrama were the rebel commanders. The French army, which facilitated Gbagbo's capture by bombing the presidential residence, remains outside the frame. Laurent and Simone Gbagbo look haggard. He wears an undershirt; she wears a slip or nightgown. The cell phone movie focuses on him while she glowers in the background, her features fixed, her hair in disarray. The plot is a charade of magnanimous protection. The com-zones help Gbagbo put his arm through his shirt like a child, then wrap him in a bulletproof vest and clap a helmet on his head before they lead him out the door. The couple are taken to the Golf Hotel, where they are filmed later, sitting calmly on a couch, clean and neatly dressed. Subsequent videos show soldiers from the Republican Forces ransacking the presidential residence and toasting victory with Gbagbo's champagne.

Abidjan was filled with armed young men, some armed by Gbagbo, others by Ouattara. Some were invisible commandos who owed allegiance to their commanders; others were just taking advantage of the chaos, out for revenge or pillage. Armed groups took over neighborhoods and defended their turf while Gbagbo's hardline supporters slipped across the border into Ghana. Charles Blé Goudé, the hip young general of the streets, never appeared on any boulevard to lead his rag-tag militias. He vanished, saving himself.

Djak said they didn't go out and celebrate, in case Gbagbo's capture wasn't true this time either. They watched television the entire day. But four days later, when I called again, people were going out. The barricade on the road had been dismantled and the inexpensive *woro-woro* taxis were running again. Already, food prices were starting to go down.

Gbagbo was quietly moved from the Golf Hotel to the walled presidential residence in Korhogo, built by le Vieux for the rare occasions when he might spend a night there. Gbagbo, who had wanted to destroy the North, was now under house arrest there. It was rumored he had only one request: to be held separately from his wife Simone.

Chékun and the children returned to Abobo. "You know what is really strange?" she asked me over the phone two weeks after Gbagbo's capture.

I had no idea.

"People. They amaze me—the way they can just go back to ordinary life! The streets of Abobo are filled with people shopping in the market, greeting each other. In some ways, if you came now, on my street you wouldn't know what we have just lived through. As soon as there is calm, people go right back to ordinary life!"

Abou the Ex-Rebel's Last War

When his soldier friends moved south with their battalions to unseat Gbagbo, Abou the ex-rebel stayed put at his house in Bouaké. Even though he knew they needed every man they could get and he wished them success, he stayed because he had left the army and that was that. His cell phone rang with updates. "We captured one of Gbagbo's tanks!" His buddies reached Abidjan, and his cell phone started ringing with pleas for help. "Serious problems here. It's not going well. We don't know the city!" They tried to take over the television station but were pushed back. "It's hot here! Hot, hot!" One of his friends was killed. When he heard that, he knew he had to go. The soldiers gave him a uniform and a gun and took him to the big intersection on the northern edge of Abidjan where he used to pull over his *gbaka* to load and unload passengers. When his friends saw him, they said, "He came, he came, our old papa is here!"

"I know these streets," he told them. "And we're going to whip them!"

The new recruits were lined up and assigned to sections, and he was pleased when he was put with his friends in a section commanded by an experienced soldier. The rest of Abidjan was already controlled by the Republican Forces, but Gbagbo's street militias refused to surrender and had gathered in Yopougon, determined to hold out. When Abou's section tried to move deeper into Yopougon, snipers fired on them and they were ordered to fall back. As they retreated, Abou saw bodies on the ground, but only after they reached safety did they learn their section officer had been killed. They made the sad trip back for his body. After a day of fighting, they had made no progress and had lost their leader.

The commanders said they would leave Yopougon for the time being—too many of Gbagbo's militias were there and heavily armed. Abou's section had heavy arms, too, but they wouldn't use them in a densely crowded neighborhood. The other side fired whenever they spotted them. "They didn't care—it wasn't their country!" He was convinced they were mercenaries from Liberia for two reasons—one, they came up so close. "A Liberian—he is not afraid of weapons!" Also, he could hear them. "When you hear that 'Go!' you know they are Liberian."

They were ordered to march toward central Abidjan. A small tank was leading the column, but at a rotary, it halted—its gun was jammed. Abou went forward, took out all the shells, and asked for a new case of ammunition. "I looked until I found the right shells, all the same size, and reloaded it. It worked. It had just been loaded wrong. After I fixed it, the driver said, 'You! Get in! You're staying with me.' It was my first time in a tank. After that, most of the places were empty when we got there. They had fled and left their weapons. So many weapons just sitting there! The little arms we loaded into the pickup trucks. The heavy arms—Gbagbo's heavy arms rolled on tires, so we lifted the guns up and attached them to pickup trucks and pulled them.

"The commanders said, first, we are going to go and talk to the other side. There was a big meeting." Two sets of bleachers were set up. "The French army was there, the UN was there—there were speeches. Everyone should put down their arms and we are going to come to an agreement. Blah, blah, blah. Gbagbo is gone, he was already taken, so put down your arms!"

In the bleachers on the other side, Gbagbo's Young Patriots chanted, "Gbagbo or nothing! Gbagbo or nothing!" Everyone rested, took a day off, and then they held another day of meetings. Around Abou the guys were grumbling: "Negotiate with them? No way! Let's finish with Yopougon and then things will be calm and we can relax." The UN and the commanders tried again to negotiate, but Gbagbo's militias refused. Abou was asleep when the officers woke the men early and said, "Get up! We're headed to Yopougon!"

"There were so many of Gbagbo's militias gathered there, all massed in that end of Yopougon, and to go forward we had to fight our way. They were shooting, shooting! We fought—to go forward! Fought again—to go forward. We slept there. The second day, it was serious. Really serious. I lost hope. I thought, I am going to die here. I said to the tank driver, 'If we get through today, we are going to live. But I don't think we are going to make it through today.' The driver looked at me. 'You are really saying that?'

"I said, 'It's hot, it's hot!'

"And he said, 'No, Abou, you have to let that go.'

"'Park the tank then,' I said. 'We need to pray.'"

The battle was ahead of them, so they could stop safely for the moment at a pump. It wasn't working, so they broke it open and water rushed out. After washing themselves thoroughly, they prayed and consumed their combat rations—a baguette, a tin of sardines, and a bottle of water. "If we don't die today, then it's over and we won't ever die after that!" they told each other. With the others behind the tank, they moved forward. Their commander walked beside the tank with his bodyguard around him. He scanned the buildings, pointing out where to shoot. "Put it there! And there!" When he gave the order, his soldiers hit the ground. His section was disciplined, they knew each other and stuck together, but many others were in complete disorder. The most disorganized were the new recruits from Abobo. "Those Abobos—heeey! They made it more dangerous because you could get shot by your own side!"

They made it to the navy headquarters on the lagoon, but the place made Abou uneasy. Anyone could paddle up at night in a little boat and start shooting, and once, they did. Human rights organizations have reported that the troops Abou was with killed prisoners. When I asked about the prisoners, Abou said he couldn't speak about what he didn't see. Inside the tank, he saw very little, he reminded me. When I asked about looting, Abou admitted that yes, that first day the guys were coming back with their trucks filled—mattresses, televisions. "Always there were thieves—they took arms, clothes. I saw that! The commanders told them you can't steal things from innocent people. The commanders blocked their trucks. If you had the commander's cell phone number and you called him and told him your car had been stolen by his men, he would send soldiers there immediately! Immediately! But cars—they took a lot of cars! So many and they didn't know how to drive. A lot of them wrecked. They were on the highway, they wanted to go back to Bouaké. Hey! I've got a car, check it out! Look at me, I'm young, tough! It was *kanbeleya!*" (This is a Julakan word for youthful masculinity, machismo). "Boom! Dead! Plenty of them! Plenty, plenty, plenty! Me, I didn't really like all that kind of thing very much. You have to get in your head that whatever you do, tomorrow-*la*, it's going to come back around to you. You do good, you are going to have good. You do bad, you will have that, too. That's clear. In our religion, that's what Allah says. If I take something that belongs to someone, isn't someone going to come and take mine? Or what?"

After the battle of Abidjan was over, Abou was assigned to guard duty. The young men went out on patrol and marched. "I didn't want to stay in the army—orders, orders. I didn't ask because if you ask, they will say to wait. They weren't giving me any money, and my family had to eat. So I came back home."

Before the fighting that last day in Abidjan, the marabouts told them what they needed to do to succeed and they bought milk and white kolas as sacrifices. They gave the milk to the children to drink. The imams blessed them. "I am here today," Abou says, "and some of my friends are dead. Some of them had *gris-gris* and amulets everywhere and they are dead. You have to have good faith and believe in God, that's what I saw and that's what I believe."

Just a Word in Our Mouths

Two months after the Gbagbos were taken from their bunker, Tom and I arrived in Abidjan. The June night was hot, damp, and smoky, a night just like the one thirty years before when I arrived in Abidjan for the first time. But I was not the same naive young woman. In thirty years, I had seen how a country ruled by a charismatic all-powerful leader will be rudderless when he dies because it has no institutions to serve as a foundation for the next administration; that a one-party state does not easily become a multiparty democracy; and that a democracy requires more than elections, that it requires a balance of powers, an independent judiciary, and healthy civil society organizations. I had realized that a free press does not necessarily act as an independent press, that it can support the powerful, and if it isn't responsible, it can spread divisive, unsubstantiated rumors. I had learned that linking your economy to one unprocessed commodity makes you vulnerable to rising and falling world market prices. I had witnessed the way harassment by their own government turns people bitter and how giving preference to one region and one ethnic group leads to resentment that expands like pressure inside an enclosed space until it explodes.

It was estimated that three thousand people died between the second round of the election and the final peace four and a half months later. I wondered who had been counted. Had they counted Old Man, who died because Abobo was under siege from its own president and he couldn't get medical care? And how about those who were murdered in violent reprisals as the Republican Forces moved south? Had the women raped by both sides been counted? After a remarkably successful election, after the vast majority of Ivorians voted peacefully for unity, the needlessness and suffering of Gbagbo's war to stay in power boggled my mind.

As soon as we arrived, a succession of people visited us. Some were old friends, others acquaintances. Each greeted us warmly, sat down, and began to talk. We didn't have to think of the right questions—none were necessary. They recounted what they had lived through between early December and mid-April. The same thing happened when Tom went to meetings. Before they discussed agricultural policy, his Ivorian colleagues told him their stories of survival. We had arrived from the outside world; therefore, we became what the people of Abidjan needed: witnesses. After they left, I wrote down as much as I could remember, but while they talked, I gave them my full attention and listened. They told us about a wealthy businessman who spent millions of CFA francs buying guns from militia members and then turned them over to the United Nations. And they talked about a radio program that had passed along vital information called in by listeners all over the city.

In addition to survival stories, they had theories: Gbagbo could not be captured until the statues he had erected around the city were destroyed because powerful fetish objects were encased inside. Gbagbo was ready to surrender in early April when the Republican Forces troops closed in on Abidjan, but his entourage, especially Simone, pressured him not to. It was Simone who dispatched the death squads into Abobo, and the killers must have been Liberians. It was critical that France intervened, something they could say to us but not to some other Ivorians. The world had to intervene, some people told us, because Gbagbo planned to retake Abidjan through ethnic genocide; they believed he had lists of Jula drawn up; some people even thought that Jula houses had been marked with chalk by young people supposedly conducting a census of households for the distribution of mosquito nets.

A Jula colleague of Tom's from Yopougon ventured out the day after Gbagbo's arrest to take medicine to his elderly mother. In the taxi with him were his wife and his adult son and daughter. But Yopougon was still controlled by Gbagbo's paramilitary groups, and they hadn't gone far when their taxi was stopped at a barricade. A militia leader made them get out and took their cell phones and cash, then another militia chief appeared and demanded the cell phones. While the two argued, a small crowd gathered. Gradually the crowd edged slightly closer, and bit by bit the family inched backward until they were absorbed into the crowd and slipped out the other side. The driver stayed by his taxi and was killed.

A professor described how one column of Republican Forces soldiers entered Abidjan through his middle-class neighborhood and took every single thing in his house except his computer, which he had hidden in the ceiling. The only thing they left was the armchair he sat on as he watched them carry his goods away. Their commander had come and apologized but his possessions had not reappeared.

Lazeni, the chauffer who received the threatening late-night visit, returned to Abidjan once the city was calm. If he hadn't left, he would surely have lost his expensive car, he told me. Anyone with a weapon could have stolen it in the chaos. When he returned to the tea shop in his neighborhood, he saw Yapo, the ne'er-do-well neighbor who tricked him into opening his door. At the sight of him, Yapo turned away in fear, as if to run. Lazeni stopped him, greeted him, and asked after his family. But the next time Lazeni saw Yapo, he couldn't bring himself to speak kindly to him so after that they passed without speaking.

Some Republican Forces soldiers told Lazeni they were going to come to his neighborhood to teach people a lesson. He didn't think it was a good idea and reminded them that Alassane said not to seek revenge. They assured him they wouldn't hurt anyone; they would just make a show of force and tell people that from now on they should do the right thing. Lazeni told them they didn't need to do that because his neighbors had already apologized and asked for pardon. The soldiers accepted this, but in fact there had been no apology. Lazeni told them this to avoid causing more tension in his neighborhood.

On many Abidjan corners, you saw young men holding machine guns. They wore armbands or thin vests with "FRCI" for Republican Forces printed on them. One, who had no identification on his uniform, not even an armband, showed me his enlistment document, a small slip of paper. He lived in Abobo and had enlisted on May 25, six weeks after the fighting ended, with the hope of a job in the army or the gendarmes. Outside the destroyed presidential residence above Gbagbo's bunker, burned-out tanks stood next to huge piles of gray cases of ammunition for heavy arms. The Golf Hotel was still sandbagged and guarded by UN peacekeeping troops in blue, and downtown, walls were bullet marked and the glass facades of some skyscrapers were cracked and broken. In the building of the Independent Electoral Commission every possible item had been looted, the doors had been taken off their hinges, and even the wiring had been pulled out of the walls.

Chékun and I had a happy reunion in Abobo, where youths in Republican Forces vests and armbands guarded every corner. From her balcony, I watched young men priming looted cars for painting in an improvised body shop on an unpaved back street. Blue cars would drive away green, red ones blue. We stopped by her evangelical church to greet her pastor, an older Senufo man with a gentle way about him. He praised her steadfastness during the crisis and asked me if I knew she was the president of the women's association at the church. I didn't know, and Chékun laughed, both pleased and embarrassed, and admitted she hadn't told me. "Of course, we had a very difficult time here in Abobo," he said quietly. "We sheltered sixty families in the churchyard. But we mustn't forget that the ones who were targeted and who were most in danger were the Muslim imams." His concern reassured me. This was the *brassage* Ivory Coast I knew and admired, the "brewed together" society where religious tolerance was the norm.

In Koumassi we went to the scrapyard to see Yaya and Djak. The last time we had seen Yaya, he was a boy in Kalikaha. Thirty years later, he was a middle-aged man in his early forties, tall, long legged, and still skinny, with a cloudy scar in his left eye and a habit of ending sentences with "Or what?" or the exclamation "Cho!" which means, "It's true!" As we walked briskly along the dirt path toward his scrapyard, other dealers called out to him in Julakan, "Yaya, what do they want to buy? What are they looking for?"

"They're not looking for anything," Yaya called back. "These are my relatives!" He led us to his open-air office. Under the tin roof were some metal chairs, a large stone for sharpening tools, and heavy wooden tables, which his workers used as benches and couches. In one corner, on a metal filing cabinet, was a small television. After he had proudly given us a tour of his scrap business, he and Djak showed us the intersection where Gbagbo's militias had set up their barricade. The large blocks of concrete had been moved to the side of the road. "A lot of people were burned to death here," Yaya said soberly. "One hundred twenty-five. We don't know exactly how many were killed at this barricade, but maybe fifty. Terrible things happened. *Cho!*"

When we reached the North, the streets of Korhogo were even more crowded than usual because so many people had fled there from Abidjan, and everyone was smiling. That was when I realized that every face in Abidjan had worn traces of the months of strain. In the North, people had worried about their relatives, but they hadn't dodged bullets or seen bodies in the streets, hadn't rationed their food and worried how much longer they could feed their children. They weren't as thin, but mostly, you felt the difference in their eyes, in the way the skin wasn't pulled tight around them.

Gbagbo was under house arrest behind the high white walls of the presidential mansion in Korhogo. In a strange turn of events, the people of Korhogo had become his *jatigis*. When they walked past the high walls of the presidential compound, passersby knew he was trapped inside, stripped of his power, while their candidate was in the presidential palace. But they didn't gloat. That would have been unseemly when Gbagbo was a guest under their protection. Many people in Korhogo had lost relatives in the violence and they hadn't forgiven Gbagbo, nor forgotten how he threw out their votes, so to express their feelings, the women of Korhogo turned to music. When Gbagbo tried to retake the North in 2004, he boasted he would destroy Korhogo and plant coffee and cocoa there. Although it might be apocryphal, his threat entered the oral history of the war and the song referred to it.

People asked me if I had heard the song the women were singing, and in response to my request, a group of women gathered to sing it. The quietest, smallest, and seemingly youngest woman sang the verse in a high clear voice and the others responded with the chorus.

Ask Gbagbo . . . is the cocoa ready to harvest?
Ask Gbagbo . . . the day the warplane came, what did Gbagbo say?

He said he would kill us all, even the children
And plant coffee and cocoa.
Ask Gbagbo . . . is the cocoa ready to harvest?

Simple words with a complex meaning. Cocoa, as the women know, was the bitter heart of the conflict. Cocoa money bought the fighter jets that bombed their town and paid for arms and mercenaries. Their song asked Gbagbo, "So that cocoa and coffee you said you would plant in Korhogo, how is that working out for you?" Kass, sitting next to me, laughed so hard that I had to start the tape over and ask them to begin again. The second verse was:

Gbagbo couldn't plant coffee and cocoa in Korhogo
If God wants, we will go plant cotton and mangoes in Gagnoa.

Gagnoa was Gbagbo country, and cotton and mangoes were cash crops of the North, the equivalent of cocoa, although not so lucrative. Then the chorus again:

Ask Gbagbo . . . is the cocoa ready to harvest?
Ask Gbagbo . . .

Kayoh, a large woman in her thirties with a deep powerful voice, added her verse:

Don't give Gbagbo any more time because
He kills people, he burns them alive, he cuts their throats.

And a woman named Fanicho added hers:

Ask Gbagbo if the dead can vote . . .
The Americans should ask Gbagbo if the dead can vote . . .
Alassane should ask Gbagbo if the dead can vote . . .
The whites should ask Gbagbo if the dead can vote . . .

Our hostess, Karidja, leader of a Rally of Republicans women's group, improvised a line: "People say to kill Gbagbo but Alassane says not to kill him." The others repeated it, then sang the chorus afterward. Other women had joined us on Karidja's porch and were singing along, and soon we were all dancing. When we sat back down, I asked why they wrote the song. They deferred to Kayoh, a large woman dressed in dark red with her headwrap tied high. "When the nineteenth of September 2002 came, we didn't know anything about war," she began in her deep voice. "We were asleep and it was raining. We went to our gardens and harvested our vegetables. At the market, we saw men with arms. They explained that some Ivorians were excluded and that seemed true to us and we joined this cause. We don't know anything about bombs or war, but one day we saw two fighter planes flying over Korhogo. We heard an explosion." Here she paused for effect and imitated the sound of the bombs. Her eloquent gestures were oversized and dramatic, and her arms flailed expressively as she made booming crashing sounds. "People died that day, not from the bombs but from fear. Some had heart attacks. We lay on the ground for hours. We were afraid to get up! We knew nothing about war. When the airplanes bombed, fortunately, the mortars didn't explode. Gbagbo said he wanted to destroy Korhogo and come here to plant a coffee and cocoa plantation." She wagged her finger and fixed us with a last question: "And if he had succeeded in destroying Korhogo, who would be here for him now?" It was that important matter again of *jatigiya*. If Gbagbo had destroyed Korhogo, who would shelter and feed him now in his hour of need, who would be his *jatigi*?

I asked what they thought about the new government of Alassane Ouattara and about reconciliation. "What we want is for merit to be what matters, not what region you are from or what ethnic group," said one of the women. Another added, "Alassane is concerned about the hungry and the sick. Gbagbo didn't care about them. We think Alassane has a good way of working with the people and we think he will work with women, too."

"We want the country to be reunited," said another. "People from the North were discriminated against. Gbagbo even killed them. Alassane always says, 'Don't kill. Stay calm. Everyone will have the place they deserve.'"

One tall thin woman who joined us on the porch was too well dressed to be a market gardener like the others. In elegant French, she told me she had lived through the postelectoral crisis in Abidjan and had just arrived in Korhogo to visit relatives. "Reconciliation," she said drily. "It is just a word in our mouths."

I asked what she meant.

"Reconciliation is a word I can say, but I can't yet feel inside. But we are determined to do it for Alassane so he can govern well."

Six months later, I was back in Abidjan at a conference. When I said, "It's good to see how things have improved here in Abidjan since the last time I was here," most people nodded in agreement, but occasionally someone said, "Actually, the difficult times are just beginning," and the conversation ceased. This was, I realized, code for a pro-Gbagbo version of events in which a Ouattara presidency was the worst possible disaster that could befall the country.

I was attending the last talk of the day by an imam about how he and a Christian abbot worked together to promote HIV awareness and treatment. The room was stuffy and we were all tired when a jolt of electric current passed through the people around me. The Ivorian men all pulled out their cell phones, and on the closest little screen, I glimpsed the back of a vehicle on an orange dirt road. When the talk ended, I heard the news: Gbagbo was no longer in Korhogo. He had been transferred to the International Criminal Court in The Hague and would be charged with crimes against humanity. The Ivorians, none of whom I knew, seemed humiliated by this news; some exploded in anger at the West.

But when I asked an astute Ivorian sociologist what he thought, he said quietly, "It had to happen. There has to be an end to impunity." He added, "There are two kinds of reconciliation, you know. Some people want just reconciliation, but others want reconciliation with justice."

In Abobo, a few days later, I asked Chékun's husband, Ngolo, what he thought about Gbagbo being tried by the International Criminal Court. He looked down and fiddled with his cell phone. This was so annoyingly 100 percent Ivorian, I thought, to avoid answering the question by pretending you had just received an important text message. The Ivorian infatuation with cell phones was making it impossible to have a conversation! Then he handed his phone to me and a miniature movie played of an Abidjan street, a fire, a person being dragged by one arm and one leg into the flames. One hundred twenty-five. That was his answer.

Chékun and Ngolo's oldest son was only ten but he was serious for his age and made excellent grades. Ngolo knew someone who worked at an elite public boarding school run by the Ivorian army, and just before the election, when Gbagbo was still president, Ngolo asked his acquaintance if he thought it was worth paying the fee for his son to take the entrance exam. "If you are lucky, and this group is no longer in power, maybe your son would have a chance, but if they are still in power, I can tell you for sure that even if he is at the top of the list, they are going to remove his name." Ngolo, thinking of his own missed chances, was for signing him up, but Chékun relished the idea that her children didn't have to leave home to go to school. Nor did she want her son to be raised by the military. Ngolo reminded her that after he graduated, their son would have no obligation to the army and she gave in. By the time he took the examination, Ouattara had been inaugurated and Abidjan had become a construction site—roads and bridges were being repaired, new buildings were going up. The boy with a northern name, son of a schoolteacher and a mechanic whose parents had no connections and paid no bribes, was admitted. It was a hopeful sign.

Chékun and Ngolo had invested in a lot on the edge of Abidjan, and bit by bit, buying materials as they could afford them, they began to build a house.

The new neighborhood had neither water nor electricity yet, but it had air and space, and when the house was finished, they would no longer have to spend a large proportion of their income on rent. Tom and I spent the afternoon of Christmas Day with them in their old apartment in Abobo. They were worn out from an all-night Christmas Eve service at their church, and another evangelical church across the street was loudly broadcasting its Christmas Day service. We arrived with gifts for the children—books to read for fun, something their home didn't have, despite the importance they placed on education. Their oldest son disappeared into the bedroom and came out dressed in his school uniform, a miniature soldier wearing a miniature beret. Wordlessly, he stood there for our approval, his back perfectly straight, his dark eyes serious and proud. He was a beautiful little boy, a studious boy, and he was going to one of the best schools in the country. "This is his chance," said Ngolo quietly, proudly. But at that moment, I completely understood Chékun's misgivings.

A French company had lit up downtown Abidjan for the holiday season with giant colored orbs, stars, and trees. Even the bridges were lined with hanging ornaments, and a huge sign spelled out "reconciliation" in flowing cursive. In the center of the rotary in Abobo, on a large pedestal, ropes of light outlined a sculpture of seven women. After dark, families flocked downtown to wander through the magical glow. Dressed in their best, their children in tow, they bought snacks and pointed their cell phones aloft to capture the festive colored lights. Knowing what kinds of scenes were stored on those cell phones, I thought what a difference one year could make.

Lasungo and the *Yala-Yala* Nurse

Lasungo, diviner and healer, rubbed his hand along the right side of his neck where the skin had healed in ropy welts. He had been sick himself, he said, looking away into the distance with vacant eyes. His problems started when a *yala-yala* nurse walked into the front yard of his small house in Korhogo selling injections. *Yala-yala* nurses, like most nurses in Ivory Coast, are usually young men, and they wear white vests and printed T-shirts or hats, which makes it hard to distinguish them from public health workers conducting legitimate vaccination campaigns. This one was selling injections guaranteed to make you feel better no matter what your ailment. An injection cost $70, an enormous sum, but he offered one to Lasungo on credit. Some friends who were there urged him to take it. He didn't know why he gave in, but he did. The sickness started on his right side, where he had the injection, which was why he was sure the injection caused his illness. The nurse kept coming back to get his payment, but Lasungo didn't have that kind of money. Now that the fighting was over, he had no customers for his bullet-proof undershirts and amulets.

One day when the nurse came to collect, a New Forces soldier happened to be visiting Lasungo. Confronted by the soldier, the nurse said he would accept whatever Lasungo could pay. So Lasungo paid a small amount and never saw the nurse again. His right ear developed pains, his neck became swollen and sore on that side, and then the pain spread down his entire right side to his foot. He went to his family's farm in Kalikaha to sacrifice to the spirits, cutting the throat of a sheep and leaving the blood near the stones the nature spirits liked to sit on. The sacrifice didn't cure him, but he felt better afterward.

He couldn't afford to go to a clinic, so he bought medicine from the women who walked through the neighborhood selling pills. As we talked outside his

Lasungo at his house in Korhogo, 2011

house, one of the *yala-yala* medicine vendors appeared and lowered the basin on her head so he could look through the bubble packets of tablets and plastic bags of colored capsules. Lasungo bought a few water-soluble aspirin, some capsules called Medik-55, which she said were for headaches, and some large red-and-yellow capsules, which might have been antibiotics. He could afford five of those, so she knotted them into a bit of worn plastic bag, took his coins, put her basin back on her head, and went on her way.

I asked Lasungo if he knew a treatment for AIDS. He said he did because a spirit in the form of a white man came to him in a dream and told him which leaves to gather and pound and had instructed him to buy a bottle of wine and mix it with the leaves. But he hadn't tried the cure because no one with AIDS had come to him. The healers who advertised on the radio attracted all the clients, but he couldn't afford to advertise. I asked him how he would know his client had AIDS, since most people didn't admit it. He would place his palm on the person's forehead, he explained, and the spirits would tell him.

That evening, Adama imitated for me how healers advertised on local radio. "I can cure hernias, liver problems, heart problems, and AIDS! I have helped lots of people and they are completely cured! I live behind the market in Petit Paris! When you get there, just ask for me, Cherko! Don't forget—ask for Cherko!" As we chatted over bottles of cold tonic water, Adama said how sad he felt to see Lasungo now. "Remember how he used to be? Everyone admired him! Now he has nothing—no wife, no children, no money. It's pitiful. Even more pitiful than the word itself." Lasungo had sparked with life when he was young, played the balafon with extraordinary spirit, won the champion farmer contests, and been chosen as a leader. The other young *poro* initiates had looked up to him. Seeing him now was like going back to your high school reunion and discovering that the boy who was captain of the football team and class president and the lead guitar player in everyone's favorite rock and roll band was now down and out, barely making ends meet selling nutritional supplements out of his garage.

Yaya and the Scrap Iron Business

In Abidjan, roads that had been ignored for more than a decade were being repaved and the potholes were being fixed. The traffic jams were still terrible, but as we inched along in bumper-to-bumper traffic, the exhausted driver of my little red taxi was smiling. A functioning government meant new rules and regulations, and Yaya had to start paying taxes on his five rental houses. At the scrapyard, his young workers were loading scrap into a shipping container for an overseas buyer. On the days they loaded containers, Yaya paid a flat fee of $60, and six of his young men were working that day, so they would make $10 each, a good salary. Yaya's nephew Young Lonala was directing the work. They carried big chunks, parts of bulldozers, car doors, and large metal sheets. Tiny bits of iron they scooped up from the ground and dumped in by the wheelbarrow-full, the shiny bits clinking as they poured them in. The container would hold at least twenty-five tons, but if they loaded it too full, the weight would sink it into the mud and they wouldn't be able to close the doors. Inside, the metal slid and resettled, an evolving assemblage of circling lines of wire, metal sheets in subtly rusted colors, and old motors and gears in various metallic hues. Every now and then, one of the younger men climbed in and stamped, and the industrial forms and painterly colors kaleidoscoped into a new arrangement. You could have taken any of it and made sculpture, but I doubt you could have improved on the random kinetic collage. It even had its own soundtrack that clinked and banged, tapped, dinged, and gonged.

Yaya and his workers were as intrigued with their metal detritus as I was, but more functionally. Yaya could identify sizes and styles of rebar with a glance, and every motor and hose was scrutinized—if it still worked, it could be resold for more money than scrap. When the rare machine or part came in they didn't recognize, they huddled over the thing and called in consultants from down the muddy alley, determined to figure out what it was for and how to make it work. The only American motor they had ever come across, they told me, they had been unable to take apart. "The Americans—when they make something, it's solid!" said Yaya. "Cho!"

A man approached with coils of shiny wire to sell and Yaya examined them, then declined to buy. Coiled wire takes up a lot of space in the container but doesn't add much weight, he explained. Wire was also tricky because it could so easily be stolen. Heavy things he could buy with confidence, things you needed a truck and forklift to move, but something light—anyone could have walked off with it—and if you got caught, sentences for buying stolen goods could be longer than for stealing the stuff. "I don't want my name ruined again. My name was ruined in the village by fighting, and that caused pain to my family."

I asked him about reconciliation in his neighborhood. "It's over," he said. "Whether you were for Gbagbo or Ouattara, we have put it behind us. We greet each other, we joke."

"Really?'

"Sure. We live together here."

"But what about the young men at the barricade?"

"Oh, no! Not them! They can never come back here. We know who they are, and they would be killed." He saw my look of surprise. "*Cho!* Them? No, no, no, never, never."

Barefoot boys were scrounging through the scrapyard for bits of rubber and plastic-coated copper wire they could resell. Yaya didn't chase them off, unless they took little pieces of iron. "That I paid for." The boys wrapped the colored wire into balls, stamped on them, put the flattened tangles inside paper bags, and set the bags on fire. The black smoke smelled toxic, but the boys clustered around their fire. One showed me a large coil with the coating burned off and said it would bring between $10 and $20, a substantial sum. Across the alleyway, a plate of rice and sauce cost thirty cents.

That Sunday, a quiet day in the scrapyard with nothing to do but wait for the afternoon soccer match to come on the flickering television in the open-air office, Djak and I took out our pencils and paper and phone calculators to work out the container's value. Loaded, it had weighed about thirty-one and a half tons, and the scrap iron had sold for 120 CFA francs per kilo. But before we had converted the tons to kilos and set up the problem, Yaya had it added up in his head. When we completed our calculations, he was right, of course.

With 500 CFA francs to the dollar, he was used to dealing in millions. He said he calculated in two steps, first the large numbers, then the small ones.

The next time I visited, Yaya soberly informed me that he had problems. Some wiring had caught fire and destroyed some of his best motor parts. Even worse, the government had decreed that scrap iron was needed for construction and could no longer be exported. Yaya said some dealers worked around the ban—they loaded the containers lightly and told the customs officials they were shipping aluminum. The officials knew better, but the buyers paid them something and they looked the other way. "Before, under Gbagbo, everything worked like that," Yaya said. "It was all *beezness*."

He had another serious problem. After the postelectoral conflict, a lot of burned metal was sitting around Abidjan, and Yaya's partner managed to score two burned-out tanks. They cut them up and loaded the chunks into three containers, which they sold to one of their regular Bangladeshi customers, who had fronted Yaya and his partner some of the money to buy them. The Bangladeshis paid them for the first container, but they owed them $14,000 for the other two. They refused to pay because when one of the tanks was put in the foundry, it blew up. "Seven stayed inside," Yaya said, using the Ivorian phrasing for death. "Two more died at the hospital." A grenade or ammunition must have been left in one of the tanks, although Yaya said he didn't understand how it had happened, as they had cut the tanks up and loaded them at his scrapyard under his watchful eye.

"Business, it's business," Yaya mused. "If there's no accident we all work together. But if there's an accident . . ." He shrugged. "I had already paid for the iron. I put all my money in it. If the government would let us work, we could repay the money a little, a little. But we're blocked from exporting now. So I really don't know what I am going to do." He was forced to sell to the Chinese-run factory nearby. He complained that the Chinese buyers didn't greet him properly, didn't treat him like a human being, didn't remember who he was when he came back, even after he had sold them a million CFA francs of scrap iron the week before. "How can you do business with someone like that? But now I have to."

Reselling a large pile of used roofing panels was keeping his household fed. Each month, he bought four fifty-kilo bags of rice and a one-hundred-kilo bag of corn. The sauce ingredients alone cost $10 a day, and he gave each woman a dollar every morning for her own little expenses. We spent an afternoon counting his household and came up with thirty-six names. People were always coming and going, and some stayed for months, others for years. "It's God that arranges things so Yaya can feed them all," said his nephew Young Lonala. "It has to be."

"I like to have people around," Yaya admitted. "Even in Kalikaha when I was young, if I wasn't working in the fields, I liked to have people around. But at my house . . ." He chuckled and slapped his thigh. "There are too many people! That's why I come to the scrapyard, even on Sundays. *Cho!*"

He didn't blame the president for the new taxes or the ban on exporting iron. Alassane was trying to get the country back in working order. Thirteen years behind schedule, construction on a third bridge across the lagoon was finally starting. The campaign was on for deputies in the national assembly, and Yaya was often at the nearest Rally of Republicans headquarters. Yaya said he knew people who would vote for the old ruling party because their candidate gave a fat envelope to their neighborhood association. "I can understand people taking the money. Take the money! But I'm not voting for them and no relative of mine is voting for them. They started all the trouble." At his party's headquarters, Yaya was in his element. "It's not a kingdom here," he declared to the younger men. "We don't want someone who will sit around and do nothing. We want to hear about his ideas and projects, and afterward, if he doesn't do it, we can ask, 'You said that during the campaign, why didn't you do it?'"

If he "knew papers," Yaya told me, he would have gone into politics; he deferred to the young people who did. "At meetings I don't speak, even if they ask me to. My French—you know—it's not correct! I learned it bit by bit in the streets." When his candidate won, he was pleased and waxed philosophical. "We were born here. Here, it's for us, *all of us*. It's not just for one person. But if there are places you can't enter or your child can't enter, you have a responsibility to get involved in politics. You have to fight. Today, Alassane has the power and now we can go anywhere. Who's going to treat us badly now and say we are rebels? It's true, no? Or what?"

Gbagbo's first hearing at the International Criminal Court in The Hague was scheduled for that day, and in Abidjan, it would be early afternoon. The city came to a halt and wherever they were, people gathered around televisions. What would he say? How would he justify shelling his own people? In Yaya's little open-air office, we sat on the tables and watched the flickering black-and-white screen, waiting for Gbagbo.

The workings of the International Criminal Court were convoluted, and technical judicial matters had to be resolved. The judges stood at their podiums in their archaic gowns making sober announcements, and eventually the hearing was postponed. Around us, the banging and clinking started up again and the afternoon soap operas came back on—nonstop drama inside the villas of wealthy Ivorian families, real estate deals gone awry, adulteries and betrayals. Yaya sympathized with the characters' real estate problems. In Abidjan, real estate was always complicated, he said. You had to keep a close eye on your property or someone would cheat you out of it.

"We don't know what's out there, afterward," Yaya mused. "Here, if you say you don't pray, you are zero. But Muslim or Christian, you can't just pray. You have to be a good person. If you are a Muslim and you leave the mosque, you can't go and kill people. Those people that do that, they are not real Muslims! And Simone Gbagbo—even we who are not Christian, even we know she is not a real Christian! *Cho!*"

Abou the Ex-Rebel and the DDR

Abou was still waiting to receive his money from the program to demobilize, disarm, and reintegrate (DDR) the former combatants. Some former combatants had returned to their villages to farm, but others, having escaped farm work and the oversight of their elders, wanted a different life and were living in cities, barely hanging on, trying to find odd jobs that would buy a plate of rice and sauce. Yellow motorcycle taxis had appeared in some towns; the moto-taxi drivers were former fighters who received the bikes as part of the program. The success of the reintegration program was critical for lasting peace because Ivory Coast had sixty or seventy thousand young men who had left their lives to become soldiers. In uniform, they had found themselves with two meals a day, a job that kept them occupied, and a weapon that ensured if not genuine respect at least authority. Some had fought with militias for Gbagbo, others with the New Forces; many had joined in 2002; others had enlisted during the postelectoral conflict.

By the time Abou came back from the battle of Abidjan, his chickens had all died. Rather than start over, he rented the chicken houses to another poultry entrepreneur. Abou had eighteen family members in his household to feed, so he did what he called little-little things—odd jobs for merchants and truck drivers he knew. He also raised corn, peanuts, and yams on an empty lot near his house, and every month his partner in the cement business in Abidjan sent him half the profits.

A large group of ex-rebels in Bouaké, frustrated by how long it was taking for the DDR program to pay them, blocked the main road, but Abou didn't join the demonstration. "Me, I earn enough to eat. We eat. For those who don't manage to eat, it's another thing. It's not the same at all." Nor did Abou want to demonstrate against a Rally of Republicans government. "I am Rally of

Republicans 100 percent. Demonstrate? I can't do that. Have a delegation and go and explain, that's good. Demonstrate? After all the suffering I saw? No, I cannot do that! I have confidence in Alassane." Even if he didn't get anything from the program, he was satisfied because things would be better for his children. "Now, northerners are not harassed or attacked," he said, leaning forward. "You put on your boubou, you leave here, you go to Abidjan, no one harasses you. You go to the army camp—there's a little mosque where you can go and pray. It's a new pride and dignity for us. If someone asks for my ID, I hold it out; they don't tear it up, they say, that's fine. Yes! It's finished, like that. See, it sorted things out for us. Already it's so much better. The war has done its work!"

Nawa on Market Day

After her health improved, Nawa had been selling fried chunks of yam next to the road in the evenings. Wrapped in paper, with a spoonful of her hot sauce on top, they were a popular snack. Then the price of cooking oil had risen. She bought a large container on credit but found she couldn't raise the price of her yams and ended up in debt. On his last visit home, Old Man had given her his savings to pay it off. Whenever she talked about Old Man, her eyes grew sad. Of her six younger siblings, he had been the one she turned to and counted on. He persuaded her not to give up when she found out she had AIDS, he made sure her younger son did his homework, and he kept an eye on her older son so he didn't run wild. Even from Abidjan, she had felt his concern.

Now she had turned to buying and reselling vegetables at a neighborhood market. Every six days, on market day, farmers and market gardeners walked into town with their produce. Nawa's day began early under an enormous tree, where the women gathered to display their produce. At lightning speed, she moved from one woman to the next, looking over the zucchinis, cabbages, and greens, greeting the farmers and asking prices. She had to be fast—if there was a bargain to be had, it would go quickly. A pile of giant zucchini caught her eye. She and the farmer negotiated, reached an agreement, and Nawa pulled the bills from the money belt under her wrapped skirt. Then she quickly bought two very large sacks of spinach. A friend had come to help, and the two women tied the sacks closed, hoisted them onto each other's heads, and took off through side streets toward her friend Assiata's courtyard. There, they paused to catch their breath and drink water before continuing. At the market, wooden tables and benches were arranged in rows under a tin roof. Nawa greeted the women around her and covered her table with an old sheet of black plastic. She arranged the zucchinis, portioning out the smallest and those with broken ends so all the piles were of equal value. The spinach she placed in bunches, stems toward her, leaves pointing toward the aisle where the customers were starting to pass. "Greens! A lot for twenty-five francs! Greens! Twenty-five! Twenty-five!" she called out.

Greens are an important part of the West African diet, and the tables were piled with different varieties: spinach, red-leaved spinach, eggplant leaves, and white bean leaves. Nutritious and inexpensive (twenty-five francs is just over a nickel), greens are cooked and pounded to make a sauce that is served over corn *toh* or rice. Although we didn't pound them or eat them as a sauce, greens—mustard, turnip, or collard—were also on the dinner table at my grandparents' house in Arkansas. They had been introduced to the southern United States by enslaved Africans, although by the time I came along, the culinary origins of greens had been conveniently forgotten. On his five acres, my grandfather planted collards in late August to harvest in the winter. Up at four in the morning, he cut the big paddle leaves and washed them in an old bathtub in the yard, and then on the way to his office job, he sold the bunches at two nearby grocery stores, one in a black neighborhood, the other in a white one.

As the morning heated up, Nawa sprinkled water over her spinach to keep it looking fresh. "Greens! Twenty-five!" she called out.

"Nawa is tough!" her neighbor teased. "I want to get my greens sold quickly and go work in my garden plot, but Nawa will stay all day if she has to!" This woman was selling little plastic bags of spinach seeds, and Nawa bought two for her mother to plant. Some vendors had cut their vegetables into affordable chunks in case you couldn't afford an entire zucchini or cabbage. One woman was selling homemade peanut butter by the scoop from a big basin. She had that panache of the experienced market woman—chatting and joking with her customers, hardly seeming to look at what she was doing, yet making each scoop exactly the same size. Women were lining up to buy from her. Pounding peanuts into paste with a mortar and pestle isn't difficult, but if you could afford the few extra cents, the peanut butter was a timesaver. Mixed with chicken bouillon, tomato paste, pounded onions, and hot red pepper, it would be simmered into a piquant sauce.

By ten in the morning, the hum of women's voices—bargaining, greeting, calling out to advertise their wares—filled the open-sided market. Nawa made her money back on the zucchinis quickly. Everything after that would be profit, except the quarter she owed for her table rent. By eleven thirty, the market was quiet again. The shoppers had headed home to cook lunch. Her older son worked as a tailor's apprentice, and since she lived right by the tailor, Nawa's friend Assiata had offered to feed him lunch every day. Nawa regretted she hadn't been able to send him to school. "The children who don't go to school will be left behind," she said. She was determined her younger son Yardjuma would go but she struggled to come up with the money for his supplies. Joining the parent-teacher association, which was obligatory, cost $8 a year, and he was sent home because he didn't have a uniform, which cost $10. To get him back in school, Nawa borrowed $20 from a friend; she asked the teacher which supplies mattered most and bought those. Nawa wasn't sure when she would be able to pay her friend back, but so far, the friend hadn't asked her to. She worried her son didn't study enough and wouldn't pass the test for middle school. If he failed, his education would be over because she couldn't afford to send him to a private school. When she had a little extra cash, she hired a tutor for $3 a month, but mostly she depended on a neighbor who helped the little boy with his homework as a favor when he had time.

At noon a woman stood up and blew a whistle insistently. This was the signal for members of the market self-help association to come to the weekly meeting. Women crowded onto two parallel benches, all business, no chatting or teasing. Every week, each of the forty-two members put in a dollar, and one of them took home the pot. A young woman who had been to school kept the accounts in a notebook, putting a check by each name as the women paid up. With a substantial sum like $42, you could invest in something to resell, buy a big container of cooking oil, or put a child in school for the year. Nawa had been at home sick when they started this round so she couldn't take part until every woman received her share and they started over.

In the quiet heat of the afternoon, Nawa and I fell into a conversation about forgiveness, the Ivorian custom of asking pardon. "The Muslims say to forgive," Nawa said, "and if it's something small, something you *can* forgive, you should do it. But if the person has killed someone in your family, you don't have to forgive that." She shook her head gently. "That is too much to forgive." I knew she was thinking of Old Man.

Her little sister was going to be married soon, and Nawa wondered who the husband would be. Adama hadn't asked me to keep his plans confidential, so

I told her that she would be married "within-the-family" to the son of her father's sister; first cousins were a preferred marriage. Her sister was obligated to accept, Nawa told me. If she objected, she would offend her father and her father's family. "Marriage is almost never easy," Nawa said quietly. The sweet part of life for her was friendship with other women. "Especially my friendship with Assiata."

At the end of market day, Nawa had a profit of $4.40. "A good day," she said happily. Since she was the only woman in her end of the market selling zucchinis, she hadn't had to lower her price. "A very good day!"

The next afternoon, Nawa invited me to visit her friend Assiata. Assiata's sister-in-law was visiting from Mali, and although she wasn't young, she was a *jeli* and a true performer, and she sailed out of the simple mud house like a star taking the stage, lit from within. She wanted to know all about Bakari Obamba, and so I recounted stories from his memoir while Assiata made pots of tea—fresh mint, Chinese green gunpowder tea, and generous amounts of sugar—and Nawa looked on happily. Assiata was a plump host in a well-worn boubou, urging tea on us while she kept a watchful eye on her children. Her daughter Khadi, born just after Nawa's husband died, was her assistant in the courtyard. Khadi was one of those girls who seem older than they are—not just smart but alert to the world around her. As she whirled by, playing, watching the younger children and carrying out her mother's commands, I could tell she was eavesdropping on everything we said. It was a lovely afternoon, filled with women's laughter, my last in Korhogo, as I was leaving the next morning for Abidjan. As we walked slowly back to my hotel, I asked Nawa if she had enough money to pay for her antiretrovirals.

"It's free for me now. The people at the clinic helped me fill out the forms. But I don't need to take the medicine any longer."

I turned and looked at her. "What are you saying?"

"I'm healthy now, you've seen for yourself how I can work all day at the market. I don't need to take the medicine anymore."

"You're not taking it?"

"No." Her voice was matter-of-fact.

I grabbed her arm and pulled her out of the stream of pedestrians, against a high concrete wall. "Nawa! You can't do that!"

She looked down.

"You can't! You'll get sick again."

She refused to meet my eyes.

"Nawa, please! Tell me you'll take the medicine! If you don't take it, you'll be sick again. You understand that, don't you? You have to keep taking it!" Droves of motorcycles, mopeds, and bicycles passed us as the people of Korhogo made their way home from work, and the whine of motors nearly drowned out my words. A red-orange cloud of dust filled the air, and the sun softened hazily. So close to the equator, dusk lasted only moments. At seven every evening, all year round, almost without warning, day slipped away and night fell.

"Nawa, please don't do that to me. What if I come back and you're not here?"

A long moment passed between us, our eyes locked together, before Nawa nodded. "I understand," she said. "I will take the medicine."

In One Ear and Out the Other

One year later, when I was back in Korhogo, Nawa said to me, "Let's go and greet Dr. Taaa—*noh*!" I could tell how much she liked her doctor by the way she turned his name into a lilting little song. But when we arrived at his office on the hospital grounds, he was away on vacation. It was the day after Christmas, which didn't mean anything to Nawa. Outside his office, a wiry little woman greeted Nawa and pulled her aside, speaking urgently in a low insistent voice. Edging closer, I overheard "your medicine" and "this disease" and "you have to learn to not mind what he says" and even the dreaded word *sidabana*, which was Julakan for AIDS. This was the first time I had ever heard anyone discuss AIDS in public. When the woman paused for breath, Nawa turned to me. "This is Masita. She talked to me and helped me."

"Very nice to meet you," the woman said to me in rapid-fire French. "I work with Dr. Tanoh and the other doctors and counsel the HIV-positive patients." She switched back to Julakan. "Nawa, you need to come to the meetings, that would help you," and then in French to me, "I'm not a doctor or a nurse, I don't have any professional training, but I know this disease because I am HIV positive myself." This was a statement I had never heard an Ivorian make. Without a pause, she continued in Julakan, "Nawa, you mustn't let it worry you, what your father or other people say." To me again, "This disease—it isn't easy, I know because I live with it myself." She switched back to Julakan. "Nawa, you've never come to my house and I'd like you to come." In French to me: "If you will wait while I take this relative of mine, this older sister has come all the way from a village for a diabetes test—it won't take long—then we will all go to my house, it's not far." In Julakan: "Nawa, my house is not far and we'll go there together to greet the children who are living with me. I want you to see them." In French: "Most of the children at my house have the disease, too.

I have taken them in because their families don't care for them properly." In Julakan: "Just sit down and wait for me. I won't be long!" In French: "It will be good for Nawa to come. She will see that she can remarry someday, even have more children."

Nawa and I found some concrete blocks in the shade of the hospital's back wall, and as if blown there by the harmattan winds, we sat down obediently to wait. Half an hour later, Masita and her relative reappeared, and she led us to a street of expensive walled villas. Masita wore a long dress made of cheap synthetic fabric, and as a purse she carried a white plastic sack with a plastic handle. "It's the next house down," she told me, gesturing to a metal gate. I wondered if she lived with a wealthy relative or worked for someone. A toddler girl, wearing nothing and badly in need of a bath, poked her head out, and seeing Masita, came running toward her. "What are you doing out here?" Masita demanded. "Get back inside!"

The house had a ceramic tile porch and a large living room, but since the only chairs were outside, we sat there, and once she had offered us water, Masita began her own story. She was working as an assistant to the midwife in a maternity clinic when she suspected she might have AIDS because she was sick so often. It was 1995. She knew some of the women who gave birth were ill, there was always blood, and they had no gloves. She told her doctor she wanted to be tested. "What good will it do you to know?" the doctor asked. "There is no treatment." Masita said she didn't want to give her children the disease. The doctor gave her a form and sent her to another clinic where there was a lab. A month passed. She signed a form saying she didn't hold the clinic responsible for the outcome of the test, but they didn't draw her blood. She went back to the doctor. "Are you ready, no matter what the result will be, to have the test? Do you understand what it means if you have this disease?" he asked. She said she did. "In case you do have the disease, do you understand that there is no medicine for it?" Yes, she replied. "Then why do you want the test? Because you will just be there dying and you will know it."

"If I have something else, I want to find out and treat it. And if I have this disease, I want to know. Either way I am going to die one day. There are plenty of people who die and it wasn't that disease that killed them," she reminded him. When they finally gave her the test, it came out positive. She believes she contracted the virus from a woman who came into the maternity clinic in labor, very ill, and losing blood. Despite their efforts, both the woman and her baby died.

Ten years after her diagnosis, Masita was very weak. As she lay on her mat waiting to die, she listened to a little radio and one day she heard there was a medicine for AIDS. It cost $10. It was 2005 and subsidized antiretroviral medication had reached northern Ivory Coast. She was so frail she was unable to keep food down. "It's too late for you," her husband said when she told him, but Masita called her grown son and he urged her to go to the hospital and offered to pay. When she began the treatment, the drugs were too much for her fragile body, but she was determined, so when she vomited up one of the pills, the next day she took two. Her doctor told her she was going to kill herself that way, so she learned to take the pills correctly, and after being on antiretrovirals for a year, "I returned to life!"

One day she went to a meeting for people with AIDS and sat in the back, hiding her face in her hands. The speakers explained how to take the medicine, how to take care of yourself, how you could and could not infect other people. "I started to have courage. You have to have a lot of courage to follow this treatment. You are tired, you are so easily tired, and it's easy to give up. In the meetings, I learned, too, what I had to be careful about. I was afraid to eat with anyone, but I learned that I couldn't infect anyone from eating with them." She decided, then and there, to take the field, to throw her own thin recovering body into the battle against AIDS. "It's the disease that trained me. I'm not a doctor, I'm not a nurse, I was a midwife's assistant and I helped women give birth, but I'm not even a midwife. But I live with AIDS and I know it! And the ones who listen to me, they are still alive! If I say it's black, it's black, and if I say it's red, it's red!"

Masita is like a stringy chicken, the kind Ivorians call a *poulet bicyclette*, going back and forth on her skinny legs, pecking here and there in search of a few overlooked grains of rice. A *poulet bicyclette* mother hen clucks constantly as she herds her chicks and tries to keep them from straying. Masita does the same. As she goes from the hospital to the clinic, to the support groups she leads, and to people's houses to educate their relatives, she keeps up a constant stream of persuasion and exhortation, drawing on her large stock of narratives to make her points. All her fables have the same moral: "The people who listened to me and followed the treatment got better. The people who didn't take their medicine are dead." The ones who died—when she told them to get tested, to follow the treatment—"Well, it went in one ear and out the other."

Masita is also part fire and brimstone preacher, and her sermons compare and contrast two possible paths. At the end of the antiretroviral path is life; at the end of the other path, the path of ignorance, is death. At frequent intervals, refrains repeat, like choruses: "The spirits won't cure you! The traditional medicines won't cure you! The medicine will. God made AIDS and God created the remedy!" The white plastic bag with the red Sir Cigarette logo, its plastic handle over her thin wrist, serves as her briefcase. In it she carries test results, bottles of antiretrovirals, her reading glasses, a few coins, the spiral notebook listing her patients and their phone numbers, a ballpoint pen, and her cell phone.

As we stood in her courtyard, kids ran around us, children she had taken in. She sent one child out the gate to buy some small bags of peanuts and told the oldest girl to start cleaning the rice for dinner; the other older children she called over to shake my hand and greet me in French while she proudly enumerated their accomplishments in school. The house, she explained, was abandoned. When she found it, animals had lived in it and people had shat in it. She and the children cleaned it with bleach, put cardboard over the broken windows, and she bought sturdy wooden front doors to replace the ones that had been taken.

Nawa recounted to Masita how she followed the traditional treatment from the kind healer but got even sicker until she couldn't eat anything but corn porridge mixed with milk and often had diarrhea. How, after she knew she had *sidabana*, she wanted her parents to know the truth. But her father had not taken it well.

"When you say you have the sickness, people say you have been out chasing men," Masita replied, "but look at that little boy over there. He takes the medicine. He has lost his mother and father. And this girl here, same thing. She takes the medicine. Were these children out chasing after men? You have to be strong and not get discouraged. His relatives thought this boy was going to die and they gave up on him, but look at him, does he look sick? When he first came, he was thin and sick. But now when his relatives visit, they say, 'Look at him, he has gotten so big, he has gained so much weight!' You should have courage and not give up, Nawa. You will get better, too, and you will have the opportunity to meet a man and marry and have more children. Look at me, I had the sickness for ten years, but I am still here and I am in good health! So have courage and don't despair." Someday, Masita promised Nawa, she would meet her father and make him understand that Nawa was not chasing men, that it was her husband that infected her. "After all, wasn't he the one who gave you to this man in marriage?"

"He says if his child had another kind of sickness," Nawa replied sadly, "he would take care of it. But me, he says I was chasing men, and I got it myself." Her eyes filled with tears. "I never did that. I don't know anything about that."

"The day I meet up with him," Masita responded, "I am going to make him understand. Even because of an old razor blade or knife, you could get the sickness. I am going to try to meet him and talk to him. You don't need to cry; wipe away your tears!" she said briskly to Nawa, then turned to me. "The day I met Nawa at the hospital and we went back to her house together, I met her mother and she understood. But I didn't meet her father, so he hasn't been exposed to this, he hasn't been sensitized."

"My mother understands, she knows I don't sleep around. It's my father." Nawa recounted how, when she returned from the healer, still very sick, her father said he had no money but her mother had a little, so they went to the hospital. The nurses gave her a transfusion and then a blood test, but after the blood test, they sent her from one clinic to another and would not tell her the result. Eventually they sent her to the small clinic where Dr. Tanoh sometimes worked.

"You should not have told your father; you should have told your mother and hidden it from him and taken the treatment," Masita scolded.

Nawa began to cry again. "I told the doctor I was afraid to tell my father. The doctor said not to tell him. But I said no, if I die, I want them to know why I suffered and what I died of."

"If you are going to cry, you should leave. Crying won't help," Masita said sternly and resumed her own treatment specialty—treatment by narrative, longform, an adroit combination of admonition and exhortation. Like most preachers, she had an endless supply of examples—those who had stayed on the path and were healthy and those who had, often unintentionally through ignorance, wandered off and suffered the consequences.

"My father says," Nawa said mournfully, "that I have the illness and the ones who have the illness are the ones who are prostituting themselves. He says, when you go to funerals in other villages, you are prostituting yourself. But

I told him, I have never done that. I don't know anything about that." She was crying quietly, her face hidden by one hand. "The things he said to me—I decided it was better just to stop taking the medicine and die."

"Don't cry," Masita told her, gently this time. "Just give that up to God." Masita turned to me. "It's hard-*dé*. It's difficult. It's ignorance. He was never sensitized about the disease. He has no notion of what it is, HIV . . ." Her cell phone rang and she fished it out of the plastic bag. "I'm coming! I'm coming!" she cried cheerfully. It was the lab technician at the clinic, Camara. That day's results were back and he needed her to distribute them. "Ay, Camara, Camara!" she responded, laughing affectionately. "I am on my way!" The patients were supposed to have a blood test every three months, and if their numbers hadn't improved, Masita made sure they were taking the medication correctly or the doctors switched them to a different antiretroviral. But I knew that Nawa didn't go for blood tests. Regular preventive care was incomprehensible in northern Ivory Coast—the clinic and hospital were places you went when you were seriously ill and had cash on hand.

Plastic bottles of antiretrovirals made in India were piled into cardboard boxes on Masita's porch, and she showed me what Nawa was taking, the twice-a-day treatment. "Thank God for the medicine. She should take it the same time every day, at eight in the morning and eight in the evening, for example. Those who can't tolerate this one can take the other, thank God." She also showed us plastic bottles of an antibiotic, for when the patients had diarrhea.

"I didn't know there were certain times to take the medicine," Nawa said.

Masita explained to her how to take her pills correctly and how to take the antibiotic for five days. "Even if the package changes, it is the same medicine and you take it the same. See, here is the old bottle and this is the new design." Masita broke off the explanation to hush a crying child. Nawa said she hadn't understood this, that when she had diarrhea she had taken only one pill. Masita explained again to take it for four or five days, and if she was still sick, to go to the doctor.

"Even if I am in the house for four days," Nawa told her, "and can't get up, my father doesn't ask how I am doing, he doesn't look in and greet me. He doesn't care one bit. He gets angry just seeing me."

Masita turned to me. "It's complicated." It was, and since the family had asked us to tell Adama, I felt implicated. Perhaps we could have explained better or insisted he come hear the diagnosis from Dr. Tanoh. One of the little girls returned with small bags of peanuts. It was a poor thing to offer guests, Masita said apologetically, but it was all she had. She wanted Nawa to come to the clinic the next morning at six to have her blood drawn so Dr. Tanoh could determine exactly how she was doing. If we walked back together, it was on our way, and she would point out the place. Nawa must be there early because the samples had to be transported to the American missionary hospital an hour away before the day turned hot. The test should be free, she added, but since the machine at the hospital was broken, it cost money to hire the driver and buy gas for his moped to take the samples to the hospital in another town and bring back the results. That was why they charged $2.

The next morning, Nawa and I met early at the little clinic, a converted house on a main street surrounded by a high wall. It was run by an Ivorian nonprofit that received government funding as well as funding from international donors, including Planned Parenthood. The clinic focused on family planning, AIDS treatment and education, and maternal health. When it was open, the big gate was ajar. The metal sign saying it treated contagious sexually transmitted diseases had rusted to near illegibility, which might have been a good thing because once an organization becomes associated with AIDS, no one wants to be seen going there. When it became known that the clinic where Nawa was first seen by Dr. Tanoh treated HIV-positive people, people stopped going even though treatment there was free, so the clinic switched to mobile testing at high schools and in nearby villages. The AIDS awareness efforts in high schools were successful, according to Dr. Tanoh, and young educated people knew how to avoid the disease and were less likely to shun those living with it. But fewer than half of Ivorians attend school, and the percentage was even lower in the North.

The clinics run by nonprofit organizations (NGOs) attracted the most experienced health professionals because they paid higher salaries than the government-run hospitals, although some medical professionals, like Dr. Tanoh, worked at both. Dr. Tanoh had a calm, low-key way of talking with his patients that made testing seem routine. But even if they had symptoms of AIDS, their acceptance of the test was voluntary.

"It's somewhat difficult here," he said. "People are afraid to get tested because they say, 'If I go for the test, people will know and automatically I will be banned from society, I will be rejected.'" One of his female patients had come to see him that morning upset because she could not convince the man she lived with to be tested. He was frequently sick but didn't believe in AIDS. In his view, God had touched him and that was why he was sick and one day he would die. If you have never heard of cells that are too small to be seen by the naked eye, if you have never heard of microscopes, germs, bacteria, or viruses, accurate information about AIDS doesn't make much sense.

As we waited on the bench outside the clinic the next day, Nawa shivered in the early morning coolness. I was wearing a wool hoodie, but she had only a cotton cloth wrapped around her shoulders as a shawl. At this time of year, the wind called the harmattan blows south from the Sahel toward the savanna, bringing hot dry afternoons and chilly nights and mornings. The men and women on the bench regarded me uneasily so I got up and poked my head inside the office to say good morning to Masita. To her usual long dress and headscarf she had added reading glasses with only one earpiece. I hoped the sound of her greeting me in Julakan would reassure the people waiting. A moped pulled up with a young girl on the back so frail she couldn't stand without assistance. The people on the bench, who all looked healthy, scooted over and made room for her, and she leaned her head wearily against the wall. The mood got heavier. Masita noted each patient's cell phone number in her worn notebook, so when Nawa's turn came, she left her father's number. "If she had a phone," Masita said to me, "I could call her when we have a support meeting coming up."

As Nawa and I walked back to my hotel, we passed vendors selling "cold clothes," used clothing from the United States and Europe. I insisted she try on jackets, and we settled on a bright-blue swim team jacket with a fleece lining. The vendor wanted $7. Nawa refused, but as we walked away, he called us back and accepted her offer of $2.50. At another roadside stall, I bought her a $20 cell phone and filled it with $10 worth of prepaid units. She had to show her ID card, and we paid $1 to register her account with a French telecommunications company, a recent requirement. At the hotel, Tom and I put our numbers into her contact list, and added her father, her brothers, and her uncle in Kalikaha. I put MASITA in in capital letters, but Nawa didn't seem worried about distinguishing her contacts. She was delighted to finally have a phone of her own. Without a cell phone, it was as if you didn't exist.

Once her excitement about the cell phone had subsided, Nawa told me about one day when her medicine was finished and she asked her father to take her to Dr. Tanoh's office on his motorcycle, but he refused. "What if someone who knows me sees me there with you? And then he will say, oh, Adama's daughter has the disease." She didn't have the fifty cents for a moto-taxi, so a friend of one of her brothers offered to take her on the back of his motorcycle. When Dr. Tanoh came back from lunch, he found her sleeping on the stone bench in the waiting room. He wanted to give her a transfusion and offered to pay for it himself if she could bring someone to sit with her. He even gave her the money for a taxi to go home and come back. Her mother had gone to her garden plot at the edge of town, but her father was home, and she asked him if he would come back to the hospital with her. He refused. She never went back that day and she felt so discouraged she stopped taking her medicine; it didn't seem worth it. She decided she might as well be dead.

When she stopped taking the medication, the virus rushed in with even stronger force. Nawa had been very ill just before I arrived. Her head hurt, her bones ached, she was too weak to get out of bed, and she couldn't eat. When her mother told her father, he said, "A disease like that you can't cure, you die." Her mother had a little money and her farmer brother was visiting from Kalikaha so he took her on the back of his motorcycle to an American missionary clinic. They drew her blood, told her she had parasites, and gave her medicine. After four days, she was better. I asked if they talked to her about AIDS or proposed the test and she said no. She hadn't said anything to them about her status either. She thought since they drew her blood, they would know she had *sidabana*. I don't know why she didn't go to Dr. Tanoh. She may have felt ashamed that she had accepted money from him for the taxi but not returned for the transfusion.

Tom and I didn't like feeling angry at our old friend Adama. Tom urged me to talk to him about his treatment of Nawa, but I wasn't sure it would do any good. "I'm willing to talk to your father," I told Nawa, "but I am not sure he will listen." Nawa wasn't sure either. "Do you think he will listen to Masita?"

Nawa hesitated. "It's complicated."

"What about Dr. Tanoh? If I get your father to go with me to greet Dr. Tanoh, would he listen to him?"

"Ahhhh," said Nawa quietly. "Maybe if it's like that, maybe."

She told me that one day her father was sitting and chatting with an elderly friend of his. Her father said, "You know the disease they get in the whorehouses? There is a medicine now for that."

The old man retorted, "Medicine! There is no medicine for that! The medicine for that is death! They are all going to die."

"But now," Nawa said quietly, a little smile breaking out, "that old man is dead and I am still here!" She promised she would never go off the medicine again, no matter how difficult her life might be.

"Masita's voice is an important one the patients need to hear," Dr. Tanoh said the next time we talked. She didn't receive a salary, but the doctors tried to help her out, and he hoped that eventually there would be funding to hire her. Testing for HIV was now incorporated into all medical visits, he explained. "It's the first thing we ask. Have you been tested? We try to make it a normal part of every visit. And if they are positive, we try to show the person and their family they can continue to be part of society. I come over and touch them, I put my arm around them. They tend to put themselves at the edge of the world, they think they have to stay away from people, so I explain, no, you can live normally with your family, touch people, eat with them."

Earlier that day, a woman wept in his office. "Of course her husband refuses to be tested, so he doesn't know he is infected." The husbands were the most difficult, he said, especially those that weren't literate. Since they refused the test and didn't know they were infected, they were convinced their wives had cheated on them. Dr. Tanoh saw about twenty positive people each month, and 90 percent were hiding the results from their families. "We try to persuade them to tell one person who is close to them so they can have someone for support. But if they tell one person, that person will tell everyone, so it's difficult." When he arrived in Korhogo in 2007 from a medical center in downtown Abidjan, he was shocked because for every ten people he saw, nine were HIV positive. But after some time, he realized the rate in the overall population was not as high as he had initially thought; it was high among the population who were sick. The rate of infection was much higher among women, but the statistics were skewed because more women agreed to be tested. When a woman came in for prenatal care or to give birth, she was concerned about the health of the child she was carrying and readily agreed to the test. In the past, AIDS had been concentrated in urban areas, but now he was worried that the HIV rate might be even higher in the villages where people had less information. Women gathered to help each other give birth, and since farmers often have little cuts on their hands, they could be infected even by helping clean up.

Nawa and my translator Clarisse were sitting with us, and Clarisse spoke up. "At the maternity clinics, the family members usually clean the table after the birth," she said.

"Well, it's not right! They don't have gloves!" Dr. Tanoh burst out. "Midwives should not ask the family members to clean up! Nor should they give them bloody clothes to wash!" It was the only time I ever saw him angry.

I asked him why Nawa's face had become paralyzed on one side. "Most likely a toxic microbe," he said, reverting to his usual calm tone, "the kind of thing we all ingest from time to time, but because our immune systems are healthy, we fight them off." Because her immune system was compromised, the microbe multiplied. "I have seen similar cases and they responded well to antiretrovirals."

Dr. Tanoh was not from the North and his Julakan was not fluent, so I asked Nawa if there was anything else she wanted to ask him while Clarisse was there to translate. "Yes," she replied, "there is one thing. I want to explain why I never came back that day for the transfusion. It was because my mother wasn't home and my father wouldn't come. Even though I wasn't able to come back, I want to thank him for trying to help me." She added blessings for the success of his work and for Allah to repay him for his good deed.

Dr. Tanoh said he understood, and he urged us to bring Nawa's father to the office. "If he comes, I will find the right words to make him understand," he said quietly. "I will tell him that it's not just through sex that you can get AIDS." We agreed to meet at his office at nine the following morning with Nawa's father.

Tom and I decided to invite Adama to the hotel for dinner that night. Over a good dinner at a secluded table would be the best way to propose the visit to Dr. Tanoh, and Tom also had some translation issues he wanted to discuss. Unsure how to broach the conversation, I began to repeat what I had learned that afternoon from Dr. Tanoh. He had explained that people didn't understand all the ways AIDS could be transmitted. For example, because of the custom of the brother of the deceased taking in his brother's widow, the brother and his other wives were sometimes infected. Midwives contracted it because they were around lots of blood, and other women who helped with a birth could be exposed, too. Women who tressed hair were supposed to disinfect their picks and combs in bleach, but if they didn't or if they diluted the bleach, they could pass the virus from one client to another. To everything I said,

Adama replied, "Uh-huh, uh-huh," in agreement. "It's true people here are very ignorant about the disease," he said. "They think you can get it from eating and drinking with the person or touching them. And if you have it, they say you are a prostitute. They are so ignorant!"

I had been afraid of this—that he would say what we wanted to hear.

"Dr. Tanoh says nine out of ten patients have problems with their families," I continued as we ate peanuts I had bought from a street vendor. The open-air restaurant was infamously slow. Since it was inside the hotel walls and didn't have many customers, the guinea fowl, chicken, and carp were frozen and had to be defrosted before they could be grilled.

Adama responded again as if he agreed. "That is because people don't understand that as long as they don't do certain things, they won't be infected. They are fearful, so they want to keep the sick person away from them."

"You know, Dr. Tanoh said he would like to meet someone from Nawa's family," I said, trying to sound light. "I went to see him today, but of course he knows Nawa has more family than me! He suggested meeting tomorrow morning at the hospital."

Tom spoke up instantly. "I would like to go and greet Dr. Tanoh."

"Well, I will go, too," Adama said, falling right into our trap. "It is a good idea to go and greet Nawa's doctor, a good thing to do." He added formally, "If Monsieur Tom is willing to take time from his work, I should take time from mine, too."

We settled on nine the next morning. Adama would bring Nawa on the back of his motorcycle, and we would meet them at the hospital. For the third time, Tom walked over to the little outdoor kitchen to ask the women about our dinner. He was convinced that his prodding would make our meal appear more quickly. "What is important," I said to Adama, "is that Nawa keep taking her medicine and follow the treatment correctly. Because she stopped taking the medicine last year, she is having health problems."

"That's right," Adama said. "I am very unhappy with her for not taking the medicine. She should not have done that!" I shouldn't have said anything more, but Adama's self-righteous tone made me angry and I couldn't stop myself.

"Adama, she stopped taking the medicine because you insulted her and called her names. She was so humiliated and hurt she decided to stop taking the medicine."

"But I never said anything to her about her illness," Adama replied. "I never said anything."

"Then why did she stop taking the medicine?"

"I don't know, but if she said that, she's lying. That's a lie."

I had spent many hours with Nawa over the past five years and did not think she was making things up. Her decision to stop taking the pills was complicated, that I understood. It was difficult to keep taking them in secret while all around her, people in her situation, especially women, were being insulted. Her father's criticism was especially painful. And it was hard for her to understand that a chronic illness can be controlled but not cured. But when Tom came back to report that our guinea fowl had made it onto the grill, we changed the subject to a dilemma of Adama's. Now that the country was reunified with a functioning government, the streets of Korhogo, which had been nearly impossible to drive, were being graded and paved, and his neighborhood was being incorporated into the town. When the bulldozers had come through and created a wide new street, they sliced his rectangular earthen house in half. One room was rubble; the other room was more or less intact. He was sleeping in the roofed shelter outside where we sat to eat and talk; the girls and Nafini were sleeping in the one room that remained standing. In compensation he had been given an adjoining half lot, but his neighbor insisted it belonged to him. The neighbor had fought with the New Forces, and he refused to back down and even threatened Adama's family. Adama had the proper papers, but he had been forced to hire a lawyer and go to court. His lawyer assured him that he would eventually win the case, that the rule of law had returned, but when would it be settled and how much would it cost? The court case was eating up the money he needed to rebuild the house. These worries were weighing him down, it was clear.

When we arrived at the hospital the next morning, Adama and Nawa were already there. Once we were called in and seated around his desk, the doctor greeted us and then turned to me and asked why we had come. Since he wanted to meet Nawa's family, we had come, and Nawa's father had come, too, I replied.

Adama added that yes, even Monsieur Tom had agreed to take time away from his work to come and greet Dr. Tanoh, and he offered a long string of benedictions for the doctor's long life, health, and success.

"Yes," Dr. Tanoh responded, "we try to meet the patient's family because some of our patients are rejected by their families."

Adama replied carefully, "We know people are rejected because of the fear of infection, but now, thanks to Dr. Tanoh and his work, people are learning that you have to do certain things to get the disease."

"It's true people don't know how it's transmitted," Dr. Tanoh said. "They can touch the person, they can eat with them. They won't catch it." In his white coat and stethoscope, he got up and came over to Nawa, shook her hand and hugged her, putting his arm protectively around her. "You can be close to the sick person and you won't get sick. And the sick person needs to feel this, to feel supported. It's very discouraging to have this illness, and that is why it is so important to keep the person within the family, not to push the person away. People are afraid to get tested because they are afraid they will be rejected." He talked about women giving birth in villages, how other women came to help, not realizing the woman in labor was infected, and then, if they had some little cut or wound on their hands and they got the blood in that wound, they were infected, too. "We want the families to support the patients and encourage them so they won't get depressed. They have a hard time following the treatment, and if they are discouraged, it makes it even more difficult for them."

Tom spoke up. "Well, the head of the family is really the model, isn't he? If the head of the family treats the sick person well, the others will follow his example."

"Yes, that's *very* important," said Dr. Tanoh. He turned to Adama. "You're the papa, no?"

"Yes, yes," replied Adama. "I am the papa."

"That's why it's so important to meet you and talk."

"Yes, well, I help her often. When she needs a ride here to the hospital, I drop her off. Once she needed her medicine, but she was sick and couldn't come, so she asked me to come here to get it. So I came. But they said they could not give me her medicine; they could only give it directly to her."

"We want all of that to be reinforced," said Dr. Tanoh.

"Very good, very good," said Adama. "Thank you very much." He rose slightly from his chair. "I think that's all then." But the rest of us didn't take his cue. We stayed seated.

Tom said to Dr. Tanoh, "The family needs Nawa. She contributes to the household. We want her to be healthy, to have a happy healthy life."

"She has two children who need her," I added.

“Exactly!” replied Dr. Tanoh. “That is exactly what we want for each person who has this illness. To live positively! A healthy life, a long life. And when people feel supported, they follow the treatment well.”

We all thanked him, shook hands and left. We had not translated this meeting for Nawa, but I had the feeling she understood the gist of it. I was the last one out and I turned and said quietly, “We will follow closely and see what happens next.” He nodded and gave me an ironic little smile as I closed his office door.

Walking past city hall later that day, I noticed two white paper signs taped to the square concrete posts. Both were handwritten in blue marker in French. “National Consultation on the Reconciliation process in Ivory Coast.”

I peeked into the large hall. Behind a long table sat four young men. Two handwritten signs were taped to their table: “CDVR National Consultation.” “Come in, come in,” they urged. Their job, they told me, was to administer a questionnaire about what sort of process the Dialogue, Truth, and Reconciliation Commission (CDVR) should follow. They would spend two months consulting their fellow Ivorians.

The commission had existed for a year and a half at that point, so it seemed late to be asking what sort of process people wanted. I had seen the head of the commission many times on television, former prime minister Banny, a short man nearly as wide as he was tall. He traveled from town to town, shook the hands of the government officials and traditional chiefs, danced a few steps to the local music, admired the performances of schoolchildren, made a speech, and accepted an outfit of traditional clothing. It was obvious the ceremonies were designed to look appealing on television rather than to reconcile divisions in the communities where they were filmed. I had expected something more like the Truth and Reconciliation Commission in South Africa with public testimony from witnesses of terrible events like the murders of the women in Abobo and the revenge massacre in the western town of Duékoué. Without public testimony, these tragedies remained contested, political, owned by the North or the South, and denied by the other side. Many southerners who supported Gbagbo were convinced that the cell phone footage of the women in Abobo murdered by the security forces was a movie created to incriminate Gbagbo. The facts about Duékoué were also contested, but according to the UN investigation, about five hundred people had been murdered by groups allied with Ouattara’s Republican Forces troops. Gbagbo’s supporters usually doubled that number. It seemed to me that in order to move on, Ivorians needed to have one credible national account of what had happened in Abobo and Duékoue, in Bouaké and Yopougon and Daloa, and in many other places. Those who had committed crimes must be held responsible. With all that running through my mind, I was shocked that the commission was doing nothing more than asking Ivorians what it should do, and doing that half-heartedly. If I hadn't walked by, I would never have known the commission had come to Korhogo, the heart of the North.

The team leader assured me their arrival was being announced on television and radio, including the local stations.

"Really? I haven't heard anything."

"Actually," he admitted, "I made a special effort to listen myself and I haven't heard the announcements either. The advertising has not been as effective as it should have been."

I asked about languages, and they proudly listed off all the ones they spoke. "We will read out the questions to people in whatever language they speak, and they can respond in that language."

"But what about people who are not literate?"

"Our job is to help them understand and respond because the process is free, inclusive, and participatory."

In response to my request to see the questionnaire, he said he couldn't show it to me, but I was welcome to participate.

"But I'm not Ivorian."

"The process is free, *inclusive,* and participatory. Everyone can take part, whether they are Ivorian or not, if they have suffered some sort of loss from the crisis. You are very welcome to participate."

I started to say I hadn't suffered, but I wanted to see the questionnaire. Also, as someone who constantly went around asking other people questions and depending on their generosity to answer, I felt sympathetic. Their chairs were empty and here I was, a live prospect. Had I suffered any losses? There was Old Man, buried on one of the last days of the postelectoral crisis. There was also my relationship with the people of Kalikaha, which had been cut off for six years. But a relationship with a community is a difficult thing to describe. We had been awarded a generous minigrant from the American embassy to buy a shea butter mill and build a library in Kalikaha and had lost that funding because of the conflict. And our house had collapsed. Those losses were more tangible.

The young men held out their questionnaire hopefully and gestured to a chair. I sat down and pulled out my notebook and pen. "If I take the questionnaire, could I write down some of the questions? So I can remember them?" Unfortunately, they could not give me permission to do that. I gave in anyway. The first questions asked me about my losses since the year 2000. I wrote down that a young man in my family had died. There was a list of possible ways he had died. Assassinated? Hit by a mortar? I said to the young men, "But the answer is none of these. He died because he was very ill and he was trapped in Abobo and couldn't get to a hospital."

"Then you write that in here," the director of the team explained gently. "In the box."

The questionnaire asked what other losses I had suffered. I checked loss of property and described my house collapsing because I could not safely go to repair it. The next question asked me to rank the losses. Which was more serious? That was easy. Old Man. I riffled through the pages. There were forty pages to go, over seventy questions in all. No wonder I was the only person doing this. The seventy questions blur in my memory, but I remember one asked who I thought was responsible for the crisis. My simple answer was the political leaders.

"Which ones?" the team leader asked.

"You want the names?"

"Yes. We want specific answers."

"Okay," I said and filled the entire box. There was no shortage of culpable politicians.

Afterward, I remembered only one question:

How will you know if someone repents of their crimes?

(a) their sincerity
(b) they relate the facts
(c) they show regret and compassion toward the victim
(d) they ask pardon

When I finally finished, I asked what they thought about pardon, the Ivorian custom of asking for forgiveness or mercy. "That is the Ivorian way of doing things," the team leader said. "We take a certain joy in it, like the pleasure we take in joking with others." He traced the concept back to the first president, Houphouët-Boigny, who stressed getting along.

I asked him about the *jatigi* network that criss-crossed the country, and he agreed it had limited the extent of the damage. *Jatigiya*, joking relations between ethnic groups, and *brassage* were important factors in unifying people and preventing worse things from happening, he felt. The team leader said he knew men from the South who lived in Korhogo and had Senufo wives. "I know some that stayed here the whole time and had no problems." That was *brassage*.

I agreed. All these, along with the way Ivorians thought of themselves as a people of dialogue, had kept Ivory Coast from going over the brink. But it seemed to me that the Ivorian custom of asking and granting pardon was a tradition intended for ordinary, daily offenses. As Nawa had said, it was hard to forgive offenses as serious as rape and murder. I feared that the country was pushing the years of trauma and division under the palm fiber mat. Could you have reconciliation without a dialogue that established and acknowledged the truth? Or was that just my American perspective? I wasn't sure.

In the afternoon, Nawa called to say she had just heard from Masita that her blood test result was in. I told her I would pick it up and explained to Adama we needed to stop by the clinic. When we arrived, Masita was standing outside the office holding the stack of papers. I greeted her and introduced Nawa's father.

"You are a Koné like me, but you must be a false Koné because you act more like a Traoré."

Adama didn't know what to say. Konés and Traorés have a joking relationship and trade pretend insults, and he was always ready to jump in and take part, but Masita's tone was sharp. Besides, she was a Koné like him.

"Why did you hang up on me when I called and told you Nawa needed someone to come to the hospital and stay with her while she had a transfusion?"

"I didn't hang up on you. The line was cut off."

"You must be half Traoré because the Konés are straight and if it's black they say it's black. If it's red they call it red."

Adama looked at her nervously.

"What would be good for Nawa," she told him, "would be to find a man to live with."

"Well, not just any man!" I interjected.

"True. A man who will support her, encourage her to follow her treatment and take care of her." She envisioned Nawa living happily with a man who was also HIV positive and on antiretrovirals. "They could even have children together," she explained to Adama, "and the children would be disease-free as long as Nawa followed the directions. I have been HIV positive for eighteen years."

He nodded, desperately trying to hide how aghast he was that she would admit to having AIDS. Masita paged through her stack of papers until she found Nawa's bloodwork. Her numbers were so low the doctor wanted to switch her to a different antiretroviral, Masita explained. Nawa's antibodies were at forty-eight. Forty-eight! That meant her immune system was not functioning. She was completely vulnerable. And here she was walking streets with open sewers and drinking well water. "Follow me to my house and I will get the new medicine for you," Masita told Adama.

At her house, she launched into her explanation of how she contracted AIDS by helping a sick woman at the maternity clinic. Adama listened with mingled fascination and fear in his eyes, and with grudging admiration for someone who told a story well. "So you see," she told him, "I did someone a service, I helped someone, and from that I was infected. We don't fear AIDS anymore. We fear diabetes, cancer, Guinea worm. But AIDS—we can live with that. God made this disease and he has made the remedy."

"But when will you stop taking the medicine?" he asked her.

"Never. I will take the medicine all my life."

Adama's mouth dropped open.

"It's like diabetes. You cannot be cured of it, but you can live with it."

"Hunnnnnnhhhhhh!" he exclaimed, staring in amazement. "So you are going to take this medicine until . . . until the end?"

"Yes. The medicine is like our gasoline. Without it, we can't go. If you don't put gas in your motorcycle, can you make it to Boundiali?"

"No." Adama chuckled in spite of himself.

"You have to understand that it's not just by chasing after sex that you can get this disease," she told him with a sharp edge in her voice. "You yourself could go to the haircutter one day and if the blade is not cleaned properly and if the man before you has AIDS and gets cut, and then you get cut, you could get AIDS. Because it is in the blood."

He drew his hand across the close-shaven gray stubble on his head.

"Look at these children," she said to him. "They have AIDS. Were they tramps, chasing after boys?"

"No."

She called over the oldest girl and told him how her neck used to be covered with sores. The scars were still visible, raised welts of skin like red ropes, but except for the scars she looked perfectly healthy. Masita pulled out the girl's test results. In the antibody column she had more than one thousand, nearly the same number as a person who had never had AIDS. "Of course it's easier for children to regain their health than it is for us," she explained. "Their bodies are young, and they regenerate new cells quickly.

"People are afraid to have the test because if it's positive, they're afraid of being rejected by their families. They are afraid of dying. But the opposite is true! The ones who are tested get the medicine and live. Those who wait and wait, eventually they die." Masita told him she had tried and tried to get her husband to get tested. "It went in one ear and out the other! This was a man who if I asked him for money for medicine or food, he said he didn't have any. Then, if I washed his clothes and found some money in his pocket, he said it wasn't his, that it belonged to someone else!" She told him how, when she was very sick and a young relative came to take care of her, her husband slept with this young girl and infected her with AIDS.

Adama looked horrified.

"She is on medication and she is fine," Masita reassured him. "But my husband refused to take the test and he died. In one ear and out the other!"

Lasungo

Ballpoint Pen Divination

When I went to visit Lasungo, his little house near the stream had been knocked down for the road construction and he had vanished. After many inquiries, Adama and I finally found him in a rented room next to an outdoor bar and restaurant. The workmen building new streets had cut down the trees around his little house, he told us, and he had been forced to move quickly and to abandon some of his shrines. The new place was too public, too close to the market and the bar, so his clients stayed away and business was bad.

He had agreed to divine for me and explain the process, and before we began, I placed two hundred-franc coins on the floor, less than fifty cents. This was his fee. "What do you want to know?" he asked. I said I was concerned about the book I was writing and wanted to know what I should do to ensure the work went well. He concentrated, placed his spit on the point of a Bic ballpoint pen, and very slowly made little marks on a sheet of lined notebook paper. He joined the marks together in a funnel pattern, then stared at them for a long time. Finally he tossed the cowries and miscellaneous objects onto the antelope skin between his legs and studied them.

"Water spirits are following you," he said softly. "They are not water spirits from here; they are from where you come from." The water spirits protected me and Tom, and that was why we had good luck. He didn't see any serious problems ahead, but if we wanted things to go really well, if we wanted to make sure to have happiness and lots of money, we should offer four white kola nuts and a few coins to the twin mothers. Senufo mothers of twins have special powers because in Senufo culture the first two people were fraternal twins, a boy and a girl from whom all people are descended. At markets, twin mothers lay out tiny double baskets for offerings. We should also sacrifice two white roosters and two ewes, white for me and copper colored for Tom. Now that he had my destiny sorted out, Lasungo grew philosophical. "When you are young and the spirits choose you and start following you, you're not yourself, you do strange things. It's an apprenticeship. But as you grow older, you learn to live with the spirits, and they calm down, too."

I asked why he had changed to divining with a ballpoint pen.

Working with the cowries often made him sick, he said. The pen method was easier on him.

Since I was leaving for Abidjan the next morning, sacrificing two sheep was too much to arrange or even consider, I told him. I would think about doing the sacrifices later, perhaps the next time I came.

"It would be better to do them now," Lasungo said in his soft persuasive voice.

"How about if I give you the money for the two white roosters? Could you take care of the sacrifice for me?" Lasungo said he could. The sheep were a big expense, and I told him I had to think it over. He said he understood and hoped I would decide to do it.

That was our last night in Korhogo, and Adama and Nafini had invited us for a farewell dinner. When I asked her, Nawa said she would be glad to buy the four white kola nuts for me and give them and the change to a mother of twins at the market. "It's no trouble for me," she said, slipping the coins I gave her into the money pouch around her waist, "and it's a good thing for you to do."

The family gave us half the road, and as they walked us to the car, I pulled Nawa aside behind a granary. "Are you going to keep taking your medicine?" I asked her. "Every day?"

"Yes. I am going to take it."

Nawa

I Am Still Here Living My Life

Six months later, I was back in Korhogo, it was early morning, and Nawa and I were once again waiting on the bench outside the clinic so she could pick up her medication. "Dr. Tanoh works here now," she told me happily, "so we will greet him."

"Hey! What are you doing on that moped with my husband?" A familiar sharp voice sliced through the early morning air; it was Masita teasing the lab technician Camara, who drove off laughing with his wife and baby behind him. She waved a spiral notebook with its cover falling off. "Let me see your prescriptions! Give them to me or you won't be able to get your medicine!" As she gathered up the worn pieces of paper, she said to me, "Nawa doesn't answer when I call, she doesn't come to the meetings, and I never see her." She explained how I could find her at a new organization where her support groups were meeting. Her phone rang and she yelled into it, "Well, where are you?" To the bench, she said in an exasperated tone, "I told him to come *here*!" She disappeared into Camara's tiny office, her plastic bag over her arm, muttering about a man who had disappeared. I had seen only one man arrive that morning, and he left again quickly, so I assumed he was dropping someone off. The other patients were all women.

When Dr. Tanoh arrived, Nawa and I squeezed into his small office. The air-conditioning wasn't working, and the files of patient information had disappeared from the computer and would have to be reentered, he said with a sigh. But about the larger picture he felt hopeful. The rate of infection was slowing. In the high schools, there were very few positives, and at the hospital and the clinics, fewer positives were showing up. He also thought the taboo was diminishing. More young people learned in school about HIV, and more families had been touched by the disease; he thought this was decreasing the stigma. With antiretrovirals, HIV-positive people were living much longer, and that was a very good thing, but it created a large population who needed to be monitored and who needed health care and support services. That was the challenge now.

He wanted Nawa to get her blood drawn and for us to come back in two days, so we could go over the results. Outside, Masita was rounding everyone up to collect their medicine at the hospital. "But where is that Seydou? He was here earlier, he gave me his prescription, and now where is he? And how am I supposed to contact him? He didn't give me his number! What is he thinking?" She set off for the hospital, her flock trailing behind. Instead of going to the crowded main entrance, she led us to a shortcut, passing easily between two concrete pillars. One after another, the women, all larger, squeezed through after her, laughing and joking about their big hips. "I just don't know what happened to that Seydou," fretted Masita as we waited in an empty room for someone to bring the pills. "He was there, and then he just disappeared without saying a word."

"It's because of me," one of the women said quietly. "He is my neighbor and he was always insulting me, saying, 'You have AIDS, you have AIDS.' When he saw me, he snuck off! He didn't want to admit he had it, too."

That afternoon, Nawa and I took a taxi to visit her friend Assiata. In the past two years, most of Korhogo's streets had been graded or even paved by Ouattara's government, but the work hadn't reached Assiata's neighborhood. Our little red taxi crawled slowly through eroded crevasses and over rocks, tipping us against one door and then the other until we came to a chasm too deep to drive through and too wide to pass around. We paid, climbed out, and walked the rest of the way.

Assiata greeted us warmly, spread a mat in the shade, and set out two metal teapots, her small charcoal burner, and the green tea, mint, and sugar. Her daughter Khadi skipped over to us and proudly showed off some little clay pinch pots she had made. "My own mother was a potter and I helped her as a girl," Assiata told me with a smile.

"Khadi! Khadi!" the younger children called, and she ran off. Assiata explained that Khadi had gone to the Franco-Arabe school last year, and the school wanted her to return this year because she was first in her class, but her father said they couldn't afford the fees, just under $3 a month. "Khadi loved school," Assiata said.

I asked about public school.

"Her father went to a Muslim school, so he wants her to go there, too," Assiata responded.

Khadi skipped over to smile at me, the way Nawa used to do when she was little. "How are you, my *terimuso*?" I greeted her teasingly, as if she were my grownup woman friend.

The next morning, Nawa and I met early at the clinic to get her blood drawn. Camara and Masita kept a register and wrote down each person's name, gender, neighborhood, cell phone number, and mother's name. Each patient, and there were about eight hundred, also had a coded number, which was entered in red ballpoint. Camara gnashed his teeth at the Senufo names. The Senufo sounds, especially the *gn*, the *ng*, and the *gb*, weren't easy. I struggled with them, too. When he misspelled a name, he uncapped the whiteout and blamed it on Masita.

"It's normal," she said with a smile, "because I am his first wife, you know."

"You're not my wife! You're my aunt."

"No, no. I'm your wife. Your first wife." This kind of teasing, with its pretend relationships and joke insults, is common practice between certain families, and Camara and Masita bantered constantly. They made an odd couple. He was a handsome broad-shouldered man, articulate and neatly dressed, married, with a good job as a lab technician. Masita's thin face was lined and everything she wore was worn. As a little girl, Masita didn't speak, and her parents worried she was mute. When she was about five, her father, an herbalist, gave her herbal medicine; she began to talk and hadn't stopped since. Her tone was sharp and sometimes shrill, but just as often she bantered, gave out blessings, teased, cajoled, and chuckled with pleasure. Each time I came, I brought something small, like a package of ballpoint pens, to help with her work, and she always said, "Ohhh, you are spoiling us!" and insisted Camara thank me properly.

Masita had just wished us a long, elaborate good-bye, complete with blessings, and was going out the door when a plump, stylishly dressed woman in her thirties came in. "Come back and write one more! Do it for me. You're my aunt!" cajoled Camara.

"No, I'm your wife! That is why I won't do it! Do a husband and wife ever get along?"

"You are hopelessly unintelligent!"

"You! You are crazy, completely out of your mind!" They glared at each other affectionately, and she sat back down and entered the new patient's information in the big register.

"The real problem here is ignorance and lack of education," Camara said, picking up our ongoing conversation once the office was empty again. "Nothing will change here until people are educated." He thought that traditional herbal medicines contained useful botanical compounds, but there was no way to control the dosage. He knew people who had even suffered liver damage from herbal medicines. "And they don't work for HIV. On some other things, yes." I mentioned the traditional healers who claimed they could cure AIDS. "Oh, yes! I see them on television! They sing, they dance, but I have never seen anyone cured."

But why did people keep going to them? I asked.

"They have faith in them. Me, for example. Nawa trusts me. If I say to her, go to this person, they can cure you, she is going to believe me. Also, it's because people with HIV are neglected at home, neglected by society, so they want to be cured by any means. They are ready to try anything, ready to listen to anyone."

I wondered aloud if the belief in herbal medicines was the consequence of a culture that teaches young people to listen to their elders rather than to be skeptical. But Camara rejected this idea. "The problem of Africa is the problem of illiteracy. Someone who isn't educated is a danger to himself and to the society." He went on, "Often I explain things about AIDS. The person listens—he knows I have been trained in this area. But afterward, the person goes into town, and he hears people say other things and maybe he likes those things better. So he is going to believe that." We parted, agreeing, as always, to continue the conversation.

When we were alone that afternoon, Nawa confided that there was a reason she didn't like to go to Masita's meetings. She came home one day to find her mother chatting with Masita and an old Senufo man in a boubou. Nawa thought he was Masita's husband and was pleased they had come to call on her. When they asked for the road, she politely got up to lead the way. Once they were away from Nawa's mother, Masita said, "Since you don't have a husband, I said I would find you one, and this elder is looking for a wife and so I brought him here to meet you, so you two could marry." Nawa was taken aback but politely replied she would have to talk to her father.

"This woman came to present this old man to me so I could marry him," she explained to her mother when she returned to the house.

"But he's old! Very old! Just because you are sick doesn't mean you should marry someone the age of your grandfather!"

The next time the pair visited, Masita suggested Nawa go to the old man's house so they could get to know each other. Nawa felt uneasy and declined, saying she wasn't well enough. "You can meet at my house then," offered Masita. But that idea also made Nawa nervous. She didn't want to offend Masita, so she said she was still sick from time to time and couldn't go such a long way. "I can see you aren't pleased," the old man said. "We will leave it at that."

"This morning at the clinic," Nawa said to me, "did you hear what Masita said to that woman about marriage? She said it to another woman, but I think she was really speaking to me. She said, 'Everyone wants to marry someone

Nawa and her mother, Nafini, 2011

in good health but if you wait for that, you will never remarry!'" Nawa's voice turned quiet. "I just want to focus on getting healthy again." Fortunately, Nawa's health was gradually improving. Her beautiful smile was less crooked and her eye closed now so she didn't feel the wind hitting it all the time. And when we went back to the clinic to get her results, her antibody number had tripled. If her levels kept going up at this rate, she would soon have a functioning immune system.

"I am always impressed by how you manage, Nawa," I said to her. "You always manage to earn a little money and take care of your children and keep Yardjuma in school."

With the money I gave her the year before, she explained proudly, she had bought school supplies and two school uniforms for Yardjuma, soap for her mother, and saved the rest for her little expenses. When she felt well enough, she bought and sold vegetables and made a little money.

"It would be good to go to some of Masita's meetings," I said. "Then you would learn how to follow the treatment really well."

"I try to be careful. When I finish with a razor blade, I throw it down the latrine. I don't want the children to get sick. If I cut myself, I wipe it off with a rag and throw the rag down the latrine. I haven't told the others about my illness, but I don't want to infect them so I try to be very careful."

"But you need to be careful, too, of your health. When the children are sick or coughing, you should keep your distance from them and wash your hands. At the meetings, you would learn how to take care of yourself."

"Don't worry. I will never stop taking the pills again."

"Is it hard to take the pills?"

"No! Swallowing a pill twice a day is a lot easier than traditional medicine—heating that water in the ceramic jar and it smells bad! It's a lot easier just to take a pill!"

Nawa carved a mark on the window every year she was sick; there were seven. She did this, she said, because if she got well and someone asked her to tell the story, she would know how long her illness lasted.

"Have you talked to your friend Assiata about your illness?" I asked.

"You think I should tell her," Nawa said slowly.

"I just asked if you *had* told her."

"I really want to tell her . . . she is so kind and we are very close, but I know her well and she talks easily to everyone right and left. She wouldn't mean to hurt me. Truly Assiata is a good person, it's just that she likes to talk." When another woman they knew went to the hospital, Assiata told Nawa, "They say she has the sickness." "She would do the same thing to me," Nawa said. "So even though I would really like to tell her, I cannot. Dr. Tanoh said, 'Don't tell anyone, just take the medicine and get better.' But I wanted my father to know because he is my father."

I asked her for the third time if she wanted to choose a name for me to use in this book instead of her real name. She smiled and shook her head slowly. "I want you to use my real name. Nawa Koné. I want to be in the book so people will understand about this sickness, so they will know that even though I have it, I am not dead, I am still here living my life. I am still alive!"

Lasungo

Two Kinds of Spirits

Lasungo moved again, to a different neighborhood of Korhogo, but didn't tell his friends. A few days later, when he lay down on his mat and was too ill to get up, his landlady knew only that her new tenant was from Kalikaha. She asked around until she found an acquaintance who knew someone from Kalikaha and then sent a message that Lasungo was seriously ill. The message reached the *jatigi* of Lasungo's niece, a nursing student in Korhogo. His niece went to see him right away and called her mother in Kalikaha, Lasungo's younger same-mother-but-not-same-father sister, to say it was too late to take him to the hospital. His sister wanted to bring him to Kalikaha where she could care for him, but before they could arrange it, her daughter called back to say he had died.

To send Lasungo's body to Kalikaha in a hearse would have cost $140, but they found a taxi driver willing to make the trip for $50. The niece and her uncle sat in the back seat, propped Lasungo up between them, and covered him with fabric. "If an old person saw, they know what's what, and they know a living person doesn't ride in a taxi like that," commented Adama dryly. Lasungo was buried the following evening in Kalikaha.

His landlady wanted his things cleared out so she could rent the house, but she didn't want to touch his carved statuettes and divination and power objects. Who knew what consequences might ensue from moving them? Lasungo's sister hired a taxi driver to bring everything to her in Kalikaha, but when the driver saw the power objects, he backed out. She had to hire another driver and pay him extra.

A Senufo funeral is a three-day event that requires advance planning, so although he died and was buried in December, his funeral was set for the following April, just before the rains began and the farmers returned to their fields. I asked Adama to go on our behalf and deliver our contribution to Lasungo's younger half sister. She ran a little open-air bar behind her house, but instead of home-brewed corn beer simmered in a kettle like her mother, Zele, sold, her beer was delivered by truck in bottles. Her bar was profitable and she spared no expense for the funeral—balafon groups came from all the neighboring villages, and Lasungo's friends, now middle-aged, danced all night. They remembered him as he used to be—champion of the hoeing contests, leader of their initiation cohort, the balafon player whose music kept everyone dancing until dawn. Kalikaha's wooden champion farmer staff was on display; it was a distinction he had earned. His sister killed a steer, as did her husband, and Lasungo's nephew also gave a small steer. All three were roasted and the guests ate well. It was, Adama assured me over the phone, a well-organized funeral and everyone really danced!

The next time I went to Kalikaha I visited his sister. She left the bar to sit with me in the shade outside her house and thanked me for the contribution. I told her I had heard it was a very good funeral. "Yes, so many people came to his burial that people thought it was the funeral. But then, when we had the real funeral, it went well. Despite the sadness and the death, everyone was happy with the way it went."

"He was lucky to have a sister like you."

"Voila!" she said, with a pleased laugh, reaching out to shake my hand. "It's true that I arranged everything!" She had wanted to take care of him, she added, and had urged him to move back to Kalikaha or visit more often, but he became solitary and suspicious and refused her help. Her clients at the thatched roof bar were calling for refills, and so she said good-bye before things got out of hand. She settled them down, collected their coins, and took their orders like her mother, Zele, used to do.

Lasungo believed his path had been predetermined by his mother's promise to the spirits and that his brother's breakdown was caused by supernatural curses. Coming from a different culture, I believed that mental illness ran in his family. A woman named Mariam who lived near Lasungo and ran the only bar in Kalikaha when I first lived there said, "Drink—that was always Lasungo's problem. All his problems went back to drinking." Perhaps it was a combination—invisible genes and two kinds of spirits, supernatural and distilled.

Nawa

What He Is Saying Is True

"It's hot, hot, hot," Masita muttered as she walked into the afternoon group meeting. A flock of women and one man trickled in after her and settled on the floor. Reaching into her wrapped skirt, she pulled out two new cell phones, gifts from her son. The last time she was sick, while she was having a blood transfusion, someone stole her phone, she said grimly. Making her way around the room, she greeted people, collecting the phone numbers of new members and entering them into both phones at lightning speed. "I don't have a cell phone," one woman told her, "but my husband has two."

I would have preferred to sit at the back, but Masita placed me at the head table and I knew better than to argue. A young woman dressed in fashionable jeans turned her back to the group and, addressing those of us at the head table in French, opened the meeting.

"You should translate that into Julakan!" a woman called out.

But the young woman continued in French. "Who should speak first?" she asked.

"Masita!" the women called out. Masita's first order of business was the incentive provided by the NGO. That day they were offering cooking oil. "Don't rush off!" she called out. "At the meetings we have gifts and those that stay will get them. Those that rush off, too bad for them! Since there are new faces, we should start by talking about how to take the medicine, and I hope the regulars will be patient. Who wants to start?"

No one spoke. A woman was crying softly, her hands over her face. She had just had the test and learned she was positive, she admitted. The women around her told her not to worry, that if she took the medicine, she would gain weight and feel stronger. "My uncle's wife won't come near me now," she said tearfully in Julakan. "When I sit down, she chases me away. That is what is making me cry."

"How does she know you have our disease?" a woman asked.

"Her son went with me to the hospital, and he saw the result and told his mother. My husband was sick and we treated him and treated him with traditional medicines, but he didn't get any better. People kept saying sorcerers made him sick, and we tried all sorts of treatments for the sorcery, but he just got sicker and sicker until he died. Now I know it was this disease he had."

When no one spoke, Masita said, "There are new people here today, so the older ones should speak. Everyone should speak. Who is going to explain what the disease has given them to deal with? Here we talk openly. You don't need to feel ashamed. And the white woman—we have known her for a long time, you can say whatever you want in front of her."

A woman stood up. "When you take the medicine, it's very good. I want to tell the new people that you should take the medicine without feeling ashamed. I took the pills and then at a certain moment, I neglected the medicine. And then I suffered! If you don't take them, the disease will come back and you will collapse again."

Masita thanked her and added, "Everyone says their booty has disappeared, but when you take the medicine your butt will come back! And then people will say, 'Oh, I thought she had the disease but I guess I was wrong!'"

A woman spoke in Senufo. "Before I took the medicine, I was very sick. But now that I take the medicine, I am doing fine. Your friend is going to say to you, 'Every day you take that pill? It's so big! That's so tiring. I heard about a traditional medicine you can take and it will cure you. I will go and buy it for you.' But I say to this person, I prefer what the doctor gave me because if I have a small sickness, if I can walk, I go to the hospital and they give me the prescription. You don't need to say, Oh, I am already taking a medicine, I can't take another. No, you go to the hospital, that is what I do, and tell them the problem and they give me a prescription and I buy it at the pharmacy and that works very well. Myself, I sold medicines in the street, but now I have seen that at the hospital before they give you medicine, they take your blood pressure, your weight, your temperature, *before* they prescribe a medicine. But when a woman comes around selling medicine, she doesn't take your temperature or your blood pressure, she just sells you a medicine and that could cause problems; she is not a doctor. So I have seen that the medicines in the street are not good. I don't sell them anymore and I never buy them. And because of that now I can walk from one end of Korhogo to the other without any problems and at night I lie down in my house and sleep well." Masita translated her remarks into Julakan.

An old woman in a white veil entered; she had come from the mosque. "Make sure we have your number," Masita called out to her. "The meeting has already started, and we are talking about how we take the medicine."

"I was so tired!" the old woman responded. "I thank Allah for the medicine."

"We are not sick," said Masita. "The sick are lying in the hospital. We are not lying in the hospital! But we have a microbe in our blood. If an animal dies, you see the maggots in their body, and we have something like that in our blood. These worms eat the animal's body until there is nothing left but bones. And it's the same for us. If you take the medicines, you will be fine. But if you don't take the medicine, the worms will eat your body, too. Often we give the medicine to a woman and she takes it for a few days, but then she says, 'Oh, I am tired of taking this medicine,' and she puts it aside. She doesn't even use the medicine we give her. Our medicine that we take doesn't kill the microbes, but it keeps them sleeping. If you take your medicine at eight in the morning, the microbe is still sleeping. He sleeps all day. Then, if you take your medicine at eight that night, he is still sleeping. But if you wait until nine, ten, eleven at night, the microbe wakes up, he sits up, at ten he starts to work. So take the medicine at the right time and the microbe will keep sleeping. If someone tells you the medicine kills the microbe, it's *not* true! But it will keep it sleeping. If you wait until nine p.m., he wakes up, at ten he sits up, at eleven he starts to work eating the body. He starts to make a baby, he makes thousands of them. It's like soldiers in a war. The microbes in your body that fight disease, you want them to be fighting for you. If you take your medicine, they can fight. If you stop taking the medicine, you know what happens. You become feeble. So don't ignore the hours! Some women say, 'Oh, I know a traditional medicine,' but there isn't a medicine that works except the one at the hospital. I see a woman here, she doesn't want to speak, but I remember when she had no butt at all and was shitting all over herself. I know because I washed her clothes. And now her butt has grown back and hers is bigger than mine! And she used to say, 'Oh medicine, it's sooo big. When I take it, I feel like I am going to vomit. Oh, medicine, whine, whine!' And now she is here and she is better, but she doesn't want to speak up. She should talk.

"Pardon me, but it's not because you are a slut that you have the disease, it's not those who run after men that have it! And those of you who have children, send the children to have the test. Send them all; the test is free. If the child has it, their body is stronger than an adult's. They take the medicine and they are healed and they can even stop taking the medicine. There are a lot of children at my house, they were so weak and sick, but now they have gained weight and their parents don't even recognize them when they come to the house. Remember—our disease is a secret. The health workers won't tell someone that you have the disease. Someone might say Masita said so-and-so has our disease, but it's not true. I don't say to anyone, and when they give the test, they are not going to tell that you were tested or that you take the medicine. Does anyone have anything to add?"

But Masita's long speech had lost them and the women were chatting and joking among themselves. At the head table, a group of literate young women were sorting the plastic bottles of antiretrovirals. Masita raised her hand. "Information!" she yelled. "Patients of Dr. Tanoh?" Two women raised their hands. "He is now at the clinic. If you want to stay at the hospital you can, but if you want to stay with Dr. Tanoh, you need to come to the clinic and register."

They brought out the cooking oil the organization provided and doled it out first to those who didn't get any at the last meeting. One woman collected coins and went out to buy plastic bags for those who hadn't brought containers. While the oil was being distributed, the young woman next to me, who had been writing names in the register and sorting the plastic medicine bottles, told me her story. She had been on antiretrovirals for six years. She was pregnant for the first time when her husband became very ill and she noticed his hair changed texture. His uncle had died of AIDS and his hair changed texture in just the same way, so she asked her husband if he had AIDS. He said no.

After her husband died, his brother told her to get tested or she would die, too. When she told the family she was going to get tested, her husband's sisters said, "Yes, that is exactly what he had!" They hadn't said anything to her before that. Her husband ran off with another woman, then returned to her. "He was a whore fucker!" she said angrily. "He suffered before he died. But I suffered, too." She lost the baby. Now she lived with a cousin. The non-profit paid her a small salary for taking notes and keeping records at the meetings, but the two young women struggled to come up with enough money for food. Before she contracted AIDS, she worked as a cook and was well paid, but her illness made it hard for her to hold down a job—she was susceptible to malaria and sometimes suffered bouts of diarrhea. Nor would she lie if prospective employers asked about her status.

Masita invited me to attend another support meeting a few days later, where I once again saw the young woman. That meeting was led by a Red Cross counselor, a young man, and was more like a class, with less teasing and haranguing from Masita. When I arrived, the meeting had already started and the counselor was stressing that when you were sick, it was important to go to the doctor and get a paper prescription, to get the prescription filled at a pharmacy, and then to take the medication the way the pharmacist said.

"But if you go to the doctor," a woman said, "and he gives you the prescription and you go to the pharmacy, maybe they are going to say that it costs twenty dollars and you don't have the money. You don't want to lie down in the house and think you are going to die. Maybe you have a quarter or a dollar at the house, so you go and buy medicine made from plants, then you feel at least you have a chance to be healed. That's why people buy herbal medicine."

"We all agree," said the counselor, "that there is no point in seeking out ceramic pots from the healers. And those medicines could make you vomit or give you diarrhea. And actually right now, lots of things are free at the hospital, but the healer will take money for his treatment. And if the doctor says to take two and you take one, it won't do the work. You have to take the medicine the way the doctor says . . . so if you are at the house and you get sick, what can you do?"

A woman in front spoke up. "If your body is hot, you can put cool water on your skin and that will help." The counselor agreed. It wasn't a cure, but it would help. You could also take aspirin, and you could boil guava leaves to make a medicine for diarrhea.

"You should just go to the doctor!" said another woman. "You shouldn't take chances with this sickness. Even if it's very late, you should go to the nurse nearest you."

"We have to be careful of places where people pretend to be doctors and nurses," a woman pointed out.

"But if you go out late," asked a woman, "what if you run into the bandits?"

"The bandits won't bother you because you are sick," replied another.

"Hey!" interjected Masita sharply. "The bandits won't care if you are sick or even dying! You had better pray to God not to run into them. They have no pity!"

The discussion moved on to what to do if you missed the time to take your medicine by a few hours or missed a dose and he asked a series of questions. "What if you forget in the morning and you forget at noon too? Should you take both?"

"If you forget," replied another woman, "you shouldn't take it. You leave it and take the next one."

"*No!*" injected another woman. "You should make sure you don't forget! If you want to get better, you have to take it at the hour that the doctor said!"

"Since I am really sick, and the doctor says take one in the morning and one in the evening, if I take two in the morning and two in the evening, won't I get better quicker?" asked another woman.

"No," said one of the men. "If you are really hungry and you take the whole fifty-kilo sack of rice and put it in the pot and cook it, can you eat the whole thing? No! And it's the same with the medicine. Do you think that after you swallow all that medicine and it's too much, they can wash out your intestines and get it out?"

When I was invited to ask a question, I asked the group what was most difficult about living with this disease. There were only two men at the meeting, and one responded immediately. "If you are the head of the family, you don't have the strength to work the way you used to and you have a wife and children, and you look at them, and you feel discouraged because you can't take care of them."

The other man continued, "And then you always have these little sicknesses and you are weak, you can't work, and you always fear you will be sick again."

A middle-aged woman spoke next. "When your husband had the disease and now you're a widow, you don't have the strength to take care of your children. But there you are, alone."

The first man added, "And if you are married and your wife dies, then you are left alone and you won't be able to find another wife. It's difficult."

Another woman said, "If you lose your husband and you have children, how can you feed them? It's true they give you the medicine free, but no one gives you food for your children. And if you are sick, you have a prescription and you need money to get the medicine."

"Then there are expenses for the students," added the first man. "You can't work, and when school starts and you don't have the money, you will have to pull your children out."

A few days later, I put my headphones on Nawa so she could lie on my hotel bed in air-conditioned comfort and listen to the recordings. When the man said there was no point in going to the healer, Nawa took off the headphones. "What he is saying is true. I wasted years at the healer, and if I had just had the blood test and started the medicine, maybe I wouldn't have had so many problems and my health would be better now. I wish I had known." When she had heard every word of three long meetings, she asked me to start the recording over and she listened to all of it again, smiling and nodding in agreement with the voices in her ears.

But one month later, on a Sunday, back at home, I received an all-caps text message from Adama. "BJ" is short for *bonjour*: "Carol, BJ. I wanted to tell you Nawa's illness is serious. She can't walk alone. Don't know what to do. Tell Tom help with money. Adama. Merci."

I knew her younger brother Djak was in Korhogo, so I called him right away. Nawa kept getting worse, he told me, and his mother had consulted a healer, but it hadn't helped. I had given Djak a bank card to withdraw his tuition and spending money each month. I told him to take money out of the automated teller for the taxi and the medicine and to take her first thing the next morning to Dr. Tanoh. I explained how to find his office.

When they got there, Dr. Tanoh took one look at Nawa and sent her straight to the hospital. They were eventually able to give her a transfusion, although it took a long time to find blood. "They really did try to help her," Djak assured me, although he wasn't sure what the other treatments were. After several days at the hospital, the family took her home. But she got worse and couldn't eat or drink. On Thursday I got a text from Djak: "Nawa's health is becoming worse and worse. She has lost consciousness and the money wasn't enough. It's why I made a second withdrawal. Pardon us for not saying before making the withdrawal."

When I called, he said she couldn't eat or drink. A friend of hers had sent a "doctor" to the house and he had put a tube down her nose and fed her porridge through it. She couldn't swallow. She had kept taking her antiretrovirals until three days before this, when she said they were too big to swallow. I asked if they could grind them up in the mortar and pestle and put them in the porridge. But really all I could do was send my benedictions for her to get well and my love to his mother, who had been crying. Djak held the phone to Nawa's ear. He thought she heard my voice because her eyes flickered.

The next day, Friday, when I called, Djak sounded worried, but he said Nawa was a little bit better. They had pounded up her medicine and put it in the porridge. Djak had no idea what she had or why she could not swallow.

Sunday morning rain suddenly came pattering down hard, and I ran upstairs to close the open windows. I heard my phone ringing downstairs, but I didn't go down to answer it. I was afraid of what I might learn. When I did go, I found a text message from Djak. Nawa had died. I crawled back into bed. By the time I reached them, she was buried and they were leaving for Kalikaha to say the prayers.

Assiata and Masita Once More

A year passed before I returned to Korhogo. Everything reminded me of Nawa. Her mother and I looked at each other sadly and didn't know what to say. Sita, Nawa's young cousin, cooked the stew for lunch. "We worried about it," she admitted. "Who will cook the sauce for Carol the way she likes it?" Nawa had taught her, she said. Sita was named for their grandmother Sita, who raised Nawa and taught her to cook. The women's hands still reached out to form a circle of pottery, cooking, and care, but I missed the way Nawa had looked on with her quiet smile while I ate and I missed resting in the shade with her after lunch.

I went to see Nawa's friend Assiata. She greeted me warmly, and after asking about my husband and children, she said, "I wondered when you would come back. I wanted to talk to you since I had no one else to grieve over Nawa with. I knew. I knew because the last time you and Nawa visited, when she left, my heart was cut in two." After I left that day, she urged Nawa to stay. Nawa said she didn't feel well, so they went inside and lay down together. She asked Nawa what was bothering her and Nawa said her whole body was aching. Assiata told her she hated to see her like that, not well. Around five in the evening, Nawa got up and asked for the road.

As Assiata watched her walk away, her heart stopped beating for a moment, as if it had been cut in two. It was a sign that something was going to happen to Nawa. A week or ten days later, she heard Nawa wasn't well. Assiata went to see her, but Nawa wouldn't meet her eyes. Every time Assiata spoke to her, Nawa looked away or down. Then she knew Nawa was going to die. "Because when you are going to leave someone, you don't want to look them in the face. You know you are going to have to leave them behind, and so you just can't look straight at them."

"Nawa wanted to tell you about her illness," I told Assiata. "She wanted to talk honestly with you because you were her best friend. But she couldn't."

"She couldn't," Assiata repeated softly. "I never knew much about her illness." When she heard Nawa had gotten worse, she went to the hospital and was told Nawa had been sent home, so she took a taxi-moto to Nawa's house. Nawa's eyes were open but she couldn't speak. Assiata squeezed her hand and said, "Nawa! Nawa!" but she didn't think she could hear.

"She died around nightfall. The family slept that night and buried her the next morning," Assiata continued. After the burial, Adama remembered he hadn't sent word to Assiata, and he sent Nawa's older son to inform her. But when Assiata arrived at the house to give her condolences, the family had already left for Kalikaha. When they returned, she went to the house again, and when she saw Nawa's parents, she couldn't stop herself from crying.

"Nawa always told me what a good friend you were," I said, "how lucky she was to have a friend like you."

"When we lived side by side, we got along perfectly, perfectly, and after Nawa moved back home, we visited back and forth. But one day Nawa said it wasn't right for me to come and see her because I was the older one." She told Assiata to stay at home, and after that it was always Nawa who came to visit.

I told Assiata that it had been hard to come back to Korhogo because I was used to having Nawa beside me when I was there.

"I was thinking about you and picturing your face and wondering if you had come back. And the children were asking about you . . ."

"It was me!" interjected her daughter Khadi, eavesdropping as she always did. "I was the one asking about you!"

"That's because you're my *terimuso*," I told Khadi. My woman friend.

"I never had a better *terimuso* than Nawa," Assiata said softly. "Even among my own people, among everyone, Nawa was my best friend. When her husband died, that was a blow. I wanted to continue to live side by side, for our friendship to go on, but life separated us. She needed to feed her children and pay the rent, so she had to go back to her family."

"She was so young."

Assiata replied, "That was why she said she should come and visit me, because the younger should defer to the older."

"I knew her since she was younger than Khadi, just five years old. And when I brought my own daughter here, Nawa played with her and took care of her and she followed Nawa to the well."

"You really have known her!" Assiata exclaimed and repeated the story of how Nawa moved in next to her and their friendship began. We put our knowledge side by side and felt satisfied when the stories lined up, like tailors sewing straight seams, making a larger piece of fabric out of woven strips. Assiata told a story I didn't know, about a time Nawa had gone to work in the fields and bees stung her. Her eyes were swollen shut. She said after that Nawa's health got worse.

She knew about the woman at the market and waking up with her mouth pulled to one side. She was pregnant with her little boy when it happened. The market woman, the diagnosis of high blood pressure—we lined up our stories and stitched them together. I shared news of Nawa's two sons. Assiata hadn't seen the older, but the younger came to greet her regularly. I repeated what the family had told me, that when his friends went on to middle school without him, he became serious about his schoolwork. He had just taken the middle school entrance exam for the second time, and everyone was hopeful this time he would pass.

"He came by to greet me just two days ago," she said happily.

"The older one left the tailor," I said, "and is working for a fish seller. His grandfather told me he likes the work much better." Assiata's son had left the tailor, too, and was working at a shop in the market that sold mattresses and motorcycles.

"I don't know why Nawa's older son doesn't come by to see you."

"He is probably afraid. Every time he came, I told him to work hard at his job, and now that he left it, he is afraid to tell me."

"Maybe the tailor was difficult," I said. "They both left."

"It's true the tailor beat them."

Assiata's husband limped toward us with his cane. "May she go to heaven," he said to me softly.

"Amina," I replied. Amen. After he limped away, I launched into new territory. "What I think, Assiata, is that Nawa's husband had *sidabana*. He didn't know it, but he gave it to her and that is why she got sick." I explained that Nawa wanted me to use her real name in the book I was writing because she wanted people to understand that she was living with AIDS and she wanted them to know that just because she had AIDS, that didn't make her a bad person. "Nawa really wanted to tell you the truth about her illness because you were her best friend in the world."

"It was God that kept her from speaking," Assiata replied quietly. "This happens."

Some other women joined us and asked me to take a group portrait with my camera. "Very pretty!" said Khadi excitedly when I showed her the image. I promised to bring back a print the next time I came.

I asked Assiata for the road, and as we said good-bye, we both began to cry. She gave me blessings for a good day and a good night. "May she go to heaven."

"Amina," I said. "*Amina* here be." Amen. Peace be with us.

I thanked her for everything she had done for Nawa and her children. And I asked her to do me a favor, that when she said prayers for Nawa, to say them on my behalf, too, since I was not Muslim.

"I will do that for you," she said. As she walked me to the car, we held hands.

When I saw Dr. Tanoh, he told me sadly that he had heard about Nawa's death.

"Maybe Nawa's family waited too long to bring her to the clinic," I said. "Maybe if she had come earlier . . ."

"Well, probably her immune system never recovered from the time she didn't take the medicine," he said gently.

I came back to the clinic a few days later, on an afternoon when Masita would be there. She looked exactly the same—long dress with a square neckline and a tightly tied polyester headscarf, her glasses with one earpiece, her plastic Sir Cigarette bag. She greeted me, sat down, and started writing the test results into the patient logbook. Finally I said, "You know I lost my younger sister Nawa . . ."

"Yes," said Masita. "She was too stubborn. She wouldn't come to the meetings. I went to her house twice but still she didn't come. And she stopped taking her medicine."

I had hoped for something more, some consoling words, some acknowledgment of my loss. But later, when I thought about it, I realized Masita had no time for grief. She was on the battlefield, in a war against a fierce and powerful enemy, and she couldn't afford to get distracted. Nawa was lost, true, but Nawa was just one reluctant foot soldier. Masita was a captain on the front lines, far from headquarters and reinforcements, and she had to stay focused on her task. She had to marshal her troops and keep up their morale; she had to make sure the supply lines stayed open and her troops got the antiretrovirals that kept them going. When one of her soldiers fell, she couldn't afford to pause and turn around. She had to focus on the others. Nawa would become a character in Masita's sermons and fables, the young woman who came to appointments with a white woman from America but gave in to dejection and stopped taking her medicine, lost her health, and could not recover. Although Masita refused to grieve for Nawa, she would not forget her. She would turn her into a cautionary tale and keep her alive as a warning.

Abou the Ex-Rebel in Peace

In 2015, nearly four years after the end of the conflict, Abou finally received something from the demobilize, disarm, and reintegrate program. He and about three hundred former rebellion soldiers in Bouaké were given motorcycle carts made in China. "The merchants always need things transported," he said cheerfully, "and with a cart like that it's not hard to make a living." The streets of Bouaké were filled with the little carts. Some were piled high with bags of corn or cashews, others transported building supplies and had rebar sticking out the back, and still others were filled with women gaily dressed up for a wedding. How long Abou's bright-blue motorcycle cart will run, I don't know, but thanks to his days working at the Centrale, the New Forces treasury, he should be set for life.

Yaya

My House Is an Intersection

I paid a dollar extra to the taxi driver for the toll and took the new Third Bridge across the lagoon to Yaya's scrapyard. Instead of sitting in traffic, my red taxi zoomed over the expressway and shot straight across the 1.5 kilometers of gleaming bridge. The contract to build the bridge had been signed by President Bédié in 1997, but construction didn't begin until 2011 and the bridge finally opened for traffic in December 2014.

Djak, Nawa's younger brother, was in his fourth year of living with Yaya and attended a professional school to study mining engineering. Yaya provided his room and board, and Tom and I paid his tuition. "He studies hard," Yaya reported. "Sometimes I go to bed and he is still awake studying. You don't need to worry he's not working." Earlier that year, Djak had been invited to move into an apartment with some other students and I asked Yaya what he thought. I felt obligated to consider the idea because it would mean one less mouth for Yaya to feed.

"Better he stays with me," Yaya said. "Who knows what these other students might try to get him into? And besides . . ." Yaya grinned. "With me, he is a little afraid."

"Afraid of you?"

"Just enough," Yaya said. "It's a good thing. I am his elder. Leave him here at my house."

Djak was one of the many young men from Kalikaha that Yaya took in. Some stayed a few months, some for years. Each was given a place on the floor to lay his mat and two meals a day. When the census workers arrived in 2014 for the first national census since 1998, Djak happened to answer the door. The two young workers with clipboards explained their mission—to count every person in the household. "Okay," said Djak. "You are welcome to come in, but you had better sit down and be patient. This is going to take a very long time!"

That day, as we lounged on the forklift and ate coconuts I bought from a *yala-yala* coconut seller, Djak and Young Lonala and Siriki, another educated young man from Kalikaha who lived with Yaya, talked freely because it was one of the rare times Yaya wasn't there. He had been called away to a meeting of the ironworkers' association. They were worried about him, they confided, because of the affair with his old friend and business partner and the Bangladeshi buyers who refused to pay for the containers full of iron after the tank exploded in the foundry. I had promised to check the internet, and they wanted to know if I had found any confirmation of the accident. Although I had searched websites that reported industrial accidents, I hadn't found one in a foundry in Bangladesh. We needed to speak to his partner or the buyers, I told them, and get clearer information. I had tried earlier to interview Yaya's foreign buyers to learn where his scrap metal containers ended up, but they had refused to speak with me.

"We don't think the accident really happened," Siriki said quietly. "We think his friend invented the story to cheat Yaya out of his part of the money." Lonala nodded agreement.

"Maybe he was taken in by the buyers, too," I said. "Maybe he and Yaya are both being cheated."

"Maybe." Siriki sounded doubtful. "But he is building a big new house. People see that and the kind of cell phone he carries and the way he dresses, and they think he underwrites Yaya, but actually, it's the other way around. Yaya is always lending him money and bailing him out."

"Even now?"

"No, they aren't working together anymore. Yaya doesn't talk about it, but I think he knows. He used to go over to his house almost every night to drink tea and talk. But now he stays home."

"This has really hurt Yaya," Djak said quietly. "This was someone he really trusted."

The next time I was at the scrapyard, I suggested to Yaya that we go and greet his friend. When he heard where we were going, Siriki quietly joined us. Despite a high score on his bac exam, Siriki, like so many other young men who came of age during the conflict, was underemployed, working at short-term jobs, growing older without gaining any serious experience, and losing hope he would ever have a full-time salaried position. When Yaya and I went into his former partner's little office and sat down, Siriki waited politely just outside the door. Yaya introduced me and said he had known my husband and me since he was a boy, that I had a house in his village, and that I had known his mother and father.

His former partner greeted me politely but grew nervous when I took out my notebook and pen. "Yes, Yaya and I are true friends," he said. "He is my older brother here. When I have a problem, I go to him and listen to his advice. He has helped me a great deal. Yes, whenever I have a problem, I go to Yaya. And when he has a problem, I go to him, too." He meant to say that Yaya came to him, but that wasn't how it came out. It seemed like a Freudian slip.

I asked him about the tank and the explosion. "Could you tell me what you know about it? What the buyers told you and what they showed you?"

"I don't know anything about a tank or an explosion," he said politely. "I don't know anything about that."

Yaya sat off to one side, his long legs crossed, his long fingers upturned in his lap, and said nothing. We chatted a bit more, but when it was clear his former friend would not open up to me, I asked for the road. The three of us walked back to Yaya's scrapyard thoughtfully.

"How can he say he doesn't know about the tank explosion?" I finally asked.

"He was afraid," Yaya answered. "He doesn't know who you are. You could be checking up on taxes or something."

When Yaya got a phone call and walked off to take it, I turned to Siriki. "Did you hear what he said when I asked about the tank?"

"Yes! How could he say that? The tank explosion—we talked about it for months! It was all we talked about!"

After the electric fire destroyed his old warehouse, Yaya had built a new locked storage room where he stored valuable smaller pieces of metal that could be resold—motors, hoses, and engine parts—and a little enclosed office where he could meet with people privately. He invited me into his private office and slyly pointed out what was on his desk—neatly wrapped and tied bundles of fresh banana leaves containing kola nuts. These were the packages Jula families exchange during a marriage. He was helping a family "tie the kola," he explained proudly. The stubborn young man who bucked the marriage system in his own village had become a trusted mediator who arranged marriages in his urban village. We shared a chuckle, and then, more seriously, I asked him if his former partner owed him money.

"If I say he owes me—the problem with the container—today, if we ask, who took that money, I could say he did because he told me something and it turned out not to be true." In a sad tone, he added slowly, "It was him."

"You think so?"

"I think so. I asked him and he said he never saw the money. I said, all right, we'll leave it to God. If what you have said is true, you don't owe me anything and I don't owe you anything. But . . . if it's true you took the money, you have a problem . . . with God, and before you die . . ." His voice trailed off. He made a gesture with his long fingers, flicking away this unpleasantness. I had never seen him so sad, not even when he told me the story of Djeneba's declining health and death after her two last two pregnancies ended in stillbirths. "I won't ask him anything more. *Probleme-la,* I am letting it go."

We walked across the dirt road to the open-air office so he could keep an eye on the scrapyard. Yaya said he hoped to move back to Kalikaha. He had built houses for his two brothers, and he hoped to save enough to build one for himself next. He had planted mango and cashew orchards, and once he was living there, he felt confident he would find a way to make a little money. "Business—it's something I understand. If you buy something for ten, you have to sell it for twenty. I paid out a million yesterday, so I have to sell for a million and a half. That's how it works. That's commerce. You don't have to go to school to understand that!"

As proof, he pointed to a man sorting through a pile of heavy rebar, examining the lengths and putting aside the straightest. Young Lonala was helping. The man wanted four tons. "People said I was crazy when I bought this," Yaya said with a smile, tapping his temple with one long finger. "Crazy in the head! You know where this rebar came from? This is what was leftover from building the Third Bridge. I paid a lot for it. Let's see . . . I paid two-fifty a kilo . . . four tons . . . I paid six hundred thousand for the four tons. It has sat here for months and months, but now he is going to pay me nine hundred thousand. That is what we call business!"

Yaya hadn't yet crossed the new Third Bridge, and yet the rebar left over from its construction had ended up in his scrapyard. "Even if I should be gone, the business is here and the children can keep it going. But I have to teach them how to do it!" He laughed with pleasure at the thought of how far he had come. "The world is amazing, isn't it?"

Young Lonala had told me proudly that he didn't work "for" Yaya, he worked "with" him. Unlike the other workers, he received no salary, but Yaya rewarded him when he chose to—with a motorcycle, and with his oldest daughter as his wife. Someday he would inherit the business.

"Young Lonala," Yaya told me, "he's solid. If I'm not there, he can buy and sell himself—but if it's a big deal, he calls me on my cell phone." Young Lonala had been sent south during the rebellion to continue his schooling. He said he saw there were few jobs for educated young men, and the family and Yaya needed him, so he left school to work at the scrapyard. Yaya, on the other hand, said his nephew made bad grades so he took him out of school and put him to work. Young Lonala insists his grades were fine. Whoever is right, it's clear the current arrangement satisfies them both.

I asked Yaya if, when he moved back to Kalikaha, he would go into business with his brothers. He sighed. Abou-lonala was too old, and his younger brother—"Well, he doesn't have what it takes. Neither of them can do what I do." He admitted that sometimes he felt annoyed at them.

I asked why.

"Because they don't work as hard as I think they should." He made a sucking sound with his teeth. "When I was there, I played around a lot." His voice turned serious. "But I don't mess around when I am working. Because I don't want to have to depend on someone else. I pray to Allah to let me make ends meet until my death. Even if it's my own child taking care of me, I don't want that. I want to be able to take care of myself."

I wasn't sure if Yaya would really leave the hustle and bustle of the city and move back to Kalikaha. Maybe his talk of retiring there was a way of holding onto his place in the world, reminding himself of the unbreakable threads connecting him to the place he came from.

Yaya always managed to make money, but what wore him out were his obligations to his relatives. "Too many expenses," he said grimly. The bags of rice and corn, the metal roofing for the new, larger house he wanted to build, the children's school expenses. "And someone," he told me with a slap on his thigh, "someone is always sick!" His cell phone rang constantly, and it wasn't always buyers or sellers of iron. Often it was his relatives in Kalikaha, needing money to care for a cousin hospitalized in Korhogo or to send someone to Abidjan for treatment.

I mentioned that the government was going to institute national health insurance.

"Yes, they are going to start it soon," he replied. "You pay two dollars per person per month."

"Is that a lot?" I asked him.

"It's not a lot, but it's a lot!"

I understood that if you had a household of thirty-four people, every expense added up. I said that was why, in my world, most people only had two or three children. They lived in towns and couldn't afford more.

"But in Africa it's not like that!" Yaya protested.

"Yes, but maybe it's going to change here."

"It *is* going to change," he agreed in a serious voice, surprising me.

"You might be the last generation to have thirty-four people in your household. In the Abidjan of today, it might not be possible."

"It's true, in the Abidjan of today, you can't do this anymore. If you have five children or four children, that's it." Yaya had nine and had raised a number of other nephews and nieces. He pointed out his youngest, a little boy. "The last," he said. "After him, there won't be any more." Yaya might not have any more children of his own, but the young men from Kalikaha would continue to arrive on his doorstep, and I couldn't imagine him turning any of them away. He would give them a place on the floor to sleep because being a *jatigi* was part of who he was. His own *jatigi*, his older cousin Moussa, who struggled to make a living, lived in one of Yaya's houses rent free because Yaya felt both grateful and obligated. "My house is an intersection," he said. "You pass through to finish school or look for a job. You can have two meals a day. But once you find a job and are earning something, then you have to move out. That's how an intersection works. You move on and other people come through. *Cho!*"

Chékun

Back to the Kalikaha School

As we walked down the main dirt road that crossed Kalikaha, Bara asked me, "When you go back down to Abidjan, will you see our little sister Zele?"

I planned to visit Chékun, I told her, and hoped that Zele would be there.

"Well, tell Zele something for me," Bara said fiercely. "Tell her not to come home because they are talking about marrying her. Tell her to stay in Abidjan!" After living with Chékun for three years, Bara admitted that she had forgotten just how hard life was in Kalikaha. If she had remembered, if she had known how difficult it would be to live as a second wife in her in-laws' courtyard, she would never have come back. "There, I was always clean and I had plenty to eat, and even money to spend." She wished she could send her two daughters to school, but her husband said they couldn't afford it.

Chékun had no illusions about her sisters' difficulties. Another sister in Kalikaha had lost three children, one of whom woke up one morning sick and was gone by nightfall. Only Chékun had been chosen for another life, boosted into the literate, French-speaking middle class through her family's sacrifices and her own years of hard work. Except for Zele, who with Chékun's help had vaulted from one life to another, her sisters had been left behind. Their resentment was something Chékun had to navigate every time she went home. And now that everyone had a cell phone, her family's requests for money followed her wherever she went. She wished she could do more to help her relatives, especially her parents, but life in Abidjan was expensive. She didn't think her family understood how much it cost to live in the city: she and Ngolo had to pay for housing, buy all their food, clothes, pay transport costs for everyone to school and back, and feed the constant stream of relatives who came south needing a *jatigi* while they looked for work or took an exam. They were also active members of the Kalikaha self-help association, and when the school needed maintenance or the town had to build a house for a government official, they were expected to make a sizable contribution, and they did. When a relative needed medical care or to take an exam, they were glad to be short-term *jatigis* for ten days or so, but Ngolo said he had no intention of taking in more people for years. They had limited their family size and were investing in their children's education. Their relatives had expectations and needs, and they acknowledged that they had obligations, but the gap between the old expectations in the North and their way of life in modern Abidjan created tension. As a result, they did not visit Kalikaha often, and their children had never been there.

They had opted out of one obligation—the occult economy. Because they were Christians, they didn't go to diviners and didn't have to worry about trying to satisfy the demands of the spirits, which were ambiguous and never-ending. Chékun said it was a big relief.

Her oldest brother was a successful cotton farmer and a community leader. He had also lost a child, a little boy who loved to dance to Tom's banjo music. Her brother regretted that he couldn't read and speak French and sent all his children to school, but they struggled at the village elementary school. Her children lived in an environment where French was spoken, and because she understood the school system, she knew how to help them. But when one of her children sat an exam, she refused to take advantage of a professional benefit—if a colleague's child was just a few points shy of passing, the teacher helped them a little by giving out a hint or rephrasing a question. Chékun refused to go into the room, greet the teacher in charge, and introduce her child, as many other teachers did. "I want my children to succeed on their own!" she said. "I want them to know they did this themselves, through their own hard work."

Chékun employed a housegirl who received room and board, a salary that went to her family, and pocket money. When her housegirl's mother called her daughter home to be married, Chékun brought Bara's oldest daughter down to help with cooking and cleaning. Bara's daughter quickly grew plump, and once she could speak a bit of French, Chékun sent her to evening school to learn functional literacy. It was something she could do for Bara.

When Chékun went to Kalikaha during Easter vacation, she walked over to the school and introduced herself, and the teachers welcomed her and gave her a tour. A row of latrines had been built behind the school, but otherwise the building was exactly the same as when she attended classes thirty years earlier. Kalikaha had more than doubled in size since then, and each year children were turned away because there were not enough places. But the community itself had to raise the money to enlarge the building. That day, the teachers invited Chékun to address the oldest class, the equivalent of sixth grade. The children were studying for the exam that would determine whether they continued their education.

"Do any of you know who I am?" she asked them. She wore a pressed and tailored outfit that looked new and her hair was fashionably hidden under a dark-brown wig. She was obviously educated because she spoke carefully enunciated French, the kind of French the children rarely heard in Kalikaha. And she addressed them with confidence, so she must be someone important. "They had no idea! Not a single one raised his hand!" she told me, laughing. "But that makes sense; it's been so long and they are so young." This moment was important for her, a rare moment when her universe of origin and her present-day universe came together.

"I went to this same school," she told the children. "I did first grade, second grade, third grade, fourth grade, fifth grade, sixth grade right here." Their eyes widened and she felt how intently they were paying attention. "I used to be where you are. This is where I started my education. I was born here in Kalikaha and grew up here and I sat on these benches just like you. I worked hard and earned my entrance to middle school and went on to school in Korhogo, and now I have a job in Abidjan and I am a teacher, just like my colleagues here who are your teachers. So if you apply yourselves and work hard at your studies, you can become someone, all of you. If you apply yourselves to your schoolwork, you may do something even greater. If you work hard, you will have a job, too, someday. You can become someone, too, every one of you."

The room was silent as the students took this in.

"Your older sister succeeded because she worked hard at her studies," said their teacher, "and if you work hard, and God willing, you can all become important people like Madame Chékun."

Several years after this, Chékun received a promotion. Instead of remaining in the world of elementary education, she chose to work in adult literacy, training volunteer teachers and organizing literacy programs for people like her own relatives and neighbors. This is her way of giving back.

Asking for the Road

Ivory Coast is still deeply divided, and the old politicians seem reluctant to step aside and let a younger generation take over the leadership of the country. Former president Laurent Gbagbo and his street general Charles Blé Goudé were tried together at the International Criminal Court in The Hague for crimes against humanity and acquitted. This leaves Ivorians to work out their own reconciliation with justice, and the Ouattara administration has been accused of propagating a one-sided victor's justice. Although this book has come to an end, this journey hasn't.

In 2014, in front of the Korhogo City Hall where I had answered the questions of the Dialogue, Truth, and Reconciliation commission, I encountered another effort at reconciliation. It came from the Ivorian photojournalists' association rather than the government commission with its made-for-television tours. The photojournalists came from different political viewpoints but had shared a troubling experience. During the postelectoral crisis, they had gone, often together in the same car, to scenes of violence and documented them. They had been forced to look closely at the worst of what Ivorians had done to Ivorians. Their reconciliation project was an exhibition of enlarged color photos that they loaded into a van and took around the country.

The photos, mounted on both sides of a portable wooden wall, were set up in the parking lot under a canvas roof, and the photojournalists took turns escorting visitors through the exhibit in small groups. "This was the headquarters of a political party," our guide explained. He didn't say which party, and there were no indications in the photo of a ransacked building. I remembered, as others must have, that it was a Rally of Republicans office. Next was a photo of blood on concrete. "We didn't want to show the bodies, but here is the blood of the human beings that died in that political headquarters. They were murdered." Other photos showed bloated corpses in a morgue, a mass grave with many unmarked coffins, and a man who had been dismembered. One photo was a group portrait of young men in one of Gbagbo's street militias. "These young men joined a militia." Our guide's tone remained gently matter-of-fact. He did not assign blame or guilt, but he did convey a sense of shared responsibility.

The photos at the end of the exhibition stressed peace and unity. In some, people held hands. Muslim and Christian religious leaders stood with their arms around each other, and a line of children held chalkboards with the syllables that spelled out *re-con-ci-lia-tion*. "In the future," said our guide, "the country will belong to these children, and how will they go to school, earn degrees, and be able to work at jobs if there isn't a solid peace in their country?" He invited visitors to sit down and talk with a psychologist if the exhibit had brought up upsetting memories.

The traveling exhibition, which could not have cost much compared to other national reconciliation efforts, had been funded by the United States Agency for International Development. I felt pleased that my government's development agency had contributed, but it was also ironic because the exhibit made me think about images of violence in my own country. We Americans are hesitant to confront the dark parts of our own history, to acknowledge that we obtained the land we love by conquering Native people, and to admit we brought Africans to our country as slave labor. Nor do we acknowledge that rather than repairing the damage done by those acts of cruelty, our elected government bodies have continued to neglect and mistreat the descendants of both groups. If the photographs in our textbooks were as honest as the ones the photojournalists exhibited, perhaps we would understand our civic responsibilities differently. As I write this, our country is trying to reckon with video images of police violence shared on social media.

Hearing northerners in Ivory Coast recount their experiences helped me understand how terrible it is to be targeted by your own country's police officers. Sworn to defend you, they instead harass and intimidate you and sometimes even kill you with impunity. In a democracy, this is a terrible betrayal. It engenders a resentment and despair that rots a country from inside.

It was painful to watch a country I loved, Ivory Coast, break apart along ethnic, regional, cultural, and religious fault lines. African political systems have often been described as "winner-take-all." Politicians want to win by any means because there is no role for an opposition party and government is a lucrative business. As I wrote about Ivory Coast, fault lines in my own country became chasms of suspicion. There are so many parallels. I used to feel that we Americans, with our longer tradition of democracy, our two-party system, and our more mature democratic institutions, would never see political opponents as deadly enemies who must be completely defeated. But now I am not so sure.

As a guest in Ivory Coast, I don't participate in electoral politics, but in my own country I feel a responsibility to vote, to speak, to act. My book *Dancing at Halftime,* about stereotypes of Native Americans, led me into activism as an ally to Native people, and for the past fifteen years, I have worked with the American Civil Liberties Union as a local activist. My ACLU work and my experiences in Ivory Coast have taught me that a democratic government is not a product you inherit and pass along; democracies must be continually made and remade, invented and reinvented. This can happen only when ordinary citizens step up to take part. My neighbors in Kalikaha had never experienced life in a democracy, and most of them were not literate, yet they were determined to have a say in how they were governed. Their example continues to inspire me.

Stitched together from the lives of my neighbors' children, this account is incomplete and partial because nearly everyone in it comes from the same northern community and because it arises from my limited perspective. My neighbors' children are not the people you usually find in books or articles about West Africa—they haven't migrated to Europe or the United States or become famous. But I believe their stories matter. Each of them took to the road—in search of education, autonomy, a way to make a decent living. Each participated, in some way, in their country's transition from a one-party state with an autocratic president for life to a multiparty democracy, a transition that stumbles on. Each wanted to live in a country at peace, where all Ivorians are equal under the law.

We visited Kalikaha in February and early March of 2020. Before we left Illinois, I had gone through our old metal boxes of slides from the 1980s and pulled out pictures of elders who had died, our neighbors' parents. Tom had scanned them, and in a suitcase we brought a double white sheet and an LED projector. We announced the slide show for the next evening at 8 p.m. That afternoon, we sprinkled water on our dirt yard to keep down the dust, and Adama picked up the sheet the launderer had pressed with his charcoal-filled iron. The village carpenter heard we needed nails and brought them, refusing our offer to pay. Our tallest neighbor brought a ladder and helped us attach the sheet to the side wall of our house. Other neighbors came with extension cords, and we strung them together and tested the projector. Exactly at eight, in a place where promptness is unusual, people started to arrive, some carrying chairs or stools. Once the crowd was settled in the yard, Tom gave a brief welcome, and then, one after another, the elders reappeared on the wall:

> Beh Tuo, who taught us local history. Zanapé carving an ox yoke. Ziékun testing the bars of a wooden xylophone he had carved. Ngolofaga on a roof, laughing and waving as he sat astride new yellow thatch. Yaya's mother, Miriam, standing next to me in her best dress. Nawa, just five, smiling her beautiful smile as she burnished a pottery jar as tall as she was. Chékun's father, Donni, plowing, his son Tenena leading the oxen.

The next day, a man we didn't know stopped us on the dirt street in front of our house. "When you showed the picture, I didn't know it was my father. It was the people around me who told me, "That's your father."

"Who's your father?"

"Yanou." Donni's good friend, his face shaded by a wide-brimmed straw hat, his face tipped toward the camera with a smile as he took a break to eat lunch during a work exchange in Donni's cotton field. I remembered the day but not his name; it was written on the cardboard edge of the slide. *Yanou.* He died long ago, and although I didn't know his relatives, I pulled out the slide.

That evening, a young woman came into our yard. "I came to see the pictures."

We told her we were sorry; the pictures were last night.

"But I wanted to see my father. I have never seen him."

"Who's your father?"

"Yanou."

Tom went for his laptop and found the picture, and we sat side by side while she studied the screen for a long, long time. When we went to town, we had prints made for Yanou's five children and his widow.

That night we so easily brought the past to life. We offhandedly referred to the future. *After the cashew harvest. When you get paid for your cotton. After we build the village library. The next time we come.* Now, a continent away, we are trapped in an uneasy present, unsure when we will be able to visit again. Nawa's and Chékun's sons, my neighbors' grandchildren, are growing up, a new generation of Ivorians with access to the wider world on their cell phones. They text me their photos, their greetings, and their hopes, and when the messages land with a ding on my phone, they lift my heart.

In Ivory Coast, before you leave, you ask for the road.

"Is it really time? You have to go?"

"Yes, it's time."

Your host understands that you must be on your way and will give you the road, along with blessings for a safe arrival and greetings for your *jatigi*, your family, and your neighbors. Or, they may just give you half, a way of telling you to come back.

It's time, you say? You need to go? You have things to do and places to be?

I understand. Thank you for coming along on this journey. I give you half the road.

Epilogue

Chékun and Ngolo now live on the first floor of a spacious house they built in a new suburb of Abidjan, and they rent out the second floor. Their eldest son received his bac and is a student in a technical program; he wants to become an electrical engineer. Chékun's youngest sister, Zele, who learned to read and write at home and insisted on going to school, is a law student, and Chékun's daughter, Desirée, is studying management. After several years of failing health, her father, our old friend and *jatigi* Donni, died in 2018. Tom was able to participate in his funeral, dressed in the green flowered fabric that family members wore. In fact, there were two funerals, a traditional *poro* funeral with music and dancing, followed by a Christian funeral and burial arranged by Chékun. We had rebuilt our own house in Kalikaha, not with earth and thatch this time but with concrete blocks, a metal roof, and running water and electricity, so Tom hosted more than twenty women and their babies, Chékun's friends who came from Abidjan to help cook for the funeral. Sadly, not long after her father's death, Chékun's sister Bara also lost her little son.

Nawa's younger son, Yardjuma, lives with his grandparents in Korhogo. He is one of the top students in his high school class of one hundred. I told him his mother would be proud and happy because this was what she wanted, for him to stay in school. "I remember her telling me that," he said quietly, his dark eyes gleaming. "I miss her every day." Nawa's father, Adama, finally won his court case and rebuilt his house. Although the new house isn't large, it is always filled with young relatives who need a place to live while they go to school in town.

Nawa's youngest brother, Djak, lived with Yaya for seven years while he earned the equivalent of a master's degree in mining engineering. When he could not find a job, he ran a little stall for cell phone money transfers in one corner of Yaya's scrapyard. Eventually he passed a civil service exam for a public sector job and was assigned to the Ministry of Mines.

Despite telling me that he wouldn't have more children, Yaya prayed for one more child, a daughter who would look like his mother and carry her spirit. His prayer was answered when little Mariam was born, fair-skinned like her late grandmother and, he assures me, with that same strong spirit filling her little body. She is his tenth child and this time, he says, he really won't have any more.

Kalikaha, their hometown, is now a subprefecture, with a government administrator and an office where you can register births and get official papers. A water tower provides clean water, although once you have paid to have the pipes and a faucet installed in your yard or house, you must pay for the water. And even at the pumps, where water was free before, there is a small fee per basin. I am happy to report that the village committee that oversees water distribution includes several women. In addition, Kalikaha has a pharmacy, a bakery where you can buy baguettes every day, and a cell tower. We can even access the internet there through our cell phones. The elementary school still turns away children for lack of space, but a new middle school has opened, so children can live at home while they continue their educations.

The main street of Kalikaha, 2020 (photo by Tom Bassett)

The challenges ahead are many. At the southern end of the south-north road, Abidjan is threatened by sea level rise caused by global climate destruction. At the northern end, Kalikaha is dangerously close to the violent terrorism spreading through Burkina Faso and Mali. And with a pandemic endangering all of us, I am unable to travel the road in person to visit my neighbors and their children. Fortunately, our cell phones connect us.

Acknowledgments

Many people have gone out of their way to help me during my time in Côte d'Ivoire, and my sojourns there would not have been possible without their hospitality. I wish I could thank every single one. My deepest thanks go to the people of Kalikaha, who welcomed Tom and me in 1981 and after. We owe a great debt to our hospitable and generous *jatigi*, the late Donnisongui Silué, his wives Gnon and Fatouma, and their children, especially Dofongnoh, Tenena, Gnéré, Baara, Tedja, and Zié, who welcomed us so warmly and made our stays in Kalikaha possible. We also appreciate the care we receive from Tenena's wives, Chéfunyo and Senyeredene. I also owe a deep debt of gratitude to Adama and Nafini Koné and their children, especially Salifou, Djakaridja, and the late Nawa and Zoumana (Old Man). Adama's translation, language lessons, cultural assistance, stories, and willingness to explain his homeland made it possible for me to learn about northern Ivory Coast. Many people from Kalikaha generously shared their experiences, and for that I remain deeply grateful. All of them could not be included, but all enriched my understanding, and without their interest and collaboration, this book would not exist. Particular thanks go to Chékun Silué, Zele Silué, Bara Silué, Na Koné, Natagoura Silla, Lasungo Silué, Kortiazana Sekongo, Yaya Diabaté, Aboulonala Diabaté, Nonlanan Diabaté, Siriki Diabaté, Wakporo Soro, Abou Traoré, Doningmé Yeo, Katienengolo Koné, Ngolo Politique Tuo, Dinaba Silué, and Chébena Silué.

In Korhogo, Masita Koné, Fadjiguiba Camara, and Dr. Ainée Honore Tanoh generously gave their time, expertise, and encouragement to this project. I am also grateful to Assiata Coulibaly. Clarisse Ouattara translated Senufo and Dyula into French when I interviewed women. Kass Coulibaly and Lanzeni Coulibaly drove me around in the most entertaining way possible and encouraged me to write honestly about the crisis. Ivorian friends who understand the country much better than I do offered their insights; for that, thanks to Francis Akindes, Yacouba Konaté, Moussa Koné, and Tiona Ouattara. Ivorian artist Tamsir Dia shared his artwork and friendship. The novels of Ahmadou Kourouma and Tanella Boni enriched my understanding immeasurably. Two friends no longer here encouraged me, the late Jerry Vogel, who loved Ivory Coast and its people, and the late Nancy Abelman, who loved ethnography in all its forms.

I was fortunate to have many American readers who shared their responses to the manuscript with me. I appreciate them all. I am grateful to Amy Hassinger, Umeeta Sadarangani, and Gale Walden of the Tuesday night writing group, and Bill Moseley, Sandra Scofield, and Tom Turino. My book club—Frances Harris, Sharon Irish, Jo Kibbee, Bea Nettles, Dana Rabin, Sally Shepherd, and Karen Winter-Nelson—is a constant source of love and support. For their insights and longtime encouragement, I also want to thank Cope Cumpston, Maria Gillombardo, Kay Grabow, Hannah Klaus Hunter, Herbert Marder, Norma Marder, and Harriet Williamson.

My agent, Laura Strachan, was courageous in the Senufo sense. She took this book on and didn't give up until it found a good home, for which I remain deeply grateful. At the University of Wisconsin Press, Dennis Lloyd, Ivan Babanovski, Adam Mehring, Sheila McMahon, Jennifer Conn, and MJ Devaney made publication go smoothly, despite the unforeseen circumstances of the pandemic. Hao Hu made the maps.

Our two children, Nick and Becca, were troopers and bonded with neighbors young and old in Kalikaha. Finally, I would not have had these experiences, nor understood them, nor written about them as clearly, without a loving, demanding, and steadfast companion in Tom Bassett. This is the life we have made together. To all, as they say in Kalikaha, "May you be given something greater than what you have given me."

Glossary

Alternate spellings are in brackets.

Abidjan (AH-bee-jahn) ~ the largest city and financial and de facto political capital of Ivory Coast

Abobo (AH-bo-bo) ~ a large commune in the northern part of Abidjan

amina (a-MEE-nah) ~ amen

attieké [also *acheke*] (AH-chee-eh-kay) ~ fermented, pressed, and pounded cassava grains

balafon (BAL-a-fawn) ~ a wooden xylophone played with mallets by Senufo men

Baule [Baoule] (ba-OO-lay) ~ ethnic group from central Ivory Coast who claim descent from the Ashanti; also their language

Bété (BET-tay) ~ ethnic group in southwestern Ivory Coast belonging to the Kru language group

bissap (BEE-sap) ~ red juice made from hibiscus flowers

Bouaké (BWA-kay) ~ second-largest city

brassage (brah-SAHJ) ~ a French word that refers to a cosmopolitan, intermarried society; brewing

cho (long *o*) ~ "true!"

dé (day) ~ a Julakan suffix that adds emphasis

Douékoué (dway-KWAY) ~ town in western Ivory Coast where hundreds of people were killed on March 29, 2011

Fulani [also Fulbe, Fufulbe, Fula, Peul] (Foo-LAH-nee) ~ an ethnic group widely dispersed across West Africa and the Sahel, many of whom are cattle herders

Fulbe (ful-BAY) ~ language spoken by the Fulani

gbaka (BAH-kah) ~ a privately owned minibus traveling a set route within a city, often gaily decorated

gris-gris (GREE-gree) ~ mystical amulets worn on the body or sewed to shirts

Ivoirité (ee-VWAR-ee-tay) ~ a philosophical/political discourse that southern Ivorian cultures and southerners are more authentically Ivorian than northern Ivorian cultures and northern Ivorians

jatigi (JAH-tiggy) ~ host
jatigiya (JAH-tiggy-yah) ~ the cultural practice of host-guest relationships
jeli [*djeli*] (JELL-ee) ~ a praise singer, historian, and mourner; also their ethnic subgroup
ji (jee) ~ water
Jula [Dioula, Dyula] (JOO-lah) ~ a Mandé ethnic group
Julakan (JOO-lah-kawn) ~ the language spoken by the Jula and throughout Ivory Coast as a lingua franca
kanbeleya (KAN-belly-yah) ~ youthful masculinity; machismo
Korhogo (KOR-o-go) ~ the largest town in north-central Ivory Coast; sometimes referred to as the Senufo capital
laykoli (LAY-koh-lee) ~ school, from the French *l'école*
marabout (MAR-a-boo) ~ a Muslim spiritual leader who may have mystical powers
mogoya (MOH-goh-yah) ~ personhood, humanity, the quality of being human, or way of life
Mossi (MOS-ee) ~ the largest ethnic group in Burkina Faso; sometimes used as a slur in Ivory Coast to label someone a foreigner
palabre (PA-lahb) ~ a conflict
poro (POR-oh) ~ the spiritual belief system central to Senufo life centered in a sacred grove of trees, and the secret society that initiates young men into adulthood and passes on those beliefs
Senari (SEN-nah-ree) ~ one of the Senufo languages, part of the Gur language family
Senufo [Senoufo] (SEN-noo-foe) ~ an ethnic group in northern Ivory Coast, southeastern Mali, and southwestern Burkina Faso, most of whom are animists and farmers
sidabana (SEE-da-bah-nah) ~ AIDS; from the French acronym SIDA and from *bana*, disease in Julakan
terimuso (terry-MOO-so) ~ woman friend
toh (toe) ~ very thick corn porridge eaten as a staple by poor households
tugubele (TU-guh-belly) ~ nature spirits
woro-woro (WOH-roh WOH-roh) ~ a shared meterless taxi that operates within a city; follows a set route and is identified by color
yala-yala [*yaala-yaala*] (YAH-lah YAH-lah) ~ to wander, stroll, or sell house to house
Yopougon (YO-pou-gone) ~ a large and heavily populated commune of Abidjan; also known as Yop City
Yamoussoukro (yah-mah-SOO-crow) ~ the official political capital of Ivory Coast